RASEM BADRAN

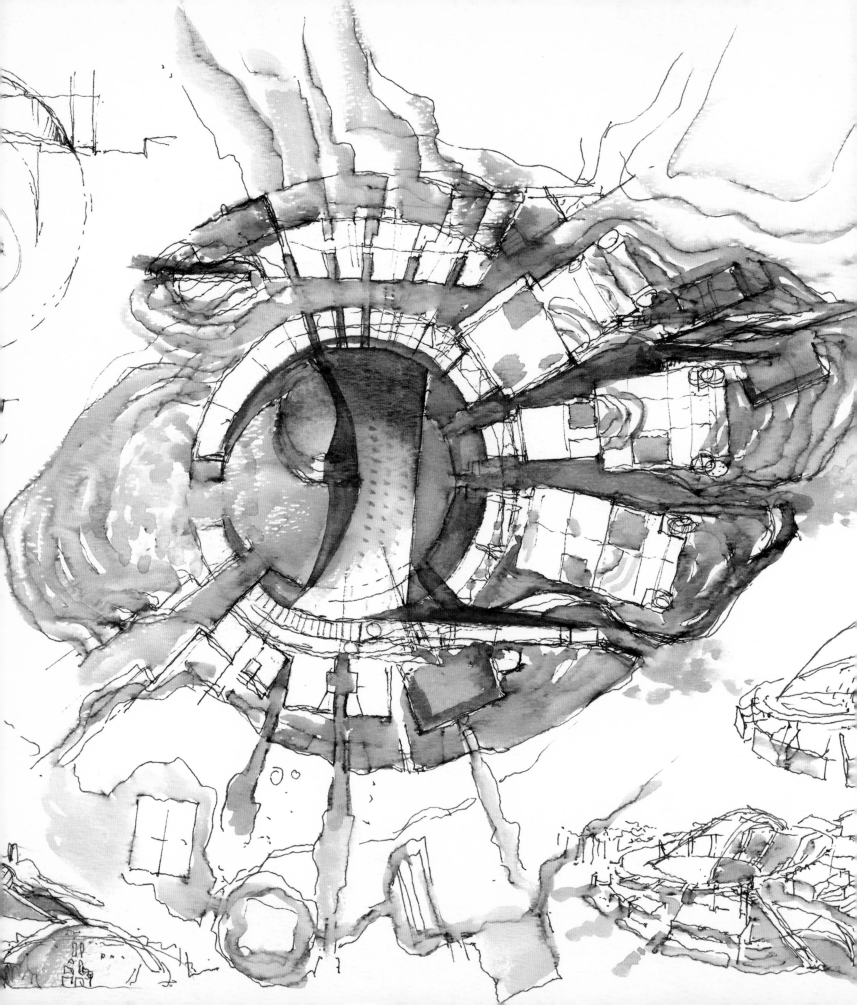

James Steele

THE ARCHITECTURE OF
RASEM BADRAN

NARRATIVES ON PEOPLE AND PLACE

With over 360 illustrations, 348 in color

Thames & Hudson

First published in 2005 in hardcover
in the United States of America by
Thames & Hudson Inc.,
500 Fifth Avenue,
New York, New York 10110

thamesandhudsonusa.com

Library of Congress Catalog Card
Number 2004110958

ISBN-13:   978-0-500-34206-0
ISBN-10:   0-500-34206-7

Designed by Christopher Perkins

Printed and bound in China
by Midas Printing Ltd.

Acknowledgments

I would like to thank Rasem
Badran for his cooperation and
support in the preparation of this
book. Thanks are also due to his
wife, Huzam Badran, and to his
founding partners, L. Shubeilat
and Anas Sinno. I would also like
to acknowledge the assistance
of Zina Sabbagh in selecting and
organizing the material available,
and Jamal Badran Jr for
coordination and graphic work.
Thanks also to others at Badran's
office, Dar al-Omran, including his
partners and management and
technical staff, as well as
members of his architectural and
design team: W. Almasri,
S. Sabbagh, M. Abbas, R. and
R. Arnaout, M. Alhiyari, A. Moamar,
Gh. Syed and Braa. Mrs Z.
Sabbagh, Ms A. Zanoon, N. Assaf,
and Mrs Wissam and Khalil from
the Autocad drafting staff. Also
former team members, among
them Dr. Y. Chika, A. Zuaiter, Mrs
Gh. Amr, I would also like to thank
the architect A. Wardat and Dr R.
Al Daher, head of the architectural
faculty of the University of
Technology in Jordan for their
contribution.

I am grateful to Jamie Camplin
at Thames & Hudson for his
guidance and all that he has done
to make this project a reality, and
to Andrew Sanigar for his efforts in
keeping the project on track.

James Steele

Above, left and right

Early watercolours, painted at the
age of four, show a precocious
awareness of surroundings and
details as well as perspective and
variations of light and shade.
Left: the landscape of rural
Ramallah. Right: Rasem Badran's
home in Ramallah.

On page 2

The entrance to the Al-Dara
Complex, Riyadh, Saudi Arabia.

On page 3

Pedestrian pathway, Abu Obaida
Mosque, Jordan Valley.

On page 4

Sketch study for the The Space and
Science Oasis Museum, designed
jointly by Rasem Badran and Dr
Abdul Halim I.A.H. from Egypt,
Riyadh, Saudi Arabia, 1989–91.

Contents

Acknowledgments   6

Introduction: Representing a Diverse Reality with a Single Identity   9

Chapter 1 A Narrative on People, Place and Culture   15

Chapter 2 Creative Heritage and the Return to the East   31

Chapter 3 Houses and Housing   49

Chapter 4 The Fourth Dimension is the Spirit   75

Chapter 5 Preserving a Living History   123

Chapter 6 An Earthly Paradise   179

Chapter 7 Rediscovering the Islamic City   203

Chronology   250

Notes   254

Bibliography   255

Glossary   255

Index   256

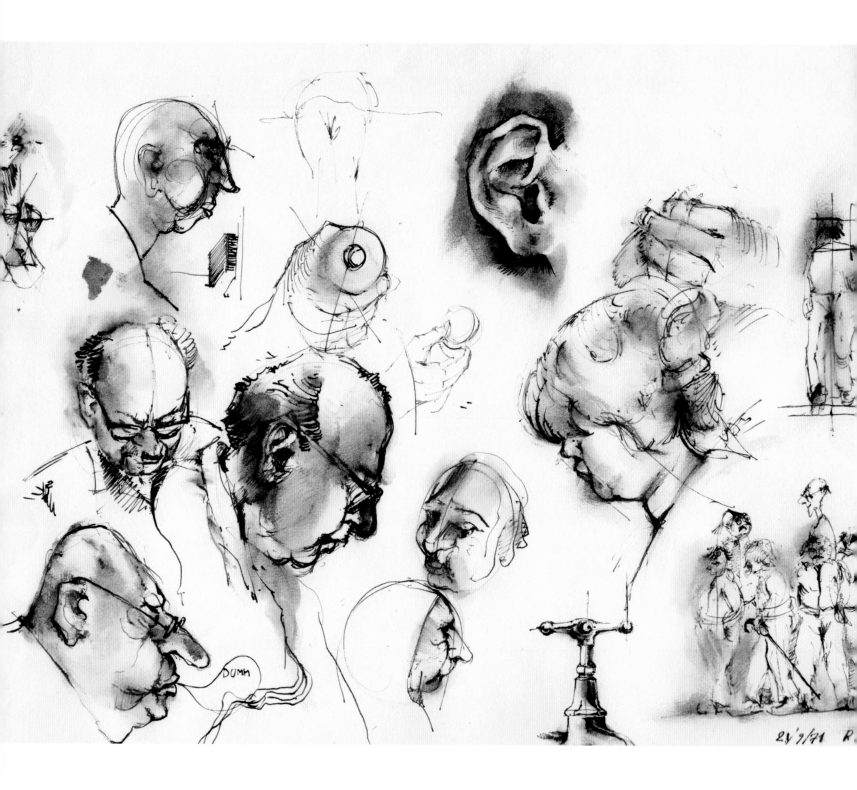

DUMM

24/9/71 R.

8

Introduction
Representing a Diverse Reality with a Single Identity

Opposite

As an artist as well as an architect, Badran has keen powers of observation that extend to the idiosyncrasies of human form. These studies, of his late father and of faces drawn from memory, elevate caricature to a higher level.

I first heard about Rasem Badran in 1983 while I was teaching at King Faisal University in the Kingdom of Saudi Arabia. Contractual restrictions forbade me doing architectural work outside of my teaching obligations, so I had decided to write a book about the Egyptian architect Hassan Fathy in 1980, which was my first year at King Faisal. I had not written a book before and had fastened on Fathy because my Saudi students seemed to respond positively to lectures about him in the history course I was teaching. I had read *Architecture for the Poor: An Experiment in Rural Egypt* (1973) on my flight from the United States to Saudi Arabia and found it compelling. Fathy had portrayed himself as the 'barefoot architect', the underdog in a malevolent establishment determined to suppress him. Everyone loves an underdog and I was no exception, rooting for him to win against the overwhelming odds, and I remember being outraged that he did not.

My book on Hassan Fathy, eventually published in 1983, has a great deal of bearing on this effort because he was the first architect in the Arab world to attempt what Rasem Badran is doing with such great success today: finding an appropriate, non-Western language, based on relevant religious, social and cultural precedents, with which to demarcate authentically a divergent identity. Luckily, I was very naive about the difficulties I would face in doing that first book. Newly arrived from America, having received a strictly defined Modernist training under Louis I. Kahn, I approached the project with that perspective, but what I found out in the course of interviewing Fathy, of researching and writing, changed my point of view and made me question much of my earlier academic experience.

A pariah

Throughout his career Fathy was treated as a pariah in Egypt because he was considered to be against progress, the most highly valued goal in the developing world. People seeking this elusive grail regard the quest for traditional wisdom as a sentimental, romantic anachronism, and view this instinct as a luxury they cannot afford. Nostalgia, as it was first defined, was considered a sickness, not merely a longing for something lost or out of reach, and Fathy was thought to be pathologically misdirected. I tasted a mild sampling of the ostracism he faced, just in lecturing about his work and undertaking to write a book about him, without really understanding why at first.

Fathy began his experiments in cultural expression before the Second World War, prior to the disillusionment with the concept of progress that we are experiencing now. The idea of a benign and beneficent future for a scientifically based society still had currency then, before the nuclear nightmare that ended and followed the war, and the environmental problems that began to emerge several decades later. In fact, Fathy's book, *Architecture for the Poor*, which brought him international fame, coincided exactly with the first oil crisis in 1973, making him a hero among ecological activists, and I believe the timing of its release was not entirely coincidental.

A different world

Just about the time I began my research on Fathy things had begun to change. The rampant development that began in Saudi Arabia and other Gulf States as a result of the discovery of oil in the region after the Second World War had begun to be questioned by a new generation. They felt that their heritage was being destroyed and they were starting to question the imposition of an alien architecture, which did not respond to the local culture, social values and environment. Those questions, which began to surface in many kinds of media, also embraced a curiosity about the past. Pride began to replace shame as knowledge about the inherent wisdom of traditional architecture started to spread. This growing awareness accounted for the interest my students showed in Fathy's work, which was in sharp contrast to the animosity with which the administration regarded it. It also explains the immense enthusiasm they showed for the work of a newcomer from Jordan, Rasem Badran.

My students first mentioned Badran to me in hushed, conspiratorial tones. Knowing of my interest in Fathy, they felt it was safe to talk to me about Badran, without threat of academic reprisal. The architectural magazine *Mimar* was like a breath of fresh air in that part of the world then, and it was publishing Badran's work, first the houses that he designed in Amman and then his winning submission for the State Mosque in Baghdad, which ranked above other entries by eminent-world-class architects such as Ricardo Bofil, Robert Venturi and Denise Scott Brown, among others.

Badran first appeared to many, including me, to be an enigmatic figure, a younger, more mysterious version of Hassan Fathy, who seemed to come out of nowhere to help the older beleaguered master lead a growing movement towards a return to tradition, renewed identity and pride in the Islamic world. Over time, as I have come to know him better, I have realized how misguided most of that first impression was.

Pre- or Post-Modern

The first phase of my learning curve, and the first issue that must be discussed in my relationship to Badran's work, involves derivation, which for someone with my Modernist training was a difficult idea with which to come to terms. Architects of my generation in the West, and in all other countries with educational systems influenced by the West, were taught that the use of historical elements in design studio, or forms that were overtly inspired by historical element, was a sin, and this attitude still persists. The Post-Modern revolution of the late 1960s – which arguably lasted until the late 1980s – tried to change that attitude. Its proponents maintained that such derivation might be a sin for architects, but that the general public really didn't care, and actually wanted a sense of historical continuity and a connection with the past. I vividly recall attending a lecture by Robert Venturi in London in the late 1980s and listening to his clearly articulated terms of surrender, a reprise of his *Plus ça change* article published in 1982. In his lecture, he claimed that Post-Modernism, or at least its architectural variant, had failed because Modernist attitudes were just too ingrained to change, and that Post-Modernists did not quote context in relevant ways, which left the public still feeling detached.

That brief experiment, however, has raised questions that still beg to be answered. Would it have succeeded if architects had been more sensitive to context and place-specific historical reference? Are Modernist attitudes so hard-wired that tradition will always be viewed as retrograde? Is derivation a dead end?

Writing about Hassan Fathy forced me to confront these questions head on and made me realize they were too simplistic. About the time I started my interviews with Fathy, Charles Jencks had just written his first book on Post-Modernism, *The Language of Post-Modern Architecture* (1977), and included Fathy's New Gourna Village as an example of what it was. His justification for its inclusion was that Fathy was a historicist because he borrowed from various periods of his own national chronology in his attempt to create an 'authentic' collective identity. This categorization seemed unfair to me at the time, devaluing the idealism that Fathy brought to his task.

I have since come to believe, for reasons that have clear relevance to this discussion about Rasem Badran's work, that Jencks's categorization was fundamentally wrong in several ways, best summed up in terms of relative cynicism and the post-global phenomenon. Post-Modernism, and the semiotically based borrowing that it encouraged, was built on cynicism expressed through irony. This cynicism was the result of the failure of the implied promise of progress, caused by environmental degradation, social malaise and a host of difficulties that brought the whole idea of scientific determinism into question.

The reasons for the social malaise are best addressed in Max Horkheimer and Theodor W. Adorno's *Dialectic of Enlightenment*, written during the Second World War, in which they describe the 'continuing struggle between rationalism and intuition', which will also often be referred to in the following pages. The essence of the dialectic they describe is that the Enlightenment, which began with so much promise for social freedom, brought about the decline of institutions and the proliferation of commodities, and the fear of deviation from facts: the 'technological imperative'. This imperative has been amplified by the digital revolution of the 1990s, which has helped to give the Internet precedence over other forms of traditional knowledge.

As a result, Horkheimer and Adorno conclude that 'the Enlightenment has extinguished its own self-consciousness', and 'meaning was lost on the road to modern science'. Today, people in the developed world have more possessions than ever before, but personal contentment seems to be in decline: more goods, but less time to enjoy life; more signs of social pathology and disintegration, less happiness.

Without the cynicism that this dialectic has bred, can historically derivative architecture be classified as Post-Modernist? If not, what is it? A sincerely idealistic search for cultural identity in a world in which meaning is being debased, social values are under threat, and in which commodities and technology – which are the legacy of the Enlightenment – are becoming more important than the people who produce them.

Badran's training in Germany has left him with an abiding respect for technology and the place it occupies in the history of traditional architecture. As a result he has no hesitation in blending together materials with different associations in what he refers to as the 'skin morphology' (stone, glass, steel). Kuwaiti National Bank (remodelling project), Amman, Jordan.

What about the post-global phenomenon, as the second qualifier of difference? Briefly stated, this relates to a new collective awareness that seems to contradict many economists' predictions of the death of the nation state in the wake of globalization. The erasure of borders by flexism – or global trading by computer – has not happened and 'nation building' is still a viable idea in the developing world.

Relative difference: the rational and the intuitive

What these qualifiers of relative cynicism and post-global identification mean for this discussion is that there are still parts of the world in which social and cultural values and identity matter a great deal, and in which architecture is seen as an expression of those qualities. Rasem Badran is trying to preserve them.

He is uniquely placed to do so by background and training, as he comes from a family tradition of Islamic arts and crafts and received his academic education at the Technical University of Darmstadt in Germany. This balance is crucial because he is the only architect of any stature in his region to have had such extensive exposure to Western ideas. This importance is perhaps best described by recalling another equally significant lecture, in London, in the same year as the Venturi dialogue. This time, the Japanese architect Arata Isozaki was talking about his opinion of the difference between East and West and how it affected his work. He explained that, in spite of his reputation as a repository of Japanese culture and tradition, 'this knowledge is as far from me as it is from you'. As part of the post-war generation of architects in Japan who rode the new wave of prosperity he explained how American influence had distanced him from his past.

I have also come to find that Isozaki's use of Platonic solids at the Gunma Prefectural Museum of Modern Art in Takasaki and elsewhere, has been his way of coming to terms with the rationalist tradition introduced by the post-war occupation: the product of an Enlightenment that non-Western countries have only indirectly experienced through the dialectic identified by Horkheimer and Adorno. Building with rationalist forms has been Isozaki's way of participating more directly in a process that has eradicated his own culture, of trying to understand why this devastation occurred. This has direct relevance to Rasem Badran because, although his culture had its own scientific renaissance a full five hundred years before the Enlightenment in Europe, it did not preclude intuitively derived, traditional knowledge and, in spite of many important contributions, it did not prevail either.

Rasem Badran may be seen here to be a complex mixture of both positions, of the rational and the intuitive, a pragmatist as well as an idealist, genuinely searching for a different, more culturally appropriate way to make architecture socially relevant. His rational side is manifested in his stress on technology, his fondness for geometrical systems, his discovery of typologies, his frequent use of the matrix and his fascination with cities as the paradigmatic repository of forms. His intuitive side is revealed in thoughts about a narrative that relates to each place, which he then expresses in his work. He bristles at being called a traditionalist, seeing tradition, as Fathy did, as 'the social expression of personal habits', which may change and may certainly include the latest knowledge, as long as that knowledge does not begin to take precedence over the people who make use of it. People, rather than technology, are the prime concern in Badran's work, and for that basic reason, among many others, he has much to teach all of us.

1 | A Narrative on People, Place and Culture

Ours is a time in which the whole notion of authenticity is being questioned and its meaning redefined. The essential connection between vernacular architecture – narrowly conceived as 'the architecture of a particular people, place or region' – and its meaning has been severed, steadily to be replaced by 'neo-traditional' configurations. These frequently attempt to replicate original settings by reproducing heritage and employing imagery that is 'authentically' fake. The result treads a fine line between sincerity and satire that is difficult to determine, especially since the introduction of cynicism by the failed Post-Modern experiment in architecture, which has left deep scars.

The digital revolution, and the speed of information transmission that it has made possible, has exponentially accelerated the pace of life, rendering the past less and less real for the latest generations most affected by this change. The present seems to become the past more quickly than ever before, which makes the distant past increasingly irrelevant. Traditional architecture derives its authority, and its social and cultural validity, largely from its relationship to a fixed moment in time and its connection to nationality or ethnicity, religion, place and function. As its historical associations have been progressively devalued, aesthetic and formal considerations have grown more significant than content to those concerned with reproducing it. Some would dispute that the link between architecture, history and contextual geography has been broken, but the danger of this dislocation occurring is inarguable.[1]

Architects concerned with tradition are increasingly tempted to envision it as a storehouse of forms, detached from their historical association with people, place and culture, which many people thought had died with Post-Modernism. Frederic Jameson, in his detailed and clear analysis of the sociological revolution of which Post-Modernism in architecture was only a small part, provides the basis for an explanation of the diversity between Rasem Badran's architecture and the progressively inhumane legacy of Modernism in the West. In *Postmodernism, or, The Cultural Logic of Late Capitalism*, Jameson perceptively characterizes the march of development that followed the Industrial Revolution as a continuum, founded on the growing importance of commodities, the technology that produces them and the support mechanisms of the media and advertising that promote them. That continuum, in his view, is both accelerating and expanding, to the point that people are becoming more and more marginalized by things and the activities that create and sell them.[2]

Jameson does not, however, account for the fact that this process is changeable and depends on the level of transition from an industrial to an information economy in the nation or region in question. This is based on the transformation from a manufacturing to a service-based financial system first described by the sociologist Daniel Bell in the mid-1970s.[3] According to Bell, computer technology and the ensuing release from Fordist, assembly-line production, rendered factories obsolete in all highly industrialized societies and ushered in the information age, in which the outsourcing and globalization of production, based on the lowest cost possible, replaced a fixed manufacturing source. The result is a worldwide layering, or constantly fluctuating weather map, of economic change, depending upon the extent of industrialization. This consequently creates a highly differentiated diagram of the cultural influence of the commodification that Jameson describes. That map is further complicated by cultural factors that are difficult to quantify.

The Islamic world, for example, which is Rasem Badran's primary area of involvement, runs the gamut from the very rich to the very poor, from highly developed to hardly developed, and from a great degree of commodification to very little, making it impossible to offer a uniform assessment of its condition on this map. But what is certain is that the influence of the factors described by Jameson is short-lived; industrialization and the fabrication of infrastructure are relatively recent, even in the most extensively developed nation in this category, which may partially account for the diversity in question.

What is also certain is that in the developed or over-developed world, architecture has become increasingly tied to theory, as well as to the commodification cycles of the society it represents; in the less developed or recently developing countries, in which Badran is most active, that link has yet to be conclusively forged. There is still an opportunity there to escape the commodification cycle that Jameson outlines.

An alternative to disassociation

This is the daunting task that Rasem Badran has undertaken and consistently addressed in his work. He seeks a valid, unquestionable alternative to these global tendencies and he contradicts the increasingly popular belief that individual identity is no longer connected to tradition, social interaction or place. He rejects the fashionable contention that history is dead, or is only now equivalent to the present, and that architectural images can be based on anything other than precedents related to context, culture and climate. He is searching for a way to satisfy the yearning that people have in many parts of the world for an architecture that represents their identity, history, religion, culture and memories.

The post-global condition: Badran's narrative in context

Badran's unwavering belief in the power of national identity may also be seen to anticipate the breakdown of the authority of globalization in the 21st century. The economists who hailed it in the mid- to late 1990s claimed that the nation state was an outmoded construct which would gradually be replaced by borderless global markets thanks to high-speed electronic networks. These experts said

Above
C. Town Mall, Amman, Jordan. Commercial retail centres have become ubiquitous throughout the world and are a reality that cannot be wished away. The question for the architect, then, is how to express local culture in such a globalized model.

that economics, not politics, would determine global alliances and that these new fiduciary loyalties would level out the peaks and troughs that were predicated upon national interest in the past. This would then create a natural defence against a worldwide depression of the kind that occurred in the 1930s. The elimination of national boundaries was also welcomed as a step towards the unfettered growth of international trade, which globalization economists maintained would benefit the developing and developed worlds alike, erasing poverty and the extreme ideologies that it engenders.

The advent of limitless financial alliances, and the decline of national political agendas that they would bring about, were also forecast to strengthen the economies of reconfigured nation states, which would then be free of the massive defence budgets they had to maintain in the past, as well as the deficit spending they needed to engage in to stay afloat. As one economic analyst explained: 'In summary, global economic forces, if left unfettered...would protect us against the errors of local self-pride while allowing self-interest to lead each individual to a better life. Together, these forces and self-interests would produce prosperity.' [4]

Several glaring inconsistencies in this prediction of a rose-tinted future began to emerge in the aftermath of the Asian financial crisis in the late 1990s and the usual, constrained – and by then ritualistic – response of international lending institutions to the economic chaos it caused. The standard austerity programmes on which the International Monetary Fund and the World Bank had insisted, to little effect, in Latin America in the 1980s, were advocated once more, but the Malaysian Prime Minister, Dr Mahathir Mohammed, refused to comply. He took the ringgit off the market, made it non-convertible, and fixed its value just low enough to favour Malaysian exports.[5] Rather than reacting to this crisis in economic terms, Mahathir saw it as a national political issue and acted in what he believed to be Malaysia's best interest. Although international lending institutions initially treated the nation as a pariah, they eventually made overtures and agreed that he had acted prudently. Events have subsequently proved that he was right, a source of great national pride.[6]

Another flaw that has brought the predictions of globalization economists into question is that, in spite of the claim that supranational alliances would eliminate world poverty, global inequality is actually rising. As Robert Wade writes in *The Economist*:

If the world's income distribution has become more equal in the past few decades, this would be powerful evidence that globalization works to the benefit of all. It would give developing countries good reason to integrate their economics closely into the world economy...and it would help to settle a crucial and long-standing disagreement in economic theory, between the orthodox view that economic growth naturally delivers the 'convergence' of rich and poor countries and alternative theories which...say the opposite.[7]

Although partly dependent on which statistical method is used to determine income distribution, new evidence suggests that global inequality is indeed rapidly worsening. This inequality has been caused by faster growth in developed nations, rapid population expansion in developing countries, slow growth in rural China, India and Africa, and increasing income disparity between rural and urban areas, particularly in China.

Wade goes on to make the critical connection between widening income discrepancies and extremism. 'Income divergence', he says, 'helps to explain another kind of polarization taking place in the world system, between a zone of peace and a zone of turmoil'.[8] This deflates another globalization claim that increased international markets would foster world peace. These discrepancies, along with questions about how democracy – which is nation-based – can become unilateral, and how resources – which are also geographically specific – can be shared, have led to the demise of global theory.

Badran has stood firm

While the storms of economic change have been raging around the globe, Rasem Badran has stood firm, making him seem like a rock of certainty in the middle of a maelstrom. He has always contended that people want to feel rooted, that ethnicity and nationality matter, and that history is not dead, but is now more relevant than ever. International events are affirming his position.

Over the years, Rasem Badran has been able to consolidate his position and hone his arguments, to the extent that he now eagerly seeks out opportunities to express them in a public forum. He has produced a lecture entitled 'Reflections on the Narrative of Place – The Infinite Conversation', to describe his theoretical position, using a dual-slide presentation to do so.

The dual-slide presentation was especially useful to academics and others because of its didactic potential for making creative comparisons. In one notable instance, a dual-slide lecture, later converted into a book, had an enormous impact on the history of architecture. *Complexity and Contradiction in Architecture* (1966) by Robert Venturi evolved out of a course he had taught at the University of Pennsylvania. The comparisons in it illustrate the point that buildings in the past with complex spatial relationships are more compelling and memorable than modern buildings which often do not have them.

A new didactic viewpoint

Rasem Badran is an avid photographer. His extensive slide collection is the result of his travels all over the world, including the Middle East. He has selected several of these last images for a presentation sequence that has been shown in many universities and public lecture venues and which explains his singular viewpoint. This presentation, reproduced here in abridged form, offers keen insights into his personal philosophy and his approach to work. It includes his accompanying text, as well as my own commentary. The sequential pairing of images is as revelatory in its own way as Venturi's comparisons were in the 1960s, because of the stark contrast it offers between his architecture, in which people are given pride of place, and the generally soulless fruition of the constructs prophesied in *Complexity and Contradiction in Architecture*.

Badran's architecture: a dialogue

In his dual-slide lecture Badran begins with a set of images depicting the weathered face of a man and a desolate landscape, in which a solitary figure stands beside a rudimentary shelter. Referring to the images, Badran describes his architecture as a narrative of, or dialogue with, a place in which he attempts to unravel its various layers of history and memory. He seeks to understand the way in which the hidden characteristics of what he refers to as the 'collective mind' are

articulated in the existing built environment, and to draw from it the lessons that he needs.[9] He refers to this narrative as a 'dynamic process over time' which begins with the research and graphic analysis necessary to familiarize himself with the formal, or material, and spiritual aspects of the place he is studying.

His recognition of the 'coexistence between human beings and the place' they inhabit as a renewing, constantly changing process is in line with the latest views on the dynamic aspects of space and time now being discussed by physicists, as well as with recent interest in the work of the 20th-century French philosopher Henri Lefebvre, whose book *La Production de l'espace* (1974) focuses on the part that the common, mundane rituals of daily life have played in the formation of the built environment. Lefebvre maintains that these everyday activities of the past tell us more about the true nature of a society than the grander institutions on which architectural history has tended to concentrate. This approach, of giving preference to the commonplace to determine how people once lived and how to compare it with social patterns today, is also evident in archaeology. The focus in archaeology has now shifted from impressive monuments to the discovery of the minute evidence of everyday life to better reconstruct the social patterns of the majority of the people that lived at a certain time and place, rather than of just the elite.

A second set of images, showing lines of buses parked side by side is compared to a similar grid of houses. Badran explains that:

Our understanding of the meaning of architectural space is organic, that is, vital and humane. It differs from the geometric, that is, repetitive and numeric. So, architectural space gains its characteristics through its connection to historical, environmental and climatic constraints, as well as traditions, habits, inherited values, religion and language. When architectural space loses these specific characteristics it becomes a purely functional setting based on utilitarian considerations, and can easily be copied and transferred from one place to another. It thus becomes

Set 2

a consumer commodity, without an intimate relationship with either its user or context. It loses the aspect of continuity, and its link to a living heritage.

Architecture can be described as a tool by which to measure time. It reflects values that relate to social structures and cultural environments, in addition to being a medium through which we can interpret dynamic human behavioural patterns over time…. Time is especially legible in sensitive spaces that envelop diverse facilities in which material and spiritual activities are mixed, and in which repetitive events have carved out profound memories. Urbanism is one such creation, due to its diverse, cosmic nature.[9]

A third pair of images captures people in a market and three young boys sitting in front of a brightly coloured mural; it illustrates Badran's view that a person is:

a vital actor, whose role alternates between active and passive composer and player, giver and receiver, with the ability to create events that join the past with the future, to discover new meanings which can be expressed here and now. I analyze the social, cultural and environmental systems, which play a role in shaping the individual's mental state, physical behaviour and performance; those things that contribute to the formation of the poetics of place. Building is a continuous process, a material framework that contributes to human self-esteem, a way of creating a living, intimate zone within a larger urban structure, or a dynamic, active part of a public space.

Badran adds that the characteristics of place, which are in symbiosis with the environment, are suggested by a poetic narrative that includes materialistic and spiritual aspects on the one hand, and time in its historical, cultural and social diversity on the other. He argues that this interpretation is generated by a constant search for formulae of coexistence or adjacencies between phenomena. This coexistence ensures the interaction of phenomena within a specific time span.

A fourth set of images pairs a village in a rocky outcropping at the top of a mountain, with a much larger, Islamic city, prompting a discussion about natural context. Badran's comments on this comparison:

The suggested narrative begins with an analytical investigation of the natural geographic and environmental phenomena of a place, including a comprehensive study of architectural behaviour, including its morphological and ecological components. This analytical study must extend to a knowledge of social trends, cultural behaviour and inherited traditions as reflected in local techniques and

handicraft. This initial reading is an attempt to identify the various components and conditions of a place and can be expanded to include similar cultural and environmental domains. This analytical reading leads to a narrative deduction, in which the evidence, deduced through the reading process, is an instant initiation. It reflects a new manifesto of predictability and generates physical, architectural statements. This reading may be ambiguous and may produce mixed feelings. It motivates our talent for discovery and a renewed reading of the surrounding phenomenon, leading to a continuous, cumulative creativity, over time.

Our configuration of that physical result is endless. It differs from linear, Euclidian science and is open to all probabilities and readings, aligning it with the new, non-linear sciences. To determine the ways in which these variables relate to the dynamic human mind, it is essential to relate them to time and space. Once this relationship is established, the human mind allows these variables to be defined, to achieve their essence and to comprehensively embrace reality. This essence is the result of a continuous mental process and a mediation between natural phenomena and their scientific reality. This produces spaces that seem both formal and familiar.

The process of understanding the method of operation creates a narrative between opposing parts, such as a hospital and recreational facilities, a museum and commercial use, government offices and a cultural centre, or a mosque and a house. Implementation is a process of interrelating and connecting both the materialistic and cosmic aspects of place, using case studies and precedents in the consideration of how it is shaped. The informal result of this implementation reflects both harmony and non-homogeneous diversity in the generation of human space. It considers dimensions, the difference between public and private uses and the relationship between the whole (macro) and its parts (micro). The significance of the spaces that are created in this way invites us to occupy and experience them. Intuition plays an important role in this process. It is a way of comprehensively embracing reality, instead of in a relative way. Intuition is a dis-

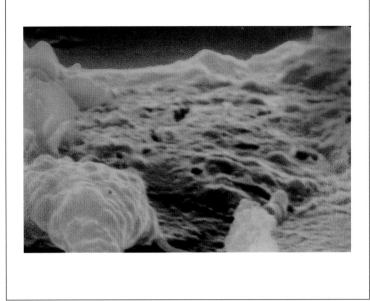

tinctive way of understanding life because life is constantly changing. Intuition allows us to understand and sense the non-homogeneous, the continuous, the interrelated and the unpredictable. Intuition is the process of activating the self through coexistence with a place and its secrets.

In the remaining part of his presentation, Badran concentrates on answering the rhetorical question: who, where and how? He introduces the next five sets of images with a discussion of what 'who' means to him:

Who is the spiritual and psychological content which is embraced by the culture of a place; which is nourished by this culture by means of all the patterns that ensure its survival and continuity throughout the generations. This spiritual and psychological content also ensures survival against competing cultures because there is both specificity and universality within the structure of the cultural mosaic.

The fifth set of images presents a starry sky (a common sight in the open desert in the Middle East, but not in the smog-obscured night sky of urban areas) and a *mashrabiya* screen. Badran uses this set to draw attention to the spiritual aspect of 'who', the various levels of contemplation that are possible, from the macrocosmos to the microcosmos.

The sixth set of images, of mountains shrouded in clouds and a crystalline structure, emphasizes the spiritual distinction in Islam between *Az-Zaher* (The Manifest) and *Al-Batin* (The Hidden), which is made possible by using what he calls the 'third eye'.

The seventh set takes an aerial view of a city, which is contrasted with a detail of a stone *muqarnas*, thus representing harmony between the macrocosm and microcosm, which Badran refers to as 'enrichment'. Elaborating on this, he goes on to explain:

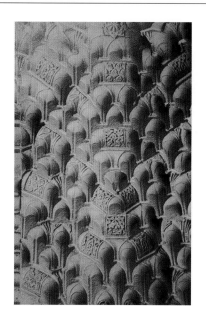

Set 7

Set 8

The mind transforms a simple abstract image into a volumetric one, causing a dialogue between surface and space, which is creation. The mind interprets living phenomenon as a form of abstract expression, joining beauty, meaning and clarity together, which is abstraction.

The eighth set, made up of a cage full of vibrantly coloured parakeets juxtaposed with a dramatic, colourful tapestry, illustrates the continuation of this process, showing transformation, the means of expression in which reality is remodelled into abstraction:

this is the way we envision universal nature, which adds a sense of variability to the physical, which is nearby, and the metaphysical, which is far removed. This is contemplation. This produces the energy that stimulates and activates human intelligence, bringing about innovation.

In the ninth set of slides built terraces defined by sunlight are set next to a picture of a flock of sheep; Badran interprets the juxtaposition of these two images in the following way: 'Energy is the light that allows us to engage in dialogue, becoming intuition. The tenth and eleventh sets represent 'where':

Set 11

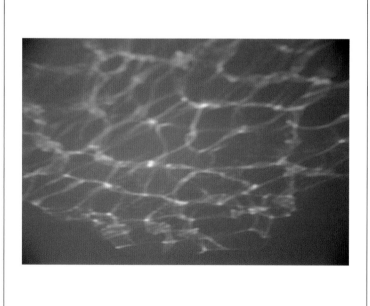

Set 12

'Where', on the other hand, searches for the spirit of the place as embodied by the social order which defines the types of relationships and behaviour patterns that are influenced by acquired and inherited customs and traditions throughout history. These are also formed by environmental, climactic, and geographic factors. This contributes directly to the building of the civilized attributes of a place.

Set 12 reproduces the patterns of the sun shining through water and the diagonal lines of a planted rural landscape; the images are used to illustrate 'what'. Badran defines it as a dialogue between the tangible and the intangible, between reality and fantasy, and an integral part of determining, or coming to an understanding of the interaction in question.

Badran's tripartite question ends with 'how', which occupies the rest of the presentation, and is identified at this point as the interaction between 'who' and 'where'. Badran defines, 'how' as a:

variable within the framework of time (when) materialized through the interaction between who, where and when. This is self-generating and renewing. It is legible in the inherited accumulation of human achievement at the macro and micro scale, seen in the following categories of the human fabric. At the macro scale, we have: (1) Street patterns, which are the social tissue of the urban fabric, (2) Urban morphologies, which are like a cosmic skin, (3) Urban elements, (4) Transformations which occur in spaces with sequential order, and in the humanizing experience of open spaces, (5) Gates, which provide a sense of privacy and maintain social boundaries.

Slide sets 13, 14 and 15 are used to illustrate the variable of 'how' at the micro level. A craftsman inscribing a wall by hand is compared to a worker in a factory, representing mass production; the surface is seen as art contrasted with the enclosure. The *maqa'ad* of the Beit Al-Suheimi in Cairo appears beside a richly decorated exterior wall in Yemen, a living wall which responds to human spiritual and physical needs, an example of 'the science of building the art of sound, technology, the art of weight and walls, the logic of material'. This can be witnessed in the interior of the Hasht Behest Palace in Isfahan, Iran, which acts as a sound filter and is compared to a water fountain that produces natural sounds. It illustrates what Badran describes as the 'technological human intervention in the environment, using elements like ventilation towers to deal with the climate.

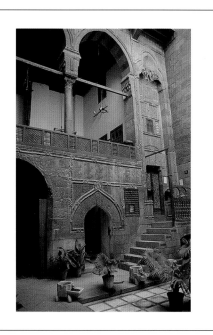

A final set of images pairs mudbrick houses in the Najd, Saudia Arabia, with an undulating roof landscape in Isfahan, Iran, as a sustained climatic roof skin:.

It annoys me, looking back at what has occurred in the past 50 years, to discover that we are living in meaningless cities built as temporary seasonal fairs replaced by other new structures, to fulfil the demands of consumers, at the expense of human coexistence and moral values.

We can assume that the creation of a memorable and valuable space is a product of cultural, environmental and social interactions, in the micro scale (with its

sensitivity), which is in symbiosis with the macro scale (in its cosmic knowledge). This is what Islamic civilization is seeking by considering the whole without denying the particular.

This hypothetical assumption leads to the understanding of human made environment through categorizing its morphology under different domains, where some structures can be dominated through specific 'climactic' constraints such as those found in the region. Others can be interpreted from the viewpoint of cultural impact, such as those seen in medieval Cairo. There is also the urban socio-economic fabric, which can be sensed in some old cities such as Sana'a, in Yemen.

The permutations seem to be infinite, and yet the methodology that Badran describes allows him the creative latitude to cope with each individual context.

2 | Creative Heritage and the Return to the East

Opposite

Jamal Badran, Art Work,
Graduation Project (1927),
College of Applied Arts, Cairo.
Jamal Badran was the
consummate artisan for whom
each of the traditional crafts
provided a creative outlet.
He demonstrated his
extraordinary skills in all areas,
displaying a virtuosity that
can now only be replicated
by digital technology.

Rasem Badran was born in Jerusalem in 1945. His father, Jamal Badran, (1909–99) was a famous artisan and craftsman, a master of Islamic art. He had studied in Britain in the mid-1930s after graduating in applied arts in Egypt, and was a pioneer in the art movement that began to flourish in Palestine around that time. When the Al-Aqsa Mosque was badly damaged by fire in 1969, Jamal Badran was chosen to conserve what remained of the *minbar* of Salah ad-Din, founder of the Ayyubid dynasty, and to restore what had been burned. Between 1970 and 1975, he also re-created the decorative patterns that had been damaged in the mosque itself. His selection was a measure of the esteem in which he was held, since the Al-Aqsa Mosque is one of the most revered shrines in the entire Islamic world.

Rasem Badran clearly recalls the influence that his father had on him as a child, and remembers spending many hours in his father's studio as well as being able to absorb the landscape of his surroundings:

The sensitivity and capabilities of my late father made a deep impression on me, especially the stories he told me, stories based on oral histories, novels and narratives to which my mother Fatima Ala-Iddeen (a poet) also contributed. His use of imagery transformed these stories, enriching my imagination and enhancing my ability to express myself. My first memories, when I was two or three years old, were of his presence and of becoming conscious of and absorbing all the details of the rich cultural landscape of Ramallah.[1]

A prodigy

Following in his father's footsteps, Rasem Badran began to draw and, in retrospect, he was clearly a prodigy. In 1948 he moved with his family from Ramallah to Damascus, Syria, along with many others from his region. He started drawing when he was four years old, trying to express the reservoir of memories and images he carried with him. He remembers this time clearly, despite being so young, sensing the need to find better ways of expressing himself graphically, to accommodate the change:

Moving to Damascus was a major paradigm shift for me and the way I perceived the environment around me. Having just migrated from the countryside, which

Above

With the charred remnants of the *minbar* of Salah ad-Din behind him, Jamal Badran uses carefully drawn sketches to re-create the missing parts of this precious historical piece in his studio in East Jerusalem.

Left

These drawings in progress show the amount of painstaking detail required in the preservation of the *minbar*.

was silent, calm and seemingly boundless, in what I now understand to be an almost metaphysical way, I found myself in the vibrant city of Damascus, which was fast paced, continuously moving and had complex levels of social interaction. In the boundless landscape of the countryside, I had no need for perspective and my first drawings there resemble Abstract Expressionism. In Damascus I had to develop new tools and means of artistic expression, to adjust to a state of mind that was different from the metaphysical environment of the countryside. My father introduced me to the concept of three-dimensional perspective when I was five years old and I learned the rules very quickly.

An eastern city by the sea

Soon afterwards, Badran moved again. In 1953 UNESCO hired his father as an arts and crafts expert and the family relocated to Tripoli (Trablus Al-Gharb), the capital of Libya, where they remained until 1967. Like Damascus, Tripoli was

Below

Like the pieces of a complex puzzle, the remaining fragments of the *minbar* provided Jamal Badran with the clues he needed to reconstruct the panels that had been destroyed.

also hectic and had just experienced the sense of jubilation that followed the end of its colonial occupation. Unlike Damascus, however, Tripoli displayed much more evidence of foreign influence, especially in the way it was planned. Known as 'the bride of the Mediterranean', Tripoli struck Rasem Badran as being:

very European in its layout, as well as in its festivals and events. It seemed to me to be very a cosmopolitan city at that time. Not only was it a lively, animated and vivacious modern city, with thriving sea- and airports, a triumph of Western civilization, but it also had all the complexity of an Eastern city by the sea.

The vivaciousness he recalls was the result of a potent cultural mix of Italians (who had remained after independence was achieved) and American and British expatriates, added to the indigenous Libyan population. Many educational and cultural events, including art exhibitions, which Badran attended, contributed to this international flavour. Tripoli was then the most cosmopolitan city in the Arab world, making Damascus seem like a 'hinterland' to Badran by comparison. 'Only then', he believes:

did I really feel and experience a different form of real urban civilization. I felt the transformations that were taking place in this hybrid, East-West environment. Due to its strong interrelationship with the outside world, this coastal city was constantly changing, with many people of different races passing through it. Unlike other inland cities in the Arab world at that time, Trablus became a recipient of many cultures and civilizations (...) because of the many ships that docked at its harbour: I embraced it passionately.

The Badran family lived close to an American airbase (Weelus), and Rasem was fascinated by the aircraft. He drew many of them in impressive detail considering his age, and began to consider the possibility of becoming an aeronautical engineer or an industrial designer. His interest in technology, which started here, is a constant theme in his intellectual development, which will be traced in detail.

His father held numerous art workshops and exhibitions of student work at the Sea Fort in Tripoli, through a UNESCO-sponsored programme aimed at fostering an appreciation of local arts and crafts and developing the skills of young people. These workshops were a further encouragement to Badran to pursue the development of his own considerable artistic abilities. These were acknowledged in 1957 when, at the age of just nine, he was awarded a silver medal for a watercolour in an International Children's Drawing Competition organized by the Shanker Institute in India.

The contrasting conditions that an artist faces, from isolation to the detached observation of social activity, are obvious in Badran's early sketches and paintings, executed between the ages of five and ten.

A constant traveller, a long-term drifter
Badran recognizes that these early experiences and relocations helped him understand that change is inevitable. 'Being a constant traveller', he believes, has enabled him to grasp:

that place is not a static reality that is unchangeable, but on the contrary, I perceive place to be continuously changing and moving forward. Being a long-term drifter, I have been able to sharpen my ability to mentally store images, with all of their contextual details, as well as events and experiences. I am able to retrieve

them later and to edit them critically when I represent them on paper, instead of literally copying or depicting a still image.

Badran likens this critical representation of a place, 'with all its complexities and contextual details' to living in a foreign land, 'where one can be detached from the scene, which allows for a new representation and imagination, especially in architectural design. This resembles oral or written stories in the way in which they establish a critical distance between the events being described and the way they are represented.' This ability to look at each region or problem with a fresh eye and to assimilate and then interpret it in a distinctly complex, graphic way, is what sets Badran apart from others who attempt to find a way effectively to translate tradition into a contemporary form.

Above
During his time at university in Germany, Badran travelled extensively throughout the country, producing evocative gouaches of many important monuments and townscapes. Above: the city of Regensburg.

Below and below left
The 'Theatre of the Future' project indicates the extent to which the technological impetus driving architecture at the time throughout Europe affected Badran as a young student.

A twist of fate

Badran's interest in aeronautical engineering and industrial design prompted him to apply for a university position in Egypt in the early 1960s, but he did not meet the entrance requirements in either specialization. He decided to major in architecture instead, and applied to the Technical University of Darmstadt in Germany where he was accepted. He looks back at this decision as an important turning point in his life, especially his choice in 1968 of Professor Joachim Jourdan as his tutor for his thesis project. For this he chose to explore the feasibility of a mobile

MOBILER SPIEL-CLUSTER

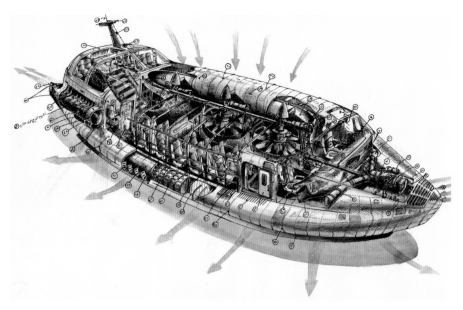

'Theatre of the Future', designed to accommodate the experimental music then being composed in Germany. In preparing his thesis, he interviewed many of the most avant-garde and creative new composers and musicians in the world at that time, such as Karlheinz Stockhausen and George Legitte. Others included Yona Friedman, who was proposing schemes for cities elevated on hi-tech, prefabricated, modular structural steel frames ('The Hanging Paris'). His theatre incorporated new staging configurations and spatial relationships to enhance vocal performances, audience participation and multimedia presentations. His design was also influenced by the Archigram group (Peter Cook), which was then publishing similarly unconventional approaches to the use of new technologies.

The 'Theatre of the Future' project led to his involvement in the set design and production of an experimental music performance in 1970. His knack for winning architectural competitions also developed at this time, with the selection of a team proposal for a low-cost housing project, Elementa 72, in Bonn, which was then the capital of West Germany. The team included Joachim Jourdan and Bernhard Müller. They established an office called P.A.S. which still operates

today, but without Badran. Between 1969 and 1972 Badran also worked on the Munich Olympia Park, designed by Günther Behnisch, who was also one of Badran's tutors, and engineered by Geiger Berger and Frei Otto.

A rational legacy

Rasem Badran's time in Germany had a profound impact on his approach to and critical vision of architecture, and helped him to formulate a systematic, typological methodology that will be described in detail in relationship to each of the projects presented here. He characterizes this as his ability to base his approach on 'critical, analytical thinking', a process which he came to understand in Germany as being:

a main characteristic of the intellectual revolution that was taking place in Europe when I was there. It is the outcome of democracy and is the legacy of the Enlightenment and the scientific and industrial revolution that followed it. The 1960s was an era of resistance and the rejection of conventional, systematic academic systems. We refused to participate in business as usual, rejecting the pillars of Western architectural thought, such as Frank Lloyd Wright, Mies van der Rohe and Kenzo Tange. We boycotted their lectures when they visited our University, because we disagreed with their extreme individualism. We disliked the fact that they were imposing their own style on international architecture, trying to dominate it by extreme personification, advocating the strict geometrical order during the post-war industrial era. They wanted architecture to become a representation of the self. Yet, some students did research these architects, only with the intention of questioning their philosophy through critical evaluation of their design approach. We focused instead on the architects who had laid the foundation for Modernism in Germany in the 18th and 19th century, such as Schinkel, Behrens and Mendelsohn; creating architecture that integrated all of the various interrelated strands of a complex epoch. I spent my free time discovering the German environment with its old cities and lush natural surroundings through sketches and drawings, in addition to technological design ideas.

A return to the East

After graduating with distinction from the Technical University of Darmstadt, Rasem Badran went to East Jerusalem to study that part of the city, before returning to Jordan. The reason behind this trip isn't clear, but it is tempting to speculate that after such an intense period of exposure to Western influences and values, he felt the need to revisit his birthplace, to rediscover his true identity. The trip may also have been due to a common reluctance among many students to enter into professional life straight after graduation, without some time to decompress. Whatever his reasons were, Badran produced many lyrically beautiful drawings of old Jerusalem during this period, as well as some housing proposals intended to alleviate overcrowding in the city.

He then returned to Amman, intent on putting into practice the critical and analytic skills he had acquired at Darmstadt, rejecting what he characterized as 'the recycling of the ideologies and the styles of others'. He refers to his approach at this time as 'contexturalism…interacting with, experiencing and attempting to enter into a dialogue with the local context'. His first opportunity to do so, as is the case with many young architects, came in the form of commissions to design several homes, between 1974 and 1975, using local courtyard and village typologies. In 1980 Badran entered into partnership with L. Shubeilat, who later retired to be replaced by engineer Anas Sinno from Lebanon as a full partner. Badran began working on larger projects, such as The Jordan Cement Factory Employees Housing project, which specifically evokes the housing studies he undertook in Jerusalem before returning to Amman. He describes the studies as being:

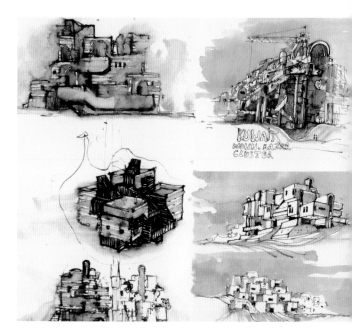

inclined toward producing a narrative, or a series of events, which provide a place with value and meaning, that enrich the mind and enable memory, creating a relationship between individual and the place that he or she lives in; contributing to an understanding of it. The Jordan Cement Factory Employees Housing project in Fuhais, near Amman, recalls the walls in the old city of Jerusalem, which I transformed into an 'Omran', a living built environment, or a 'living wall', which was my first impression.

Badran won a competition to design the Al-Beit Foundation (The Royal Institute for Islamic Studies) in Amman in 1985. He proceeded with a historical analysis and in-depth study of the architectural heritage of Islam in an attempt to determine a local, regional identity. This narrative approach, shown in his early houses of the 1970s, also played an important role in his selection to design the State Mosque in Baghdad between 1980 and 1981, which may be considered a second major turning point in his career, after his exposure to the potential of high technology at the Technical University of Darmstadt.

His house designs, completed soon after his return to Jordan, were published and came to the attention of the well-known Iraqi architect, Rifaat Chadirji. He invited Badran to participate in the State Mosque competition, which included other internationally known firms such as Ricardo Bofil and Robert Venturi and Denise Scott Brown. Badran's commitment to achieving a deeper understanding of the history of Islamic architecture was underscored in this design by his appointment of the Islamic art historian Professor Oleg Grabar as an advisor to his team, and his decision to incorporate references to the many various periods of Iraqi history into the project. This included the earliest Mesopotamian phase, which is described in greater detail in Chapter 4.

The issue of what actually constitutes Islamic architecture continues to be hotly debated, with no resolution in sight. The question is bracketed by those who maintain that it does not exist at all, and others who contend that it is comprised of recognizable symbols, which have been validated and venerated over time. Badran, in consultation with Oleg Grabar, obviously struck a chord in his design of the Baghdad State Mosque, which appealed to both the jury and the international audience who reacted positively to it when it was published. Badran's winning scheme appeared, along with the other premiated entries, in *Mimar* magazine, which was supported by the Aga Khan and had worldwide distribution. Badran describes how he came to determine the nature of Islamic architecture:

I attempted to arrive at an understanding of a sense of place, especially in the spiritual dimension, since the competition involved the mosque; the sacred place of worship; one of the most obvious physical manifestations of Islamic culture. My understanding of Islam is that it is built upon a fixed set of principles and values and yet it accommodates dynamic change over time. It accepts various

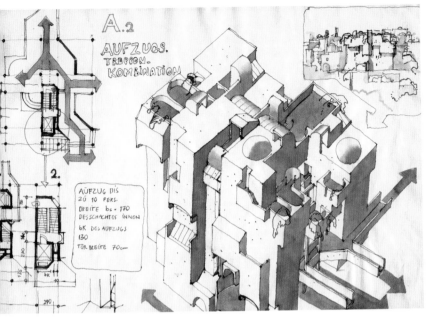

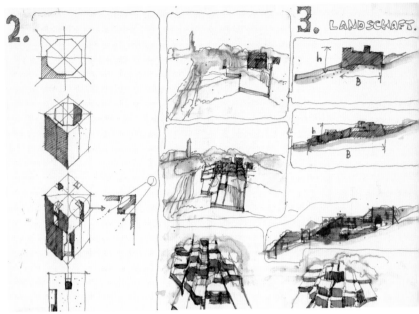

Opposite top

A series of studies illustrating the concept of covering an existing living fabric through an active skin. Kuwait (1969).

Opposite centre

A talent for internalizing traditional urban landscapes through drawing them has been a key to their contemporary translation.

Opposite bottom

Study for a passageway in the Al-Alami housing project, East Jerusalem.

This page

After returning to Amman, success in the Al-Beit Foundation competition in 1985 led to intense research into vernacular forms. The ability to produce quick vignettes of plain views helps both the architect and the client to visualize the design.
Because of its steeply hilly terrain, Amman has a distinct architectural character not found anywhere else in the Middle East.

possible interpretations of how values change and evolve as part of this notion of dynamic transformation, which can result in new manifestations. This idea of constant fixed principles coexisting with transformative realities has a bearing on how to deal with the concept of place and the way that personal authorship can take contextuality into consideration. In this way, new interpretations can arise that venture beyond familiar styles and norms.

Badran's fresh reading of both the material and spiritual history of Iraq – which includes what he refers to as 'deep time', or antiquity, as well as the contemporary context of a profound civilization – was startling and positive because he avoided the trap of being restrained by conventional styles, or of reproducing prototypical forms. Post-Modernism was rampant at the time the competition was decided, and Venturi and Scott Brown – who are widely credited with almost exclusively introducing that position into the architectural discourse – exhibited this tendency to recycle well-known symbols and forms in their entry. Badran, on the other hand, presented a sensitive, penetrating reading which avoided the use of monumental historical precedents in favour of what he calls 'a poetic authorship that is aimed at the revival of and granting a voice to the forgotten memories of a place'.

By avoiding the habit of misrepresenting context in the Baghdad State Mosque design, and in every project before and since, Badran escapes being classified as a Post-Modernist; his social, cultural and contextural interpretations are sincere and accurate, directly addressed to the people for whom he designs.

While subsequent events prevented the Baghdad State Mosque from being realized, the submission gained Rasem Badran an international audience and made it possible for him to participate in much larger projects outside his main sphere of influence in Jordan.

A third turning point in Riyadh

The most significant turning point to appear, soon after his State Mosque success, was the opportunity to design the Great Mosque and Palace of Justice in the historic district of Riyadh. This represents a third milestone in Badran's career, because of the project's national and regional significance, its scale, and the recognition it received in winning the Aga Khan Award for Architecture in 1995. It was sponsored by the Riyadh Development Authority in Saudi Arabia, under the direction of Dr Mohammad Al-Sheikh, a technocrat and intellectual leader. This acclaimed commission gave Rasem Badran an even higher degree of local and international visibility and consolidated his reputation as one of the most important, if not the most important architect in the Islamic world.

After Riyadh, the deluge

Following the revitalization of the Qasr al-Hukm district, the old centre of Riyadh, which was one of the largest projects undertaken by Badran and his office Dar al-Omran at that time, several other opportunities arose for architectural commentary in Saudi Arabia. These included the King Abdul Aziz Mosque, Al-Kharj, which responds sensitively to its lush, oasis-like setting, and the National Saudi Museum, which is near the Qasr al-Hukm Complex. The project for the old district incorporated the master plan for the King Abdul Aziz Historic Centre in Riyadh in collaboration with a local Saudi architect. Badran was also to

Above

The site of Qasr al-Hukm makes the project a prominent landmark in central Riyadh, blending in seamlessly and harmoniously with the rest of the city's historic core.

design the Al-Dara Complex, which plays an important part in his exploration into the correct, contemporary translation of the local Najdi tradition, rendered in new materials rather than the mudbrick, palm trunks and tamarisk of the past. As Badran describes this museum:

It was built in the ruins of an old, historic neighbourhood in the middle of Old Riyadh which was built of mud; not far away from the Grand Mosque project, which was based on a poetic reading of the historic, social and cultural reality of the place. The design of the Al-Dara Museum was also based on such a reading. The museum's concept, however, expanded on it, recalling the ruins of the past (as a destructive statement) and opened new channels of communication with history, through what I call the phenomenology of the unfolding. It is intended to allow anyone attempting to interpret this heritage to unfold or unravel the secrets of the past as well as the local knowledge of craft techniques. It attempts to reintroduce these realities into contemporary life by making use of state-of-the-art technology and knowledge.

These new opportunities did not dampen Badran's enthusiasm for competitions, or his ability to win them. He submitted the winning scheme for the Museum of Islamic Arts in Doha in 1997 (see p. 130), which represents a further development of the process of arriving at a place-specific reading through a narrative synthesis. Although it did not win a prize in the Al-Azhar Mosque Garden competition, sponsored by the Aga Khan for a site in Cairo, his scheme provides an extremely illuminating primer on Islamic garden design and represents a valuable documentary of the potential of landscape to transform urban life.

His entry into the Jabal Omar competition (2002) is equally instructive of his approach to intervention in a fragile urban context. It involved the redevelopment of the old part of Makkah al-Mukarramah, near the Haram al-Sharif and the sacred Ka'bah, and aimed to provide housing in an overcrowded area. In 2004 Badran and the Dar al-Omran team won the Al-Shamiya development scheme, a mega development scheme in Makkah. He was also invited to enter competitions for the redesigned Khor Dubai in the United Arab Emirates and the historic city of Sidon in Lebanon, in which he was successful. He won a contest to design a housing project in Sana'a, Yemen, Al-Beit Al-Kamal ('the complete house'), a textbook case study of his systematic, typological approach.

Local recognition

Unlike his famous predecessor Hassan Fathy, who was the first to attempt a contemporary translation of Islamic architecture, Badran has begun to receive recognition in his own country during his lifetime. In addition to Saudi Arabia, Egypt, Kuwait, Iraq, Jerusalem, Morocco, Yemen, Qatar, the United Arab Emirates, Malaysia and Lebanon his 'narrative' now includes Jordan. Queen Noor of Jordan, the wife of the late King Hussein, commissioned him to design their royal residence complex near Amman, based on an Andalusian garden metaphor. Badran spent more than two years in extensive dialogue with Queen Noor (who is also an architect). He was further asked by the former Crown Prince Hassan to research and design studies for his residence in the Royal Court in Amman. Badran has also designed the City Hall of the Municipality of Greater Amman, in collaboration with another Jordanian architect, as well as Al-Yarmouk Univer-

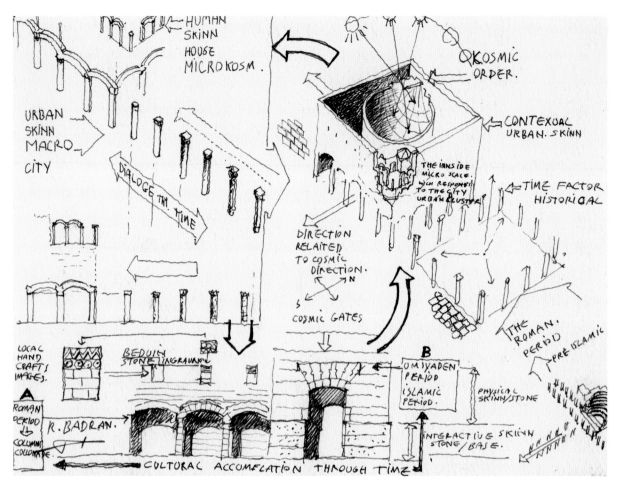

The following text labels appear within the sketch:

HUMAN SKINN HOUSE MICROKOSM.

KOSMIC ORDER.

URBAN SKINN MACRO CITY

DIALOGE TH. TIME

CONTEXUAL URBAN. SKINN

THE INNSIDE MICRO SCALE. WICH RESPONSIL TO THE CITY URBAN CLUSTER

TIME FACTOR HISTORICAL

DIRECTION RELAITED TO COSMIC DIRECTION.

N

S

COSMIC GATES

THE ROMAN. PERIOD

PRE ISLAMIC

LOCAL HAND CRAFTS IMAGES.

BEDUIN STONE INGRAUNON

B

UMIYADEN PERIOD ISLAMIC PERIOD.

PHYSICAL SKINN/STONE

ROMAN PERIOD COLUMNS COLLONADE.

R. BADRAN.

INTERACTIVE SKINN STONE/BASE.

CULTURAL ACCOMELATION THROUGH TIME

Left

Amman City hall. Analytical study of the morphology. The passage of time has been a constant theme in Islamic culture. Cultural accumulation is described here. Time is expressed visually and stylistically, through historical progression.

Left and opposite, top and bottom

Amman City Hall. The cosmic plaza. A sundial mounted on the wall becomes an integral part of the spatial experience, intentionally making a cosmic connection then is extended into the placement of architectural elements.

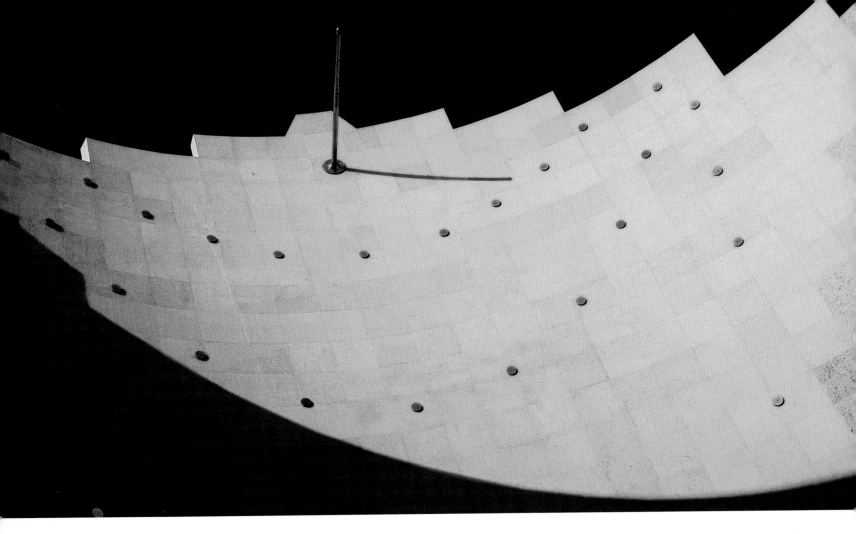

sity Central Library in Irbid. Symbolically, Badran has also redesigned a proposal prepared by Hassan Fathy for the residence of the late Khalil Al-Talhouni in Jordan. Jordan University of Science and Technology in Irbid awarded Badran an honorary doctorate in architecture, in recognition for his contributions to local heritage; he is the first to receive such an award as a non-official figure.

A continuing heritage

The creative legacy that Rasem Badran has inherited from his father, Jamal, is being perpetuated by his sister Samina Badran, who studied at the Leonardo Da Vinci School of Fine Art in Florence and now has her own studio in Barcelona. Rasem's son, Jamal, is studying architecture in London, where his daughter Ola is pursuing theatre design at Central Saint Martin's College of Art and Design.

A dialectic

This remarkable story, of a journey that began in Jerusalem and has taken Rasem Badran to Ramallah, Damascus, Tripoli and Darmstadt before a return to Jerusalem and Amman once again, is made even more compelling by the single-mindedness he has shown, in the decisions he has made, and in the enduring quality of his mental focus, apparent even when he was a child. He is a mixture of Eastern and Western influence, of intuition and rationality, of poetry and science, of the pre-industrial and post-Enlightenment tradition, which has uniquely qual-

Top, left
Stage set design by Ola Badran,
Rasem Badran's daughter.

Top right
Art work by Samira Badran, Rasem
Badran's sister.

Bottom, left
The computer is now part of the
architect's repertoire. Jamal
Badran Jr, fifth-year project,
Bartlett School of Architecture,
University College, London.

Opposite
Al-Yarmouk University Central
Library, Irbid, Jordan.

ified him to interpret his own physically diverse, but spiritually unified legacy. Important milestones along the way, such as his exposure to advanced architectural philosophies and technologies during his student years, the recognition of his singular talent by an influential organizer of the Baghdad State Mosque competition soon after he returned home, and the subsequent media exposure that his success in that effort brought him, are legible in hindsight. So is his selection as the designer of the most prestigious project in his sphere of influence in Riyadh, along with the Aga Khan Award it brought him. These were not the result of coincidence, luck or fate. Ken Yeang, who was also one of the invited participants in the Jabal Omar competition, has described luck as 'the intersection of preparation and opportunity', and Rasem Badran has been preparing for his opportunities since he was five years old. He has described his singular approach to his work by saying:

My work has been characterized by a continuous dialectic between notions of contextualism on the one hand and poetics of a sense of place on the other. In certain instances, one has dominated over the other, depending on the temporal and spatial conditions or the specific requirements of the projects I have dealt with over the years. This dialectic analysis of hidden realities has evolved, shifting from a focus on reading the clear and the obvious, to my current concentration on finding the hidden, destroyed or subjugated reality behind context.

As far as Islamic architecture is concerned I can say with confidence that I have adopted an Islamic approach...I do not see history as having a fixed, specific label entitled 'Islamic architecture', but rather see it as something changeable that accommodates the needs of the contemporary community. It is a process that represents a freedom from any form of confinement or constraint; returning to the balance of basic, natural instinct.

This page and opposite
Al-Yarmouk University, Irbid, Jordan. Until recently, there has been little opportunity for projects by Badran to be built in Amman, for various reasons which are now changing. This project, completed in 2002, converted the conventional library framework into an urban city-like event.

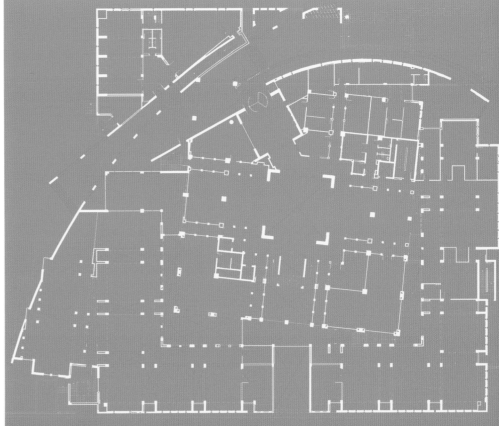

3 | Houses and Housing

Opposite

Layering is a timeless technique in a part of the world given to wide cultural and environmental variations. Prince Assem's residence, Amman, Jordan.

Badran's first residential design, for the Khouri family in 1972, relects his early awareness of the issue of privacy and the changing behaviour of people, which has historically been central to Islamic architecture. The refinement of this idea would dominate more than a dozen homes he designed over the next decade after arriving back in Jordan. The Khouri residence is modest and barely visible from the street. It is built of the rough local limestone from which most of Amman seems to be made, and so seamlessly blends in with its surroundings.

Freedom from constraints

As the capital of Jordan, Amman lacks the significant historical context of other larger cities in the region, such as Jerusalem, Damascus or Cairo. This was an advantage for Badran in many ways, because it allowed him more latitude and also forced him to look elsewhere to satisfy his interest in relevant design elements with which he could work. The first of these, which he uses consistently in the early houses, is the *maqaz* or L-shaped, indirect entrance which prevents a direct view into the house from the street. He starts by updating this, straightening out the 'L' into a diagonal that leads into a small central hall. In the Al-Sa'ed house in 1974, Badran replaced the rough stone of the Khouri house with concrete, but continued his translation of the *maqaz*. Stone appears again in the Madi residence (also of 1974), an appropriate choice of material because the triangular roofs that the architect uses skilfully create the illusion that the house is growing out of the ground.

The anti-grid order

The Khouri and Madi residences, as well as the Handal villa, begun in 1974, all present a diagonal *maqaz* and a shifted grid-like module, the first evidence of the complicated cultural layering of East and West that lies behind Badran's approach. He is often viewed, or inaccurately labelled, as a strict traditionalist, but he denies such categorization and defies simplistic description. The rationalistic influence of his years as a student in Germany is evident from the start and becomes increasingly so in the orthogonal ordering systems he employs, in his emphasis on typologies, in his fascination with technology and its basis in tradition, which is all part of the dialectic described in detail in Chapter 2.

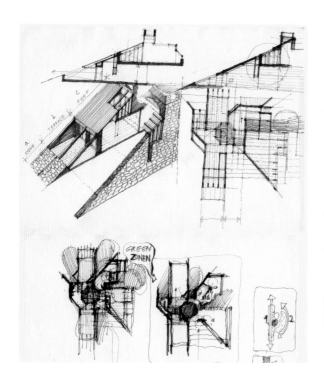

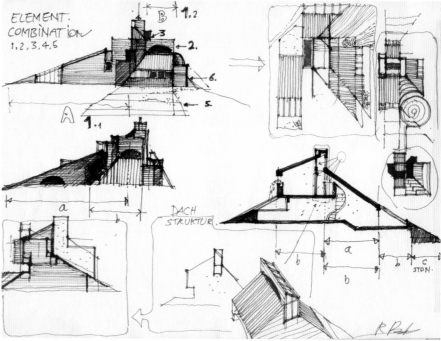

Above and left

Madi Residence, Amman, Jordan. The first work that was available to the young architect in Amman, as is usually the case elsewhere, was residential design. In these early attempts, the wish to update traditional forms, while still using local materials, is clearly visible, with the interiors combining the old and the new.

The drawing above left illustrates the impact of the local environment and inherited culture in defining the spatial elements of the living enclosure: the metaphor of the tent as skin, the cosmic space (the traditional courtyard), the ecological balance and the internal garden (paradise). Above right: transforming a cultural understanding into a physical statement (three-dimensionality).

Right and below right

Low-income, multi-family
housing scheme, Amman, Jordan.
In addition to the arcade,
the courtyard is also a venerable
design approach throughout
hot arid regions because,
when combined with vegetation,
it provides cool breezes that
can be directed indoors.
The courtyard also allows for
privacy, which is an important
requirement in Islamic culture.

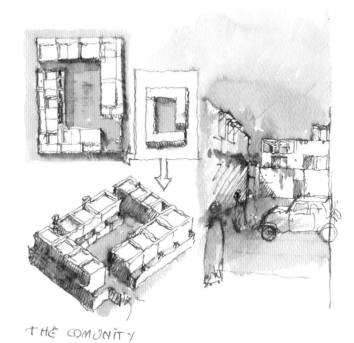

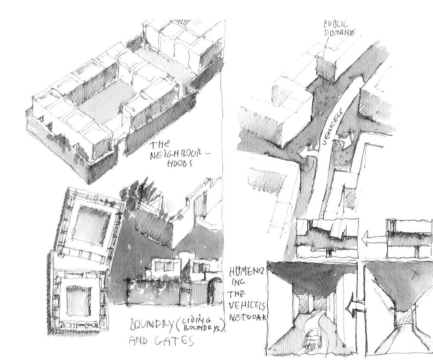

A system that Badran refers to as an 'anti-grid order', which is clearly visible in his early residential designs, was also the central organizing device of his award-winning and life-changing design of the Baghdad State Mosque, and much of the other work in the first phase of his career. The overlay of influence is obvious in his houses, in the way in which he cleverly uses the geometric system of the shifted grid to allow entrances, courtyards, gardens, ventilation and views to soften his Modernist framework.

A turning point

By the beginning of the 1980s this 'softening' had reached a stage in the residences of 1983 to 1985 in which the traditional typologies such as the *maqaz* and the courtyard, begin to expand, proliferate and become living spaces in their own right, acting as multiple buffers between the public and private zones in each house. The entry axis, which introduces this sequence of spaces, also begins to shift in a way that recalls the entrances of older mosques in a dense urban fabric, such as those in medieval Cairo.

This concept of the house as a mosque expands on the frequently expressed notion of the house as a small city, transferring it from a secular comparison to an implied spiritual responsibility, expressed in less form and more space. The change of the decade between 1979 and 1980, was also important for Badran in terms of his involvement in low-income, multi-family housing. Rather than having relatively free rein, as he had done in designing residences for individual clients, he was now introduced to the restrictions that are typically enforced by

Above and opposite

The Jordan Cement Factory
Employees Housing built in
Fuhais, near Amman, Jordan.
This project, completed in
1985, required the architect to
overcome severe programmatic
and budgetary restrictions,
which are not evident in the
final expression.

institutions. He nevertheless managed to transcend them in the Jordan Cement Factory Employees Housing in Fuhais near Amman, in 1983, an example of the large-scale use of concrete and rectilinear forms by an architect who is supposedly a strict traditionalist. In this scheme Badran was encouraged to choose concrete by the client who manufactured it. This complex is rendered less monumental through clustering, in ways that are reminiscent of the studies Badran had carried out in Jerusalem ten years earlier. The modular units in this case are terraced on a slight slope, creating covered pedestrian 'streets' and meeting places beneath the units, with cars mostly restricted to the periphery of the complex. Private balconies contribute to the overall image of a Greek island or a traditional Mediterranean village on the hills above the Amalfi coast.

The Jordan Cement Factory Employees Housing project represents an unfinished morphology that allows the inhabitants to define their own surroundings through their personal additions, creating a more celebrative form and one that evolves over time.

26/9/84

CAIRO
CITADEL OF.
SALAH ED DIN

SULTAN HASAN COLLEGE MADRASA
MOSQUE CAIRO TYP.

SULTAN
GHARI
MADRASA.
CAIRO

WALLS.!!

The Al-Beit Foundation

In 1985 Rasem Badran won a competition to design the Al-Beit Foundation on a hilly site near Amman, for an institution dedicated to the dissemination of Islamic culture. He skilfully accommodated a complex programme that included a library, media centre, press headquarters and housing zone, strung out along a curving humpbacked ridge.

The organization of the Foundation is remarkably similar to that used in the private houses he designed between 1973 and 1985, in his application of an ordering system, a shifted grid-like framework, intersected by a diagonal entrance axis, which introduces people into the building from the side. There is also the separation of public and private zones, which are divided by an open courtyard, like those found in all of his early house designs.

The entry at the Al-Beit Foundation acts as a knuckle that allows the private zone and the housing attached to it to be separated from the library, located in the middle of the tripartite, segmented scheme. It also facilitates a turn in the library so that it can remain aligned with the ridge on which this fortress-like complex sits. The press section, which is the last of the three parts, is similarly articulated for the same reason.

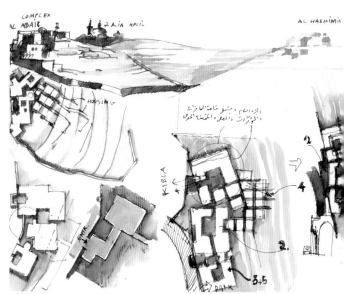

Above and opposite

The debt that the final design for the Al-Beit Foundation in Amman owes to the composition of the *madresa* of the Mosque of Sultan Hasan Mosque of Mohammad Ali, the Citadel in Cairo and the Mosque of Mohammad Ali is evident when comparing them to Badran's design.

Opposite above: the historical references show the rich variety of architectural urban elements.

Opposite below: the power of the site's physical and environmental constrains formulates the geometric order of the overall concept.

The public zone with its housing component, and the library each possess a central courtyard; the library courtyard features an *iwan*, an ancillary space, on each side. This is an obvious reference to the Sultan Hasan Mosque in Cairo, which is also a *madresa* or religious school. The preparatory research and sketches of the Al-Beit Foundation indicate the first extensive exploration of such references, which were soon to become the mainstay of Badran's approach. His far-reaching scan is impressive because it demonstrates a thorough knowledge of the history of Islamic architecture and a willingness to consider all of it as relevant for this project.

The final image of this research institution with its diverse mixture of administrative offices, lecture halls, exhibition halls, computer rooms, multimedia facilities, library, housing and mosque could have been monumental and impersonal, but Badran has managed to give it an individual identity and render it less imposing. His sketches of Cairo are instructive of his intentions. One in particular, of the Mosque of Mohammad Ali and the Citadel grouped with the Sultan Hasan Mosque, obviously inspired his clustering of elements along the ridge, since he also uses the small dome and minaret of the mosque as a visual anchor at the highest part of the slope.

Watercolour rendering of the
Wadi Saleh Housing project,
showing the urban mountainous
clusters of the living quarters.
The level of detail of which
Rasem Badran is capable in his
sketches is impressive, especially
considering the fact that he
works so quickly and does not
use overlays.

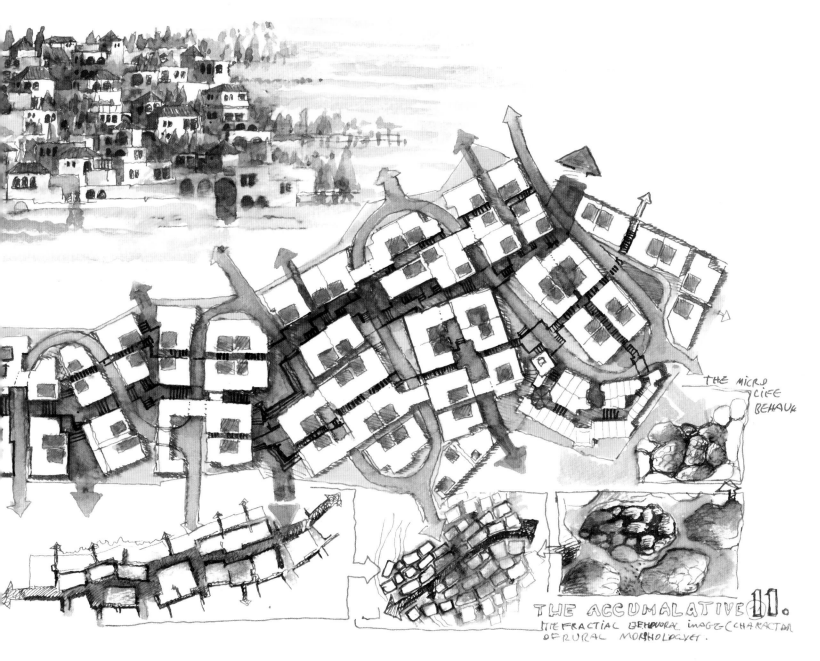

THE MICRO CLIFF BEHAV.

THE ACCUMALATIVE **11.**
THE FRACTIAL BEHAVURAL IMAGE CCHARACTER
OF RURAL MORPHOLOGY ET.

Above

Wadi Saleh Housing Project, watercolour rendering in plan view. The rural culture defines the urban issue. Badran's zoning provides privacy while still maintaining social continuity and integration – a difficult balance to achieve.

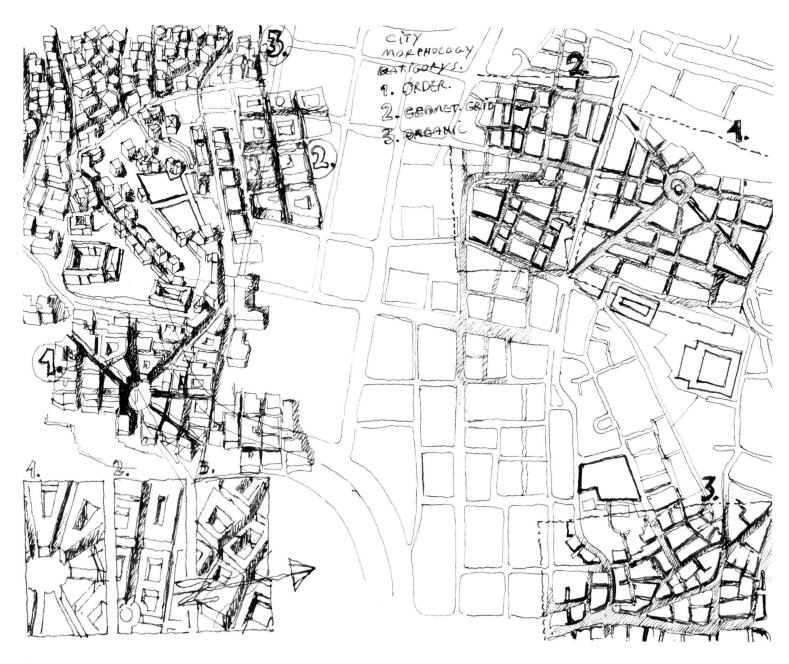

From the general to the specific

After Al-Beit and the Baghdad State Mosque competition Badran's references become less general, relating more specifically to a particular region or context. This is clear in his housing project in the historic core of Sana'a, Yemen (discussed in detail in Chapter 7), which focuses on Badran's planning efforts. This specificity is even more concentrated, in his studies for the Wadi Abu Jamil district in Beirut, (begun as part of the restoration effort in that city in the late 1990s), in which the façade of some of the units consists of series of stacked balconies overlooking the street, once typical of the houses in this area. Badran introduces a 'multi-skin morphology', an accumulation of wall elements, and organizes them in three different categories which he terms 'the functional mass' (the living cluster), the social skin (the balconies) and the cosmological skin (curtains).

Above

Drawings for the Wadi Abu Jamil Housing project in Beirut. Diagrams often include notations that reveal intent, as the historical reservoir of the city's layers and its morphology do here.

Opposite

The site as a collective memory of the city's layers. Various urban conditions are described in three-dimensional studies that indicate spatial experiences and landmarks.

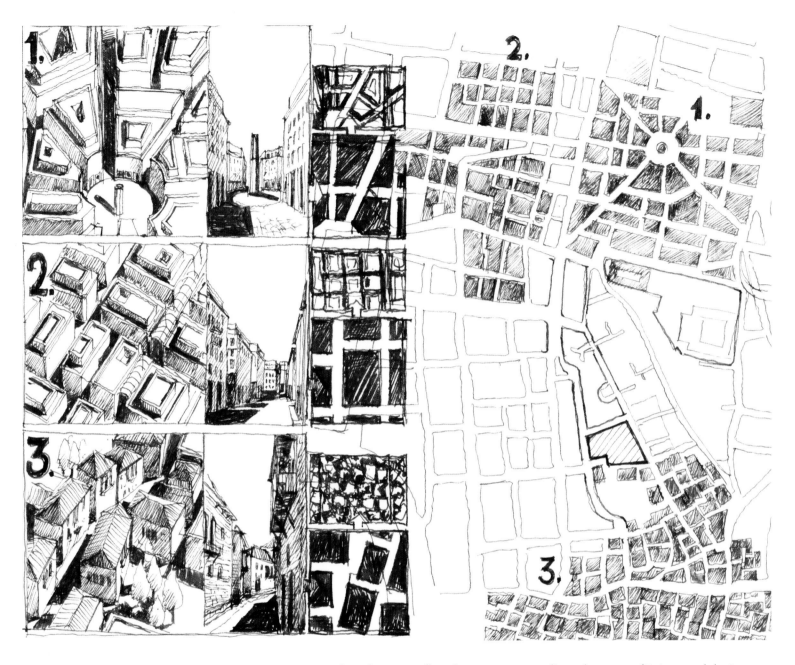

These features reflect the more cosmopolitan character of Beirut, and the interaction that takes place between residents and people in the street. Interior spaces, however, continue the tradition of the different kinds of courtyards and pedestrian pathways that connect the internal areas with the surrounding network. Badran refines them in a series of options that each have clear precedents in this area. Tower blocks are clustered around a park-like central courtyard, separated from the street by gates, which have now become an effective part of Badran's design vocabulary. This project was sponsored by the Solidere organization. Solidere is responsible for the reconstruction of central Beirut and promotes a sensitive contextual approach within the existing city fabric. This high level of contextuality can also be noticed, not only in macro scale but also in micro scale, in other private residences designed by Badran in the area.

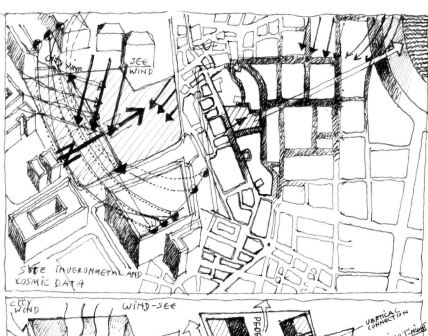

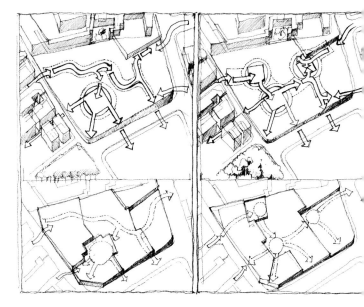

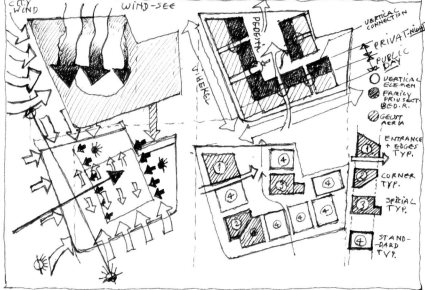

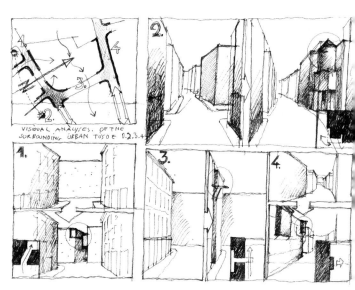

Above and right

Drawings for the Wadi Abu Jamil Housing project in Beirut, Lebanon, showing the physical and metaphysical constraints of the site. Sequencing and environmental factors are both important factors in the establishment of pedestrian and vehicular pathways.

Intersections received special attention because they offer the best opportunity for orientation and place-making in addition to forecasting the future development of the surrounding urban network (contextualism).

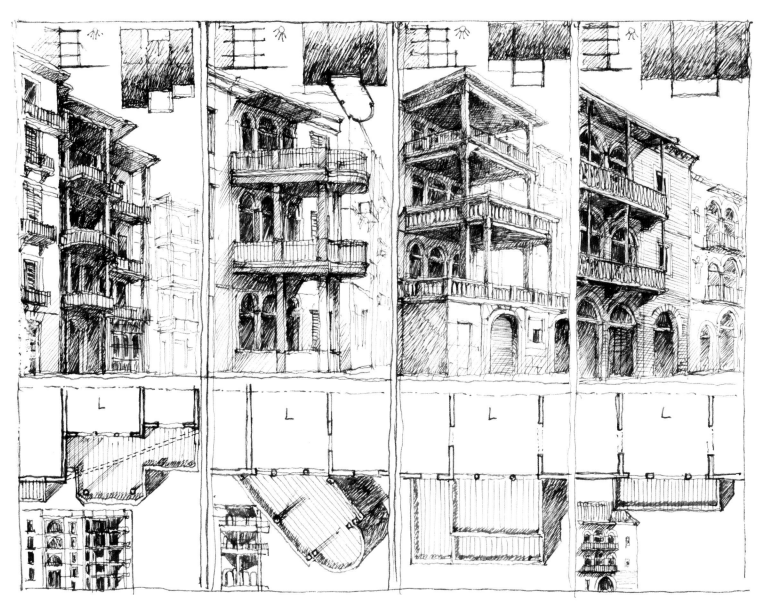

Above

Drawings for the Wadi Abu Jamil Housing project in Beirut, Lebanon. Various balcony types recall the typologies found in these neighbourhoods before they were destroyed. They bear witness to the extrovert social behaviour of Beirut's citizens.

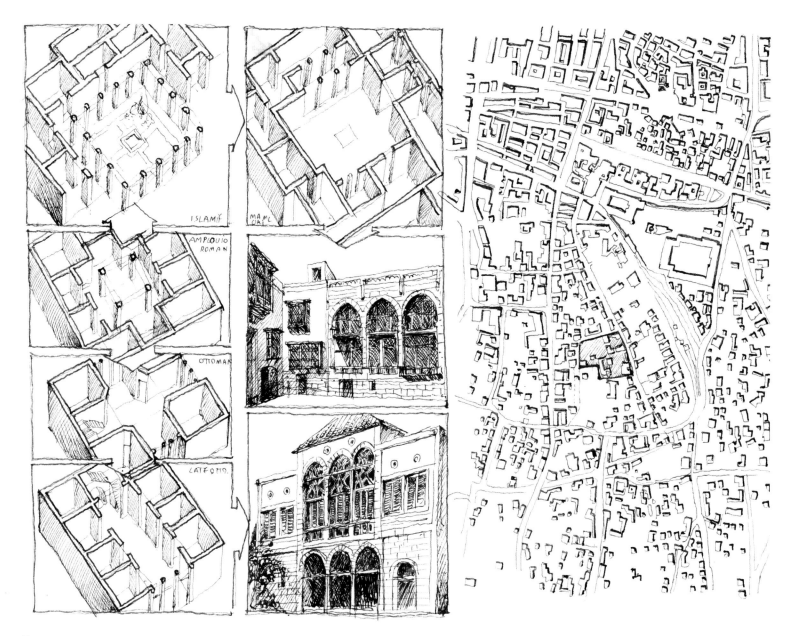

Labels on drawings:
ISLAMIC
MAML
AMPLOUIO ROMAN
OTTOMAN
LATEOMO.

Above

An understanding of the
morphology of traditional façades
and living spaces was essential
in order to apply a contemporary
living model that would relate
to Beirut's coastal culture,
a culture which differs from
its inland counterpart.

Above

Drawing for the Wadi Abu
Jamil Housing project
in Beirut, Lebanon.
Re-creating the previous
conditions found in various parts
of the city being reconstructed
without pastiche requires
great sensitivity.

Right

Drawing for the Wadi Abu
Jamil Housing project in Beirut,
Lebanon. The projected staircase
typpology. The variety of vertical
element configurations
encountered in the traditional city
calls for an equally inventive
approach when they are to be
replaced with new construction.

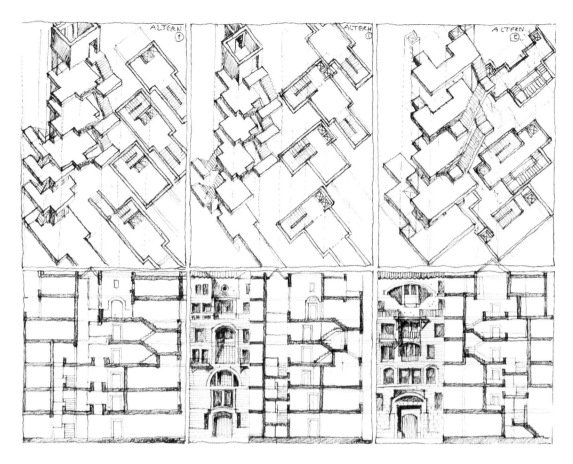

Right

Drawings for the Wadi Abu
Jamil Housing project in Beirut,
Lebanon. To provide such variety
necessitates a great deal of
research into local conditions in
the past, and knowledge of the
particular history of a place and
its powerful impact on the
inhabitants' memory. Shown here
is the staircase morphology as a
social node.

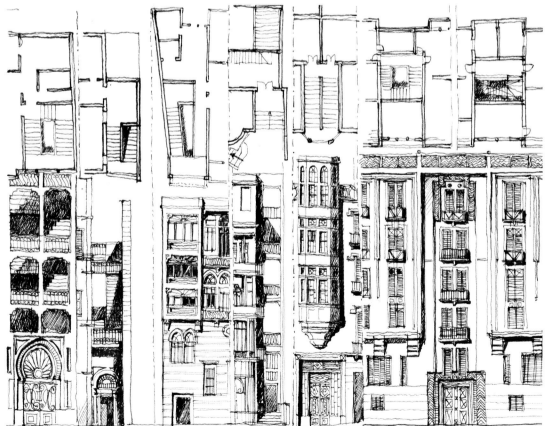

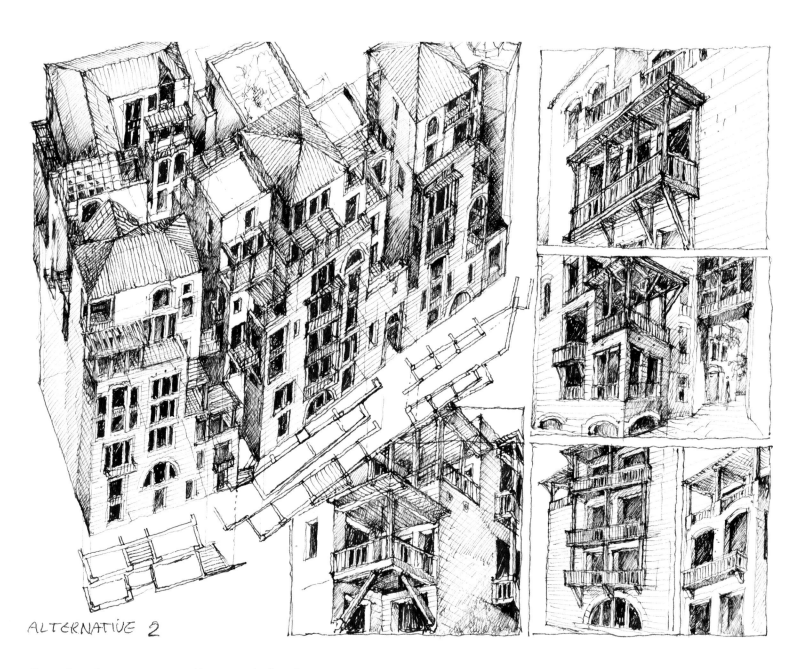

ALTERNATIVE 2

Above and opposite
Wadi Abu Jamil Housing
project in Beirut, Lebanon.
The overall image of the project.
Placing balconies on the street
as part of what is called the
penetrated walled skin is unique
to this context, and enlivens the
urban experience. Various kinds of
braces and bracket supports
enrich the visual expression of
the balconies, which can
be considered a changing,
living skin.

ALTERNATIVE
1.

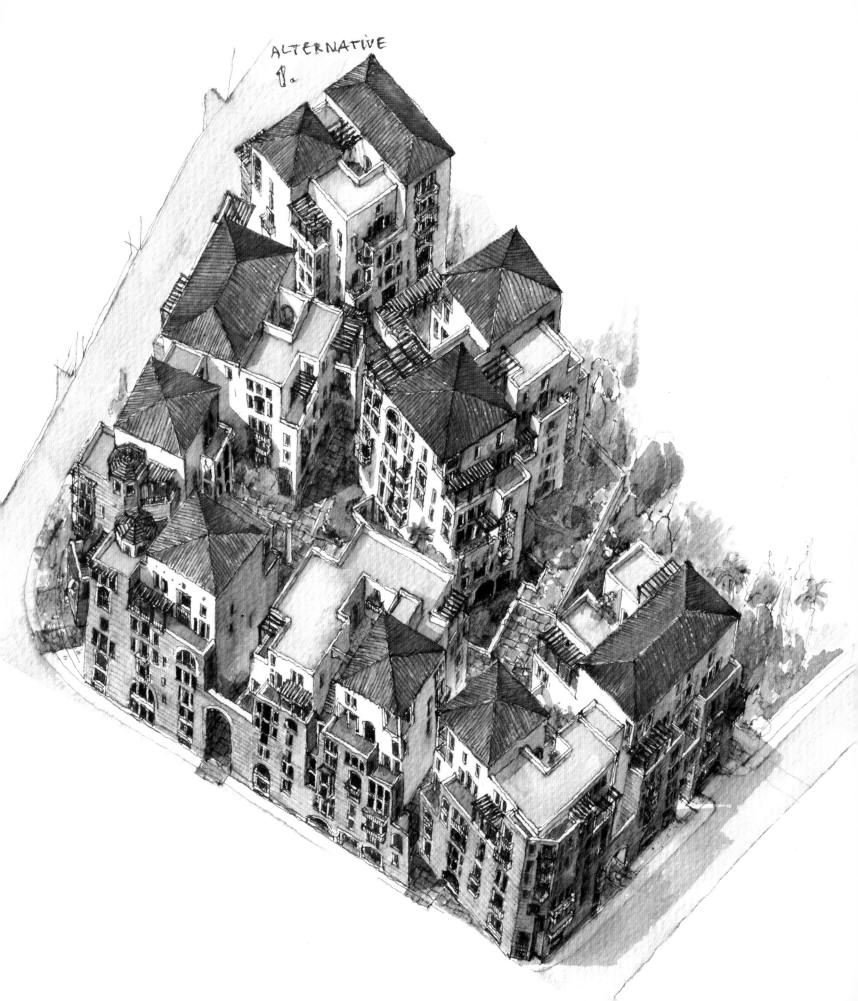

Left and below
Wadi Saleh Housing Project, Beirut,
Lebanon. Badran enthusiastically
accepts the challenge of interior
design, believing that architecture is
a continuity without distractions.
Even the streetscape (bottom left),
which could be incorrectly labelled
simply as 'external' space, requires
a comprehensive vision of internal
and external spaces.

The results of Badran's Beirut studies provide a valuable reinterpretation of past conditions through the cumulative multi-layer skin methodology.

Left and below

The Wadi Hanifah, near Riyadh,
is a unique environment and this
residence was designed closely to
integrate into it. A series of bridge-like
interventions tie the valley and the house
together, benefiting from being attached
to an old city defence wall, which has
influenced the overall morphology. VIP
Rest House, Saudi Arabia.

1. RESPONCE TO NATURAL CONSTRAINS

2. ENRICHING THE NATURAL CONSTRAINS

3. THE LIVING NATURE BY RESPONDING TO ITS CONSTRAIN

NATURAL CONSTRAINS ECOLOGY   MAN-INTERACTION - ARCH. ELEMENT RESPONDIN THE NATURA   THE MORPHOLOGICAL COMP.

Bridging the Wadi Hanifah

Two private residences, in Saudi Arabia and Jordan respectively, bring the story
of Badran's efforts in designing house and housing design around an invented
narrative. The first of these projects, intended for a member of an important
family in Saudi Arabia, is set out along a ridge overlooking the lush valley of the
Wadi Hanifah, near Riyadh, the ancestral family home. This closes one cycle of
residential design because the house is topographically and typologically place-
specific, and has a clear relationship to the historical village of Darriyah nearby.
The references here are very finely tuned to the client and the location.

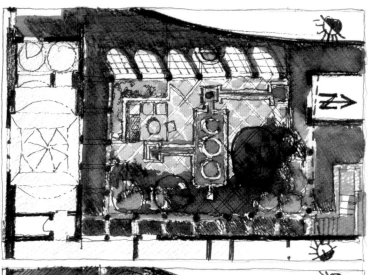
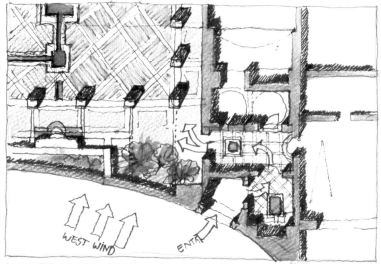
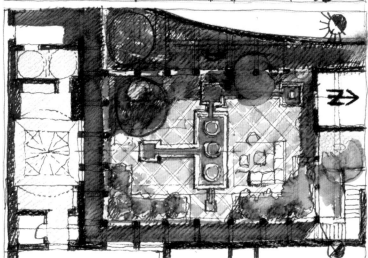

Above and right

Al-Talhouni residence,
Amman, Jordan.
The orientation of each courtyard
must be carefully adjusted to
permit maximum airflow, with
sectional proportions adjusted
accordingly. The carved water
fountains (right), designed by
Rasem Badran's late father, Jamel
Badran, serve an environmental
purpose as well, cooling the air.

The second residence, for the Al-Talhouni family near Amman, bears symbolic significance, as the family had originally approached the well-known Egyptian architect Hassan Fathy to design a rest house in the Jordan Valley, based on traditional mudbrick technology, just before Fathy died. This wish underscores their desire for a second stone home in Amman, rooted in this tradition, the dialogue between mud and stone, soft and hard. Badran's approach involves the remodelling of their existing house and an addition to contain a reception hall or *majlis*, a dining room and a kitchen and service area. This addition, or *diwaniyah*, is configured to create a protected courtyard, filled with lush vegetation and water features on a patterned paved floor. All the windows of the remodelled house and

Opposite

The beauty of nature and the art of reflection (water).

Above

Badran frequently uses local materials, such as stone, to provide continuity between his architecture and its site. This reveals his understanding of the local environmental constraints and specificity. Al-Rahji house, Riyadh, Saudi Arabia.

Above right

The stone culture of the hilly of Amman lends itself to a powerful interplay of shades and shadows. Al Sa'ed residence, Amman, Jordan.

addition that face the court are covered with *mashrabiya* screens for privacy. The courtyard acts as a natural exterior extension of the *diwaniyah* and is usable most of the year.

The houses and housing described here represent most, but not all, of Badran's work in this category and are logical extensions of his early interest in this area, which dates from his student days in Germany. His area of concentration spans the developing and the developed world, both of which are undergoing rapid growth, especially in urban areas. Unlike most architects who either focus exclusively on housing or residences, he continues to include these in his broader agenda, as part of his total cultural contribution.

4 | The Fourth Dimension is the Spirit

The mosque is unquestionably the most important building in Muslim society, representing shared principles regardless of cultural conditions or nationality; it offers a lodestone of identity in a diverse world. Historically, it has never been an isolated monument but has been tightly knit into the urban fabric, occurring at predictable intervals throughout the city. Nezar al-Sayyad, in his doctoral dissertation on medieval Cairo, has shown that this interval was determined by the reach of the muezzin's voice, since the call to prayer was made from the top of a minaret; a community using a particular mosque was defined by the circumference of that sound. This meant that minarets, as the vertical markers of these mosques, were not positioned randomly, or for aesthetic reasons alone, but for the functional purpose of projecting the human voice. This became clear to me one unforgettable morning when I visited Abha in the western part of Saudi Arabia for the first time. I was standing at the top of one of the mountains that encircle the city, just as the call to prayer started at dawn. Because of the individual timing of each muezzin, it did not begin in unison and the style of each prayer call was distinctly recognizable. As other muezzins joined the chorus, the echo began to swell, until it seemed to be one multi-layered sound.

The most important part of a city

The mosque is integral to the Islamic city and the first among the four main building types that define it, including the market or *suq*, which is typically attached to the mosque's domain, the palace and the house. There are several kinds of mosques, but the most visible is the *Jumah*, congregational or Friday mosque, which may be compared to the cathedral in Christian societies. Since the beginning of the Islamic faith, the *Jumah* mosque has been an urban phenomenon and landmark, tightly knit into a compacted city fabric. Unlike the cathedral, however, it rarely had a *parvis* or public open space in front of it, and instead more commonly featured a large courtyard inside. For this reason the great *Jumah* mosques of the past are barely visible from a distance in the city, and only their distinctive minarets identify their location, as is the case with the Al-Qarawiyin Mosque in Fez, Morocco. In the beginning of the faith, there was no stylistic prescription for this building type except for the minaret, which was necessary for the call to prayer. But conventions and traditions began to emerge to refine the central courtyard typology, which was a direct extension of the form of the House of the Prophet. This house was also the first mosque, to be used as a place of prayer.

Semiotics

Tracing these building traditions is a fascinating exercise in the power of semiotics in architecture and the way in which certain forms, which begin as predilections, become prescribed or mandatory. The minaret is the most obvious example of this subtle shift. Once a functional necessity, it was eventually made redundant by the loudspeakers more frequently used today. However, the minaret continues to be an obligatory formal requirement because of its symbolic value. The reason behind this significance has been a source of debate among historians. One of the most compelling arguments is that the form began as a light tower, erected to guide the *Hajji's* (pilgrims) from place to place. The Arabic word for tower is *manara*, which was eventually corrupted into minaret.

The dome, which now also seems to have become an obligatory formal requirement for any mosque, was not initially a necessary part of the building type either. There is a relatively small dome over the *qibla* wall of the Prophet's Mosque in Madinah, however, which provides a persuasive historical image; Turkish congregational mosques, built after the fall of Constantinople in 1453, generally display domes similar to that covering the Hagia Sophia. It was arguably a powerful influence on Ottoman architects, such as Sinan (1489–1588), who concentrated on designing this building type. What began as an aesthetic option has now become an unspoken social requirement based on the cumulative authority of historical example, as well as the semiotic power of a selected number of the most influential forms.

The mosque in the urban fabric

The *Jumah* mosque is the most visible and historically significant variant of this building type, but it is not the only one. As the distinguished Turkish historian Dogan Kuban commented:

From a purely religious and spiritual point of view, it remains the insignificant masjids, *with their simple* minbars *and* mihrabs, *which are more intimately related to the devotional practice of the common people. The great mosques with eminent forms are symbols of their time, more important for their cultural and aesthetic experience, but I cannot accept them as pure expressions of the faith.*[1]

Whether large or small, each mosque is generally part of the cityscape. The *Jumah* mosque in particular was usually surrounded by the *suq*, made up of narrow streets or walkways with commercial stalls on either side, which may have been built against the outer wall of the mosque itself. Whereas commercial activity may have been confined to the cathedral *parvis* in the past, because of the feeling that it would defile the sacred precinct, no such prohibitive sensibility seems to exist in relation to the mosque, allowing it to be tightly woven into the fabric of daily life. This proximity, however, did prompt the development of a transitional zone called the *ziyada* to define movement from the secular to the sacred world. One of the best examples of this transition exists in the Mosque of Ahmad ibn Tulun in Cairo, though there are apocryphal accounts of the horses of the ruler and his retinue being tied up there while they prayed inside.

The palace of the ruler, as the third of the four most predominant buildings after the mosque and the *suq*, was usually located at a distance from each to separate secular from spiritual authority and to ensure security. In Fatimid Cairo the palace was erected inside the walled enclave, near the Beit Al-Kadi, or courthouse, to underscore the authority it symbolized. In Istanbul the Topkapi Palace is also situated at a relative distance from the Hagia Sophia (which Mehmet converted into a mosque) and the Blue Mosque close by, to maintain the difference between the secular and sacred realms. It could be argued that Mehmet wanted to take advantage of the view from the Serai Burnu Palace, and to appropriate the authority of this location, where the palace of the first Greek founder of the city once stood, as well as the palace of Constantine himself. But the argument for the separation of sacred and secular realms is more convincing.

Houses, the fourth predominant building type in the Islamic city, vary tremendously depending on income level. Cairo offers a good range of examples, since houses of medieval vintage run the gamut from the *rab*, which consists of many small connected units surrounding a court, to the *manzils*, or mansions of the rich, which were usually multi-storeyed and had several courtyards, as well as servants' quarters on the ground floor.

Neighbourhoods, called *harat*, constituted the social framework into which these building blocks of the city were organized, based on family, clan, ethnic or trade relationships.[2]

The smaller neighbourhood mosque or *zawiya* remains the core of this urban unit. As the distinguished scholar Ismail Serageldin has described it:

As the city grew, the organization of the neighbourhoods meant that the local mosques, as distinct from the Friday congregational mosques, played a major role in identifying the community and giving it a focal point. Indeed, within this urban context different types of mosques emerged. These ranged from the massive state mosques used for Friday congregational prayer to the tiny zawiyas. All were integrated into the townscape and many were associated with community functions such as schools and charities.[3]

Basic elements

Some regional variations to the mosque exist, but the basic parts are now relatively well established. These are, firstly, a prayer hall in which the worshippers face Makkah. The direction of prayer (*qibla*) is indicated by the *mihrab*, a niche built into a wall indicating the direction of Makkah. If the prayer hall is covered it is referred to as a *haram*, if it is open, a *sahn*. There is a raised platform or pulpit (*minbar*) from which an imam leads prayers and delivers an oration, or *khutba* to the worshippers. The prayer hall can be surrounded by an arcade (*riwaq*) and in this case the colonnade facing Makkah is called the *riwaq al-qibla* and is usually larger than the others. Sometimes there are vaulted squares or rectangular spaces open on one side which face into an open courtyard. There is a requirement to perform an ablution (*wudu*), to wash before prayer at the mosque, and the place to do this is the *wodo*. In many older mosques, the *wodo* was a fountain in the middle of the *sahn*. Whether or not the muezzin actually gives the call to prayer (*adhan*) today or it is merely a recording over a loudspeaker, a minaret is usually featured just the same.

A simple beginning

The development of the mosque has been fairly simple. The House of the Prophet in Madinah was located within an irregularly shaped fenced compound, forming a courtyard for prayer. This constitutes the birth of the first mosque in Islam. It represents a physical, democratic model that allowed interaction between the leader and his people. Even the Prophet's wives could listen to the deliberations and discussions in the mosque because the Prophet's living quarters were attached to the mosque. A low platform, which was the first *minbar*, allowed the Prophet to address the congregation. As Serageldin explains:

This simple design did not ascribe any complicated mystical significance to the structure or the layout, and underlined the simplicity of the radical monotheism of Islam, where the bond between God the Creator and his submissive subjects is direct, without intermediation. Thus any space is suitable, provided that it is clean and functional.

As Islam began to grow and spread under the Umayyad dynasty (AD 661–750), the mosque became more formalized. The Great Mosque of Damascus, which was built on the foundation of the Roman Temple of Jupiter, demonstrates the use of new elements prompted by the growing stature and power of the faith. It has a rectangular plan, divided on the long axis into a covered prayer hall and open court, with an ablution fountain in the centre of the *sahn*. It has four *riwaqs*, the *riwaq al-qibla* being the deepest. There is a small dome just above and in front of the *qibla* and a tall minaret. Tradition holds that the *maqsura* (a privileged enclosure near the *mihrab*) was also introduced at this time by the first Umayyad caliph, Mu'awiya.

Mosque design did not change too dramatically under Abbasid rule (AD 750–1258) but several innovations in the minaret form emerged at this time, as in the Great Mosque at Samarra and the Mosque of Ahmad ibn Tulun in Cairo, which was influenced by it. The spiral stairway around the huge minaret that forms the centrepiece of the mosque at Samarra, built between AD 842 and 852, is believed by some to recall the Tower of Babel.

The next stage of development occurred under the Mamluks in Cairo, most notably in the use of the *iwan*. The Mosque of Sultan Hasan near the Citadel has four of them aligned on a cardinal axis, with the open ends facing into a central courtyard (AD 1356–62). This development also coincided with the emergence of the *madresa*, or religious school, throughout the Islamic world, especially in the Middle East and North Africa.

The dome is a relatively recent addition to this evolving formal vocabulary, and it was not established on a large scale until the 16th century, at the height of Ottoman power. Sinan, who is primarily responsible for the evolution that saw almost the entire prayer hall of the Selimye Mosque in Edirne covered with a dome, also expanded the number of minarets to two or more and made their profile thinner and sharper.

The contemporary mosque: the big debate

In spite of this straightforward evolution, there is a great deal of debate today about the proper form of the contemporary mosque. In Malaysia, for example, a large *Jumah* mosque at the centre of the new capital city of Putrajaya, defines the

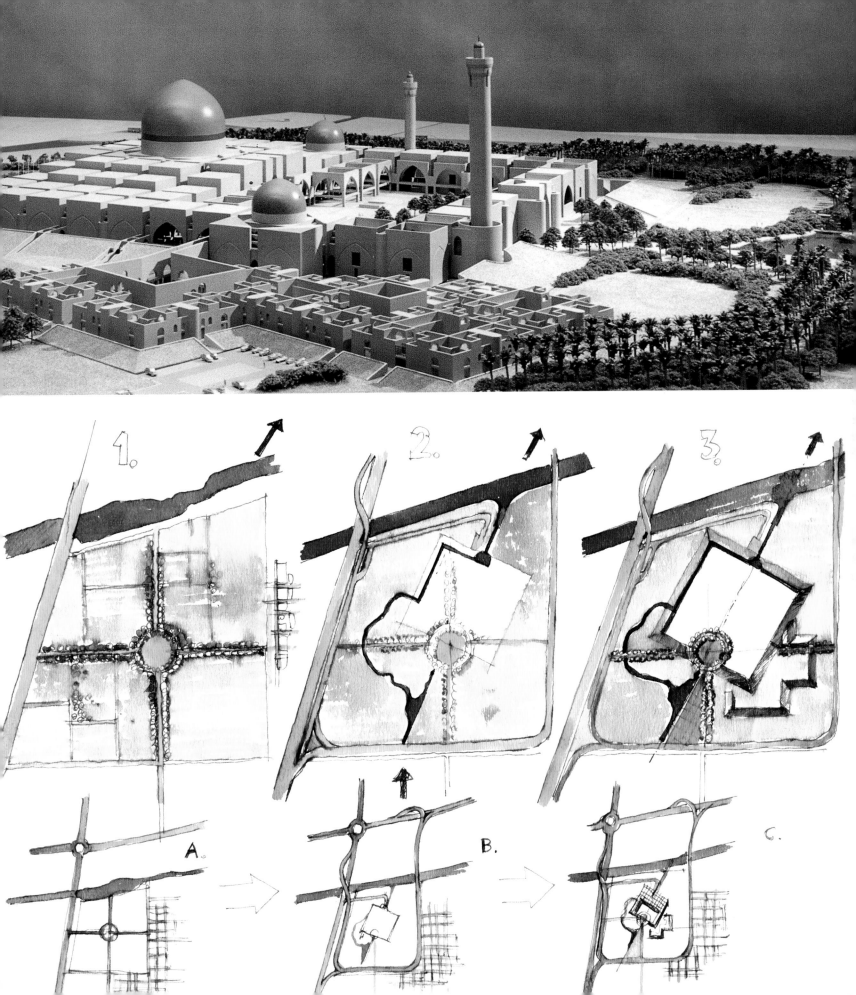

1.   2.   3.

A.   B.   C.

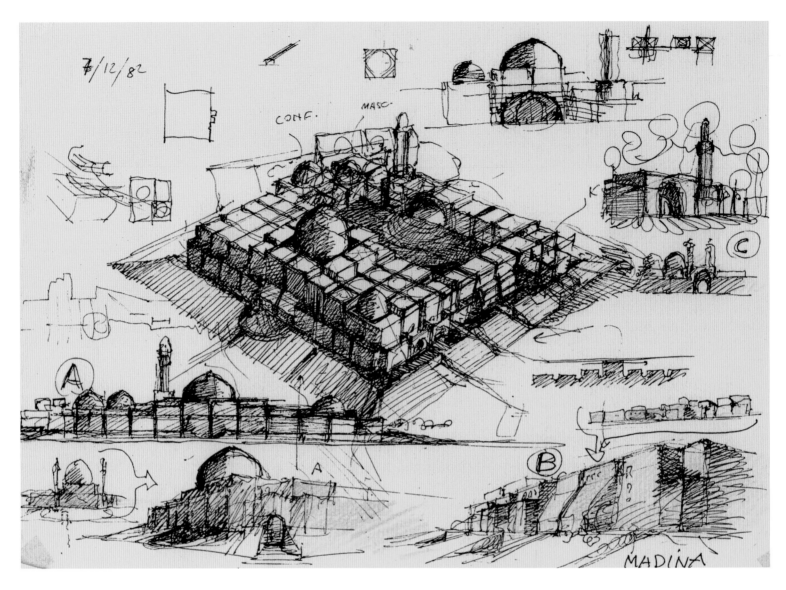

issues. It has a large dome and several minarets in addition to a paved *sahn* surrounding the covered prayer hall. Since the innovative State Mosque (Masjid Negara) in Kuala Lumpur was built in the early 1960s without a dome, few examples exist of mosques that have followed suit. The debate is joined on one side by those who believe that a mosque should have a prescribed set of parts, and on the other by those calling for innovation. This polarization between what many mistakenly call 'tradition' and 'modernity', precludes another fertile area of research, which Rasem Badran has been exploring.

The Baghdad State Mosque: a major turning point

As previously mentioned, the early houses by Badran that received media coverage brought him to the attention of the Iraqi architect Rifaat Chadirji, who is well known throughout the region and was one of the organizers of the competition to design a state mosque in Baghdad. Chadirji invited Badran to enter the competition, which included other internationally known offices. The Iraqi government, in this instance, was represented by the municipality of Baghdad, which had developed a programme for a large landmark intended to demonstrate the technological achievements of the nation. The programme requirements called for a mosque with an area of 30,000 square metres, to accommodate one worshipper per square metre. These 30,000 worshippers were to be sheltered in a covered prayer hall, with an additional 20,000 worshippers allocated to an open courtyard. Other functions, such as a *madresa* and a library, were included, as well as a residence for the imam, accommodation for those working at the mosque and reception facilities for VIPs.

Establishing a pattern

Working in a way that he has followed ever since, Badran immersed himself in the history of the nation, but, significantly, did not restrict himself to the Islamic part of its profound chronology. Iraq, along with Egypt, has one of the oldest civilizations in the world. It differs from its counterpart in the Fertile Crescent in the effect that its topography has had on the development of its civilization. Iraq and Egypt were each the product of rivers, but in Iraq, the Tigris and Euphrates were not constrained by a fixed channel like the Nile. After crossing the Hit-Samarra escarpment on their way south from their source in the Taurus mountains, the twin rivers were free to meander across broad, flat mud plains, which created an intricate network of irrigation ditches necessary to transfer water to the fields. Unlike Egypt, this also imposed the requirement for mudbrick in the construction of everything from houses to religious structures, since stone and wood were rare. The flat topography also prompted high monuments, to interrupt the tedium of an unbroken horizon, and the mudbrick platform (such as the one used under the

Right

Baghdad State Mosque. The orientation of the huge mosque complex was determined primarily by the *qibla* direction with the result that integration with other facilities required had to be carefully resolved.

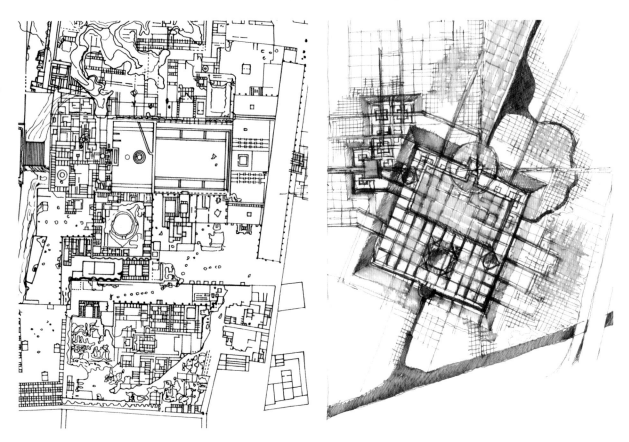

White Temple at Warka) was the first attempt to do just that. Eventually, the platform temple evolved into the much larger scaled ziggurat; the Sumerians strengthened the mudbrick with a bitumen admixture and a different tapered profile to handle the added load.

Baghdad was founded as the Abbasid capital at a time when the locus of power of the growing Islamic empire shifted eastwards out of Arabia, to represent more effectively its expanding constituency. It was a circular city with a gate at each of the four cardinal points, and the mosque and palace of the Abbasid ruler Al-

Above and opposite

Baghdad State Mosque.

The scale of the dome, compared to the rest of the mosque, was a difficult design issue. Too large, and it would overpower the worshippers. Too small, and it

would not balance the rest of the composition.

The sketch oppposite shows the structural support of the dome and the interior clusters of the prayer hall.

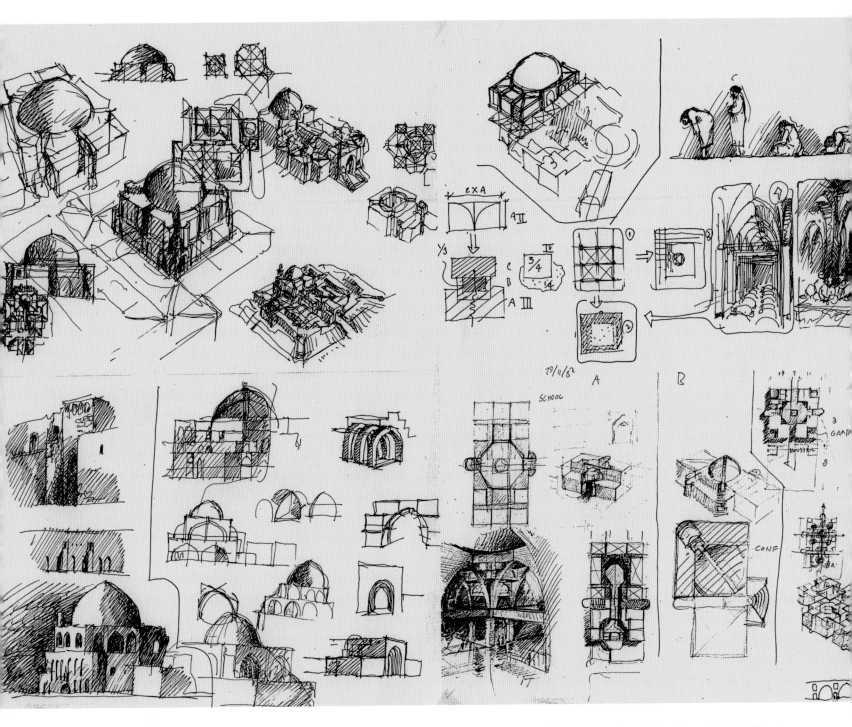

Mansur were situated in the middle. It was also built of mudbrick, like the Mesopotamian monuments before it. The same material was used in the construction of the Great Mosque at Samarra and its famous minaret.

Finding clues

Confronted with an extensive, flat, square site, far away from the centre of Baghdad, Badran looked for clues, or what he terms 'narratives and events', on which to hinge a design concept and fastened on the platform temple, the circular

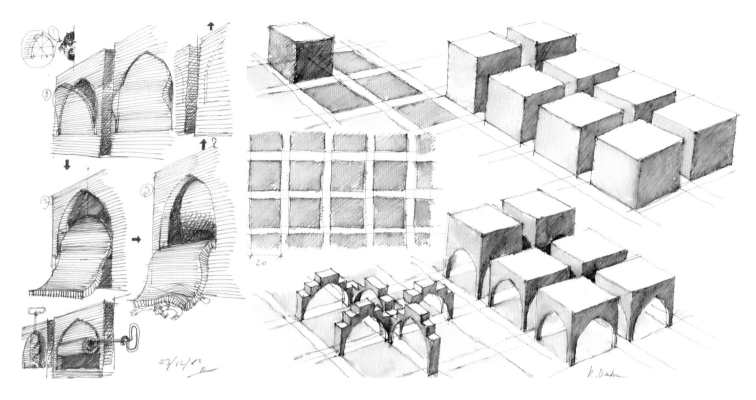

city of Al-Mansur, the Ukhaidir Palace, the Great Mosque at Samarra, the Khan Mirjan, and the ingenious environmental strategies used in old Iraqi houses. He also looked to pan-Islamic examples of mosque design for inspiration, primarily those in the early phases of the faith. From the circular city he derived the inscription of the square implied by the circle, as a linear boundary, as well as the recognition of the cardinal points, with the north predominant. The city itself had a dense fabric of courtyards piercing the residential zone and radial streets.

The Ukhaidir Palace provided more detailed information about a possible architectural vocabulary, since its towers, pointed arches and intricate brickwork are still remarkably intact. The Khan Mirjan, a hotel and storage building in Baghdad, offered valuable lessons about ribs, vaults and beams used as a composite roof system that incorporates devices for natural light penetration and air ventilation. Traditional Iraqi houses showed how convective cooling could be utilized to offset the extreme heat and humidity that is prevalent in this region for most of the year. These houses use courtyards, as do others throughout the Middle East, but they also possess a masonry subterranean chamber with a large trap door that is opened in the evening to allow the cooler, heavier night air to collect inside as the house heats up during the day. This cooler air rises in channels, or ducts, cut into the walls, providing natural air conditioning in each room.

Breaking the structural bays down into spatial units helped to approximate the hypostyle typology and to maintain a human scale, which breaks down the massiveness of the interior.

Interpretation, not literal copying

Badran's initial design sketches for the Baghdad State Mosque reveal that these precedents were clearly instructive, but were not adopted literally. His analysis covers a great many historical references from both inside and outside Iraq, which have been selectively distilled in relation to their relevance to this particular design problem. This process is interpretive rather than descriptive, in much the same way as Filippo Brunelleschi's evaluation of Roman monuments, which

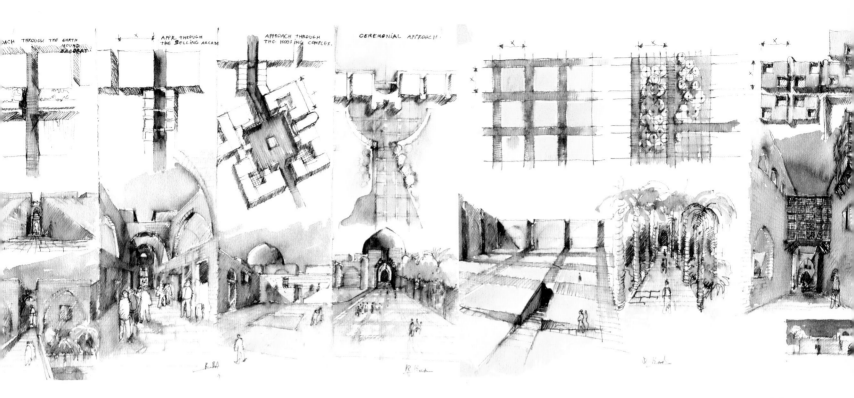

The impact of the geometrical order organizes the physical and the natural elements of the site. Views to and from the proposed scheme were also of particular importance, to ensure it would not be too imposing.

he carried out as a precursor of the Renaissance. His approach, continued by Michelangelo and other Renaissance architects, was to immerse himself in the principles, materials, proportions and details of Classical Roman construction, through on-site surveys, documentation and inspection, before attempting his own interpretation. His reading conveys the spirit of Roman architecture without being a literal description of it.

Rasem Badran achieved a similar transformation in his Baghdad State Mosque design, synthesizing many precedents from Iraqi and a more general Islamic history without specifically describing them, but abstracting and modifying them as necessary to fit the programme and site circumstances.

Strategies to deal with scale

Badran dealt with the dual difficulties presented by the requirement for a monumental state symbol and an anonymous suburban site by adopting several strategies to help him break down the huge scale of the mosque and to provide context where none existed. He began by asking himself how a person would react while standing alone inside such a large enclosure. As his diagrams show, he first created a Warka-like platform as a base for the building. This is counter-intuitive, but it works, since it conceals the main part of the mosque from visitors approaching it and creates a mound, as part of a new, natural context, reminiscent of the ziggurat. A second strategy for reducing scale was to lay a grid over the square footprint of the mosque, which he divided equally into a covered hall and open *sahn*, and then to them extrude that grid into 15-by-15-metre cubes. As he describes this approach:

To counteract the colossal impression that the programme requirements had made me decide to provide an urban texture and character to the project. This approach would also help to make up for the building's isolation. We used the building required for the ancillary functions of the mosque to provide a composition that approximated that of a city. The complex was conceived as an urban cluster, to achieve what I saw as the deconstruction of the monumental.

The cubes, as the literal building blocks of this mosque as a city, were carved away until only sets of stepped interlocking arches remained; this created a contemporary equivalent of the intricate, hypostyle hall of the Great Mosque at Cordoba. This strategy of city making is even more pro-active than it seems. In addition to providing context, it was also intended to guide future growth, as the edge of Baghdad grew out to surround it. This tactic is reminiscent of nationalist intentions, raising the question of Badran's alliance with this school of thought. It is not far-fetched conjecture, considering the impact that his educational experience in Germany had on him, as well as his preference for precedents and typologies. In planning his city, Badran harked back to Al-Mansur's circular model once again. He noted that the mosque and palace were at the centre, and that this *Dar al-Khalifa* was surrounded by layers of ring-like residential and commercial urban fabric connected by radial streets, reflecting the social and political structure of a relationship between the rulers and the people. Inspired by this model, he initially envisioned translating the main programme requirements into layers around a central area occupied by the mosque. The VIP reception space is part of the first layer around the core, which also includes ablution facilities. The second layer incorporates cultural facilities embedded in the ziggurat-like structure or earth mound; the third outer layer, which was liberated from the main geometrical system or shifted grid methodology, was given over to residential use.

Gates and pathways

The gates of Al-Mansur's fabled circular city were surmounted by golden-domed viewing platforms which looked out towards the focal points of the Abbasid Empire and were named accordingly. The Khorassan gate faced the northeast, the Kufa gate the southwest, the Shami gate the northwest and the Basra gate the southeast.[4] Badran extended these to seven and named them, as shown in his sketches, to open up the site to different Arab countries and regions. Each gate was designed differently to reflect its connection to the city or country with which it was linked. This association continues into the pathways that lead inward from each gate, so that each entry sequence is unique. This kind of identification is further applied to the landscaping, in which palm trees like those that fringe the banks of the Tigris and Euphrates, predominate, an evocation of reason behind Iraq's ancient history.

The dome

The earth berm mound, which paradoxically reduces the scale of the mosque, performs the same perceptual function for the dome, located above the *qibla*, as it first was at the Great Mosque of Damascus during the Umayyad dynasty. The cubes are transformed into a roof structure by a vaulting system derived from the Khan Mirjan, in which arches allow natural light into the sides of the main space. They are elevated as they approach the dome, a reinterpretation of a *riwaq al-qibla*. This prevents the prayer hall from being static, which it could have been because of its gridded framework.

One of the most compelling formal evolutions in the history of architecture has involved the transformation of the space under a dome and the structural innovations necessary to bring that about. In Roman examples, such as the Temple of Minerva and the Pantheon, the space below the dome is circular, like the drum, since the Romans either didn't know how to make the transition to a square or rectangular space, or knew how and chose not to. The Byzantine architects Isidorus and Anthemius are generally credited with making the breakthrough at the Hagia Sophia (AD 532–37), by putting in place sloping triangular pendentives between the curve of the drum and the orthogonal base below. Stepping these sloping triangles into squinches made them even easier to build, and pendentives and squinches were subsequently used in Ottoman and Mamluk architecture, and elsewhere, in order to carry a hemispherical dome over an orthogonal prayer space below it.

In Badran's design, the dome is supported by a brick drum, which adapts to its square base through a network of intersecting arches and beams resembling a three-dimensional squinch. In early Islamic architecture the straight steps of the Byzantine squinch were softened by a geometrical construction called *muqarnas*, which are not unlike stalagmites. The intricate facets are difficult to build and the knowledge of their construction was lost until recently. Badran uses these *muqarnas* niches here to soften the squinches under the dome, creating yet another link to the pan-Islamic past. The surface of the dome is shown as being covered with glazed ceramic with gold-plated accents, as Abbasid domes were.

A rule-breaking success

Rasem Badran won this competition and, in retrospect, he did so in spite of rather than because of his adherence to the brief. As is the case with many notable competition-winning schemes, he achieves excellence by violating, rather than following the unspoken rules, most obviously in his basic design strategies. This contradiction begins with his effective method of breaking down the monumentality of what was intended to be a symbol of national and presidential power, to make it more human and sympathetic to the common Iraqi. This is most obvious on the perimeter of the project, which is reminiscent of a traditional Iraqi village; the residential portion of his reconstructed city. A second obvious contradiction is his historically stratified selection of references that reflect Mesopotamian as well as Islamic references, including the landscape. He saved an existing circle of trees on the site and used it to frame the main ceremonial entrance; palm trees continue to flank the processional route into the mosque itself. These trees evoke the origins of civilization in Mesopotamia, which relied upon water provided by its twin rivers for agriculture and survival. Thus, trees are an evocation of the very beginnings and long history of life in this region, not just its relatively recent past.

Lastly, by imposing a Modernist shifted grid ordering system over the entire footprint, Badran unequivocally declared a break with the pre-industrial past, or at least his intention of setting up a tense dialectic with it. The sub-grid systems that constitute the different fractions inform all traditional prototypes, such as the hypostyle hall, with much larger spans, which are rendered in concrete and replace the forest of columns found in older mosques.

Although it was unfortunately never realized, Badran's winning entry in the Baghdad State Mosque competition was published in *Mimar* magazine, sponsored by the Aga Khan, which had worldwide circulation and a large subscription list.

It also appeared alongside the entries by notable firms such as Robert Venturi and Denise Scott Brown, and gained instant notoriety by comparison. Badran's penetrating reading had an overt, as well as a subliminal impact and brought him immediate international recognition.

The Great Mosque and Palace of Justice (Qasr al-Hukm) in Riyadh

It would be pure conjecture to speculate on the role that Badran's success in the Baghdad State Mosque competition played in his selection as the architect for the vast Qasar al-Hukm development project in Riyadh three years later, after winning first prize in an international competition for the redevelopment of Riyadh's old town. But his increased stature both inside and outside the region were unquestionably instrumental in some way. The brief for Qasar al-Hukm is remarkably similar in many ways to that of the Baghdad project, in the sense that both contain a mosque and palace, the interface of the sacred and the secular, as well as a more general popular component. The client for Qasar al-Hukm was the Riyadh Development Authority, a municipal office responsible for the planning and redevelopment of the centre of the old city. The programme given to Badran's office, Dar al-Omran, defined a mosque for 20,000 worshippers, divided between a covered prayer hall to accommodate 14,000 and an outer courtyard for 6,000. The new mosque was to replace an existing one that had been built over the ruins of another ancient mosque. In addition to being at the very epicentre of the capital of the Islamic heartland the site is overlaid with many levels of memories, which Badran, with his customary thoroughness, was determined to uncover.

A time capsule

Since the discovery of oil in Saudi Arabia soon after the end of the Second World War, development in the Kingdom has expanded rapidly, reaching a peak just at the time the project was commissioned in the mid-1980s. Riyadh was chosen as a capital for several reasons, the most important being its strategic location near the middle of the heart-shaped Arabian Peninsula, in a more easily defended, isolated region with a very hot, dry climate for most of the year. In the Najd a distinct mudbrick architecture had evolved in response to the heat, and development had been slower; but large swathes of the old city and the vernacular architecture in it were still being bulldozed daily. The wholesale destruction of all evidence of the past throughout the Kingdom, as in other Gulf States, and its replacement with Modernist, Western buildings that did not reflect the religion and culture of the nation, had just begun to ring alarm bells, as pride in the speed and scope of infrastructure growth was replaced with concern about the threat to tradition that such growth was causing. Articles began to appear in newspapers and other media and the highly respected local architectural journal *Al-Bena'a* began to print stories about the destruction of the national heritage, particularly in the Najd, and the virtues of mudbrick. Such articles would have been unthinkable just a few years before, in the early the 1980s, when the past was seen as evidence of backwardness and anyone who recommended conserving or respecting it in new architecture was seen as retrograde and opposed to modernization.

Seemingly small details, such as where a large congregation can put their shoes before they enter the mosque, are handled skilfully, showing the users' instinct (interactive skin), which both evokes and responds to the people's imagination. Great Mosque, Riyadh, Saudi Arabia.

An architect whose time has arrived

In such a climate Rasem Badran was the right architect, at the right time, in the right place. The site he was given to work on is near the Musmak fortress, which

A remarkable historical photograph of the previous mosque and Palace of Justice, which represents the social, urban structure of the mosque's morphology, inspired Badran's design for the new complex and was a lucky find.

The photograph led him to premiate certain design directions over others, based on the historical references of the urban infill. The proposed scheme also sought to maintain the place's sociability.

played a central role in the foundation legend of the nation, since King Abdul Aziz Ibn Saud had captured it almost single-handedly in a key victory that led to his ascent to power. It is also near the main square in Riyadh, the Mosque of Iman Turki Abdullah, as well as the central *suq*, but there were very few historical, Najdi-style buildings there when Badran began his design.

The Riyadh Development Authority wanted this new great mosque, Palace of Justice and cultural centre to reflect Islamic culture and to be a new focal point in one of the fastest growing urban areas in the world. Badran immersed himself in the history of the region and its architecture. He uncovered rare, old photographs of the previous mosque and Palace of Justice on the site and, among other clues, noticed that a bridge had existed between the two, and that the tented stalls of the *suq* were directly attached to the wall of the old mosque. He reconstructed the proportions of each building, paying special attention to the relationship between the *sahn* and the lowered area of the prayer hall in the old mosque, and the details of its massive hypostyle structure, all built in mudbrick.

He also found a historic mosque in Darriyah, the ancestral home of the ruling family. Darriyah itself is now in the process of being painstakingly restored along with the lush valley, the Wadi Hanifah, which once sustained it. The old mosque in Darriyah is a remarkable time capsule of Najdi construction skill and was of great help to Badran in enabling him to understand the intricacies of scale, proportion and detail in relationship to the material used. He also conducted many studies of the minaret, especially taking note of the angled stair that allowed the muezzin to reach the top.

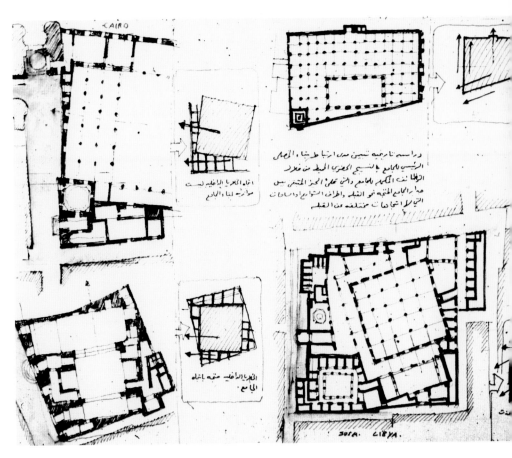

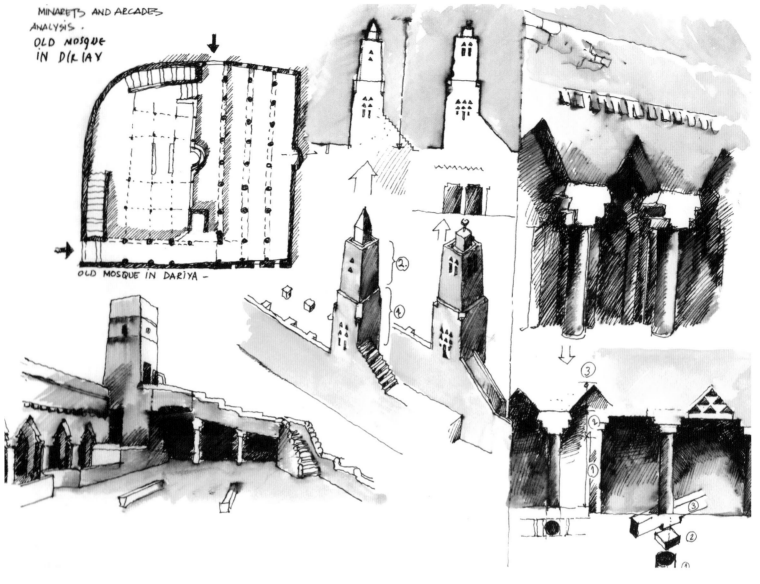

MINARETS AND ARCADES
ANALYSIS.
OLD MOSQUE
IN DIRIAY

OLD MOSQUE IN DARIYA -

The old mosque in Darriyah
(above), the ancestral home of the
Sand, also provided an important
precedent for the Riyadh mosque.
Shown on the left is a dialogue of
the interrelationship between the
mosque's functions and its site.

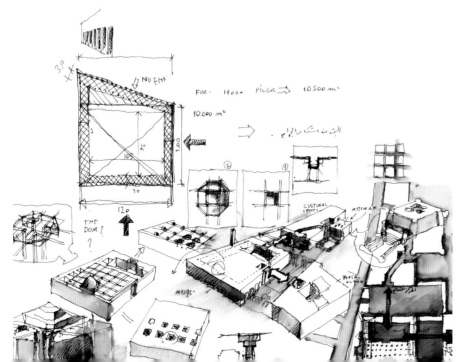

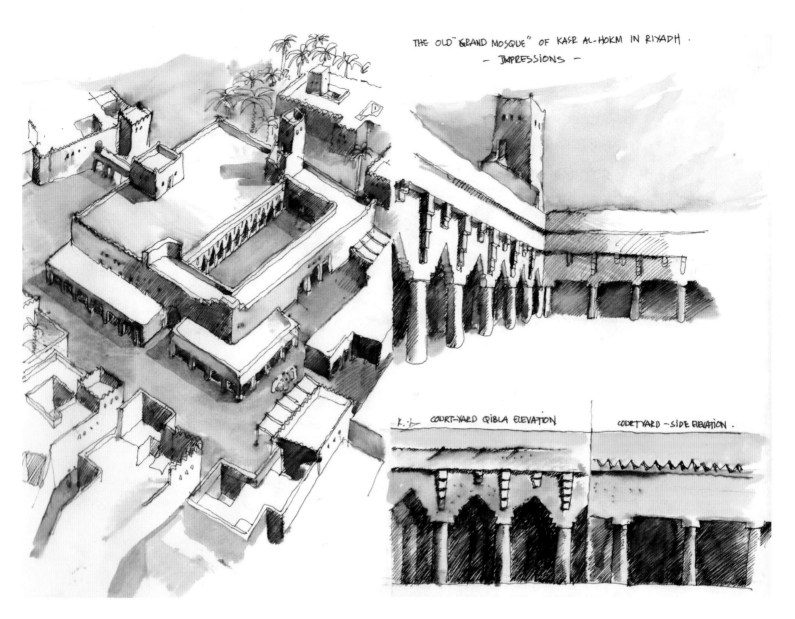

THE OLD "GRAND MOSQUE" OF KASR AL-HOKM IN RIYADH.
— IMPRESSIONS —

COURT-YARD QIBLA ELEVATION   COURTYARD — SIDE ELEVATION.

Early sketches of the Riyadh Great
Mosque reveal the influences of
historical photographs and local
precedent studies. On the right is
a study of the site's geometric
order, a first impression.

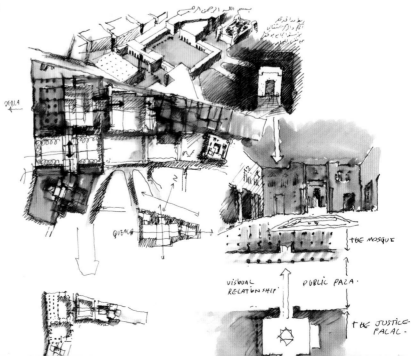

QEBLA

QUENA

THE MOSQUE

VISUAL
RELATIONSHIP   PUBLIC PLAZA.

THE JUSTICE
PALACE.

Qasr al-Hukm Complex, Riyadh, Saudi Arabia. An aerial view shows the vast scale of the project, which has been adapted to various uses that existed around the site. This is a contemporary expression of the historical values and behaviour pattern of the overall concept of the mosque.

A productive dialogue

During this initial stage of background study and research, Badran also held many discussions with the Riyadh Development Authority about his intention to re-establish the historical connection between the mosque and the Palace of Justice, to underscore the link between the religious basis for law in Islam, as a guide to the governing body and a focus for inspiration. The architect stressed the similarity of the link between the mosque and the *madresa* in the past, and his intention to highlight that parallel by looking at the new museum as a contemporary model of the *madresa*, which was part of the original brief. He began to consider several other design factors, such as how to translate the intimacy of the Darriyah mosque in one that was much larger, what form the space should take, what structure and material would be appropriate given Najdi precedents, what the response to environmental factors should be considering the extremes of the local climate, how handicraft could be reintroduced into the architectural vocabulary, and how natural and artificial lighting should be balanced.

The final design

The evolution of Badran's design sketches for the Qasr al-Hukm Complex show that he was wrestling with several critical planning issues. He had made the key decision to link the mosque and the Palace of Justice, but struggled with the difficult question of how far apart they should be. He also progressively re-introduced the connection between commercial activity and the mosque that had existed here, as elsewhere in the Islamic world, before the tendency to isolate the mosque in the middle of a large parking lot became the norm.

To solve the problem of distance and interrelationship, he introduced a series of formal *midans*, or plazas, beginning with the 11,200-square-metre Iman Mohammad Ibn Saud Plaza in front of the proposed Palace of Justice. This leads to the smaller Al-Safa Plaza, which acts as an intermediary space between the palace and the mosque. Both plazas are formally landscaped, and an arcade that holds the bridge connecting the palace and the mosque acts as a filigreed gateway

Qasr al-Hukm Complex, Riyadh, Saudi Arabia. Variations in surface texture help to reduce the prospect of overwhelming monumentality.

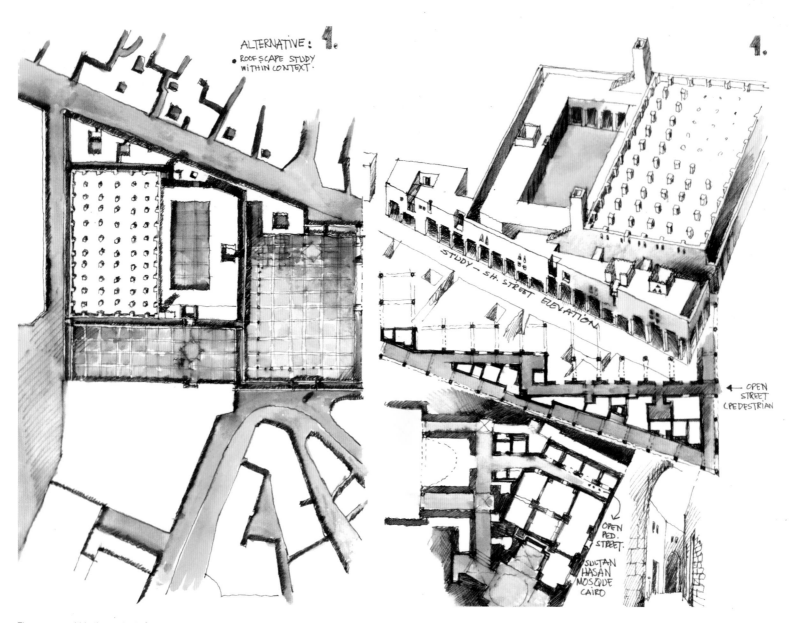

ALTERNATIVE: **4.**
• ROOFSCAPE STUDY
  WITHIN CONTEXT.

4.

STUDY - SH. STREET ELEVATION

← OPEN
  STREET
  (PEDESTRIAN)

OPEN
PED.
STREET.

SULTAN
HASAN
MOSQUE
CAIRO

The mosque within the context of
its surroundings. An important
feature of the Qasr al Hukm
project was the architect's
decision to return the mosque to
its original function in urban
integration, using commercial
facilities as a buffer.

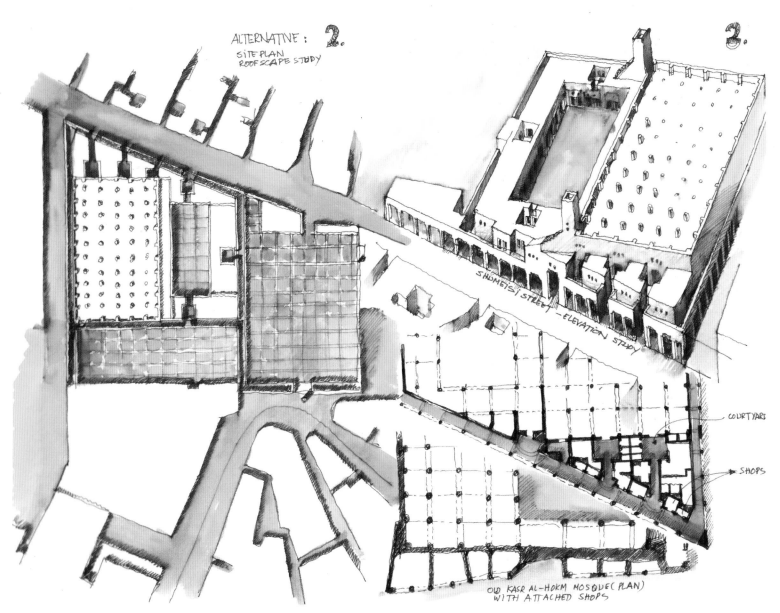

ALTERNATIVE: 2.

SITE PLAN
ROOFSCAPE STUDY

3.

SHOMEISI STREET - ELEVATION STUDY

COURTYARD

SHOPS

OLD KASR AL-HOKM MOSQUE (PLAN)
WITH ATTACHED SHOPS

Various alternatives for the
commercial buffer were studied
before a final decision was made
on the present configuration.

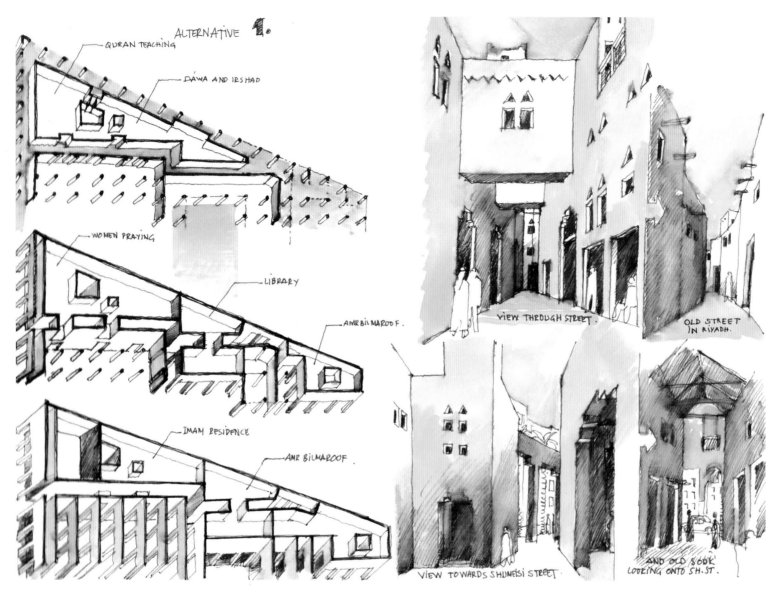

ALTERNATIVE 1.

QURAN TEACHING

DA'WA AND IRSHAD

WOMEN PRAYING

LIBRARY

AMR BIL MAROOF.

IMAM RESIDENCE

AMR BIL MAROOF.

VIEW THROUGH STREET.

OLD STREET IN RIYADH.

VIEW TOWARDS SHUMEISI STREET.

AND OLD SOUK LOOKING ONTO SH.ST.

between them. The commercial area acts as a hinge between the mosque and the street, which runs at a diagonal along its public edge, and is intentionally reminiscent of the democratic model of the Prophet Mohammad's way of life. Numerous studies show that Badran considered various options, finally narrowing these down to three: to separate the triangular area of commerce from the mosque with a service street between them, to connect this wedge to the rectilinear wall of the mosque but to keep the functions separate, and to allow the prayer hall to extend all the way to the street, taking over half of the commercial wedge. In the end, the second option of letting the commercial space connect to the mosque wall but retain its own integrity won out; this also most closely reflects the character of commercial use in the past.

An important decision

The decision to reintroduce commercial use in this way is not insignificant, and may be recognized as a strategy that Badran has used in many of the mosque

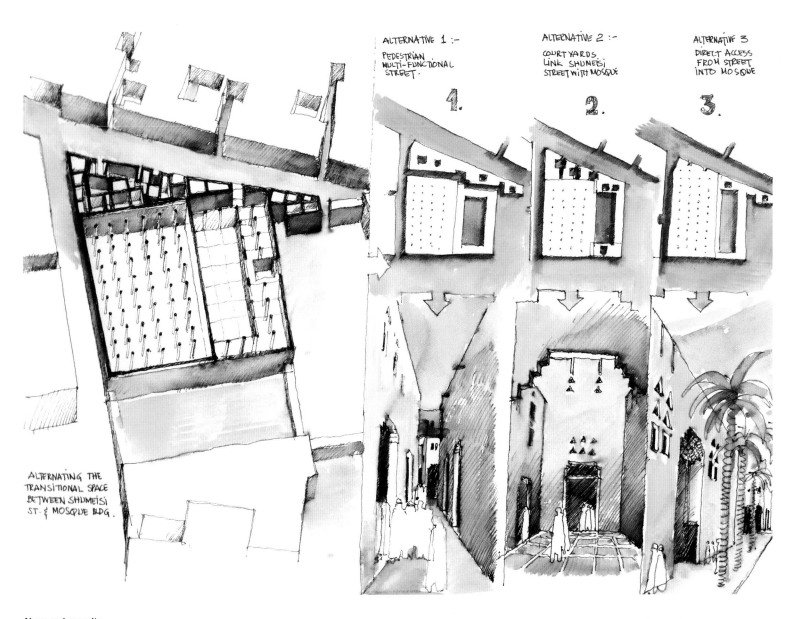

ALTERNATIVE 1 :-
PEDESTRIAN
MULTI-FUNCTIONAL
STREET.

ALTERNATIVE 2 :-
COURTYARDS
LINK SHUMEISI
STREET WITH MOSQUE

ALTERNATIVE 3
DIRECT ACCESS
FROM STREET
INTO MOSQUE

1.

2.

3.

ALTERNATING THE
TRANSITIONAL SPACE
BETWEEN SHUMEISI
ST. & MOSQUE BLDG.

Above and opposite

The refinement of the urban infill
elements with the surroundings.
The various uses in the
Qasr al-Hukm project prompted
a compartmentalization of
external spaces to ensure
progressive levels of privacy.

This compartmentalization
required different spatial
expressions.

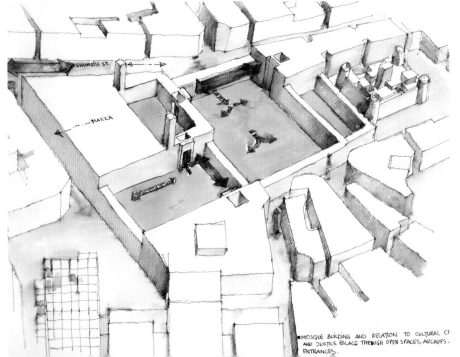

SHUMEISI ST.

MAKKA

• MOSQUE BUILDING AND RELATION TO CULTURAL CF
AND JUSTICE PALACE THROUGH OPEN SPACES, ARCADES.
ENTRANCES.

projects presented here with different hierarchies. Renewing this traditional connection restores a source of urban energy that had been eliminated in the recent past; it finds its parallels in Western New Urbanist theory, which encourages mixed use to revitalize the city. Both strategies of introducing gradually decreasing plazas that decompress public space into a semi-public realm, and of reconnecting religious and commercial uses has succeeded beyond anyone's wildest dreams. The Qasar al-Hukm Complex is enormously popular and full of visitors day and night; it is a true urban success story. The plaza strategy was part of the client's brief, which was initiated through the suggestions of experts such as Professor Stefano Bianca in Switzerland, director of the Historic Cities Support Programme, which is part of the Aga Khan Trust for Culture.

The mosque

As in the Baghdad State Mosque, Rasem Badran initially decided to organize the large prayer space in Riyadh with a geometrical system that allowed columns and arcades to be repeated, running parallel to the *qibla* wall. These arcades recall those of the Darriyah Mosque, and are sized to humanize the vast scale of the space. The columns also act as conduits for the mechanical ventilation system, so that the prayer hall can remain open. The system used in the Baghdad State Mosque, which allows natural light into the prayer hall, reappears here in the Riyadh Mosque in modified form.

The columns in the prayer hall were prefabricated in concrete, following the architect's belief that innovation is in the spirit of Najdi accomplishments in this region, and is evident throughout its traditional architecture.

The mosque has no dome because of its mausoleum connotation, which is frowned upon in Sunni Islam and by the locally based Wahabi sect in particular. The dome element was replaced by an increase in roof lighting in the dome area. Rather than having one large minaret, Badran chose to use two smaller ones framing the direction of Makkah, which means they stand parallel to the main street. Their sloping base and rectangular shape recall the form, if not the scale, of the minaret on the Darriyah Mosque.

The Palace of Justice

Badran wanted to avoid any feeling of singularity in the design of the Palace of Justice. He sought once again to recall the morphology of the old city of Riyadh, through the use of walls, gates and towers. Internal functions are organized around a main reception hall, or *majlis*, a vital feature in Saudi society as the place where the public, by tradition, can meet the government representative. The two-storey-high *majlis* is surrounded by an open space to allow in natural light. This space is linked to an open courtyard connected to the Al-Safa Plaza, as part of the interlocking strategy of public, semi-public and private spaces that Badran has chosen. The hall is encircled by arcades on the lower level and a water channel that acts both as a demarcation line separating it from the other areas of the palace and as a natural cooling device for the *majlis*.

The palace has an an inner block containing the *majlis*, which features a tower on each corner to recall the Musmak fortress nearby, while an external arcaded part follows the edge of the street and houses the public functions. This outer wrapper serves as a continuation of the wall of the mosque, conveying the visual impression that the palace and the mosque belong to the same architectural family.

Qasr al-Hukm Complex, Riyadh, Saudi Arabia. Harsh climactic conditions require a closed-down exterior elevation, with few openings, responding to the existing urban infill.

Unlike the Najdi style, the walls of the Qasr al-Hukm Complex are made of local sandstone rather than mud, which gives it a sharper profile against the sky.

The entrance into the palace from Al-Safa Plaza is flanked by two towers, which are again reminiscent of the gate to the Musmak fortress. The upper portion of the palace elevation is distinguished by the vertical slits and triangular openings typically found on traditional Najdi architecture. The 'form within a form' concept of the palace evokes what Badran calls the 'hidden' architecture of Islamic tradition, in which the interior is not immediately apparent, but is slowly revealed to the viewer.

Balancing values and needs

In evaluating the Qasar al-Hukm Complex after its completion, Rasem Badran believes it is one of the clearest examples in his career of 'a balance between inherited values and changing contemporary needs. The mosque and Palace of Justice are an attempt to awaken the values and memories of an important historical place with rich cultural, economic, social and political legacies. This balance is evident in four general areas: culture, morphology, ecology and technology. In each case, tradition was updated.

Culture

Badran has described his initial reaction to the Qasar al-Hukm site as one of permanence, sensing it was a sacred historic place:

When a Muslim performs prayer, whether in a mosque or not, the ground where this prayer takes place becomes sacred during that act. This prayer is held five times a day at fixed times related to the cosmic solar system and is based geographically on one single orientation towards a fixed point (qibla). This unity of prayer time and orientation gives the city's urban fabric a kind of 'fluid' sacredness due to the ever-changing places of prayer outside the constant physical domains of the mosques themselves. Thus the sacredness of a place becomes deep-rooted and more profound when successive generations agree to the permanence of a particular place in spite of the passage of time, giving rise to the 'sacred historic place'.

His task, as he saw it, was to retain this sacredness, and to reinforce its historical connection with the personification of secular authority that has been an essential part of the cultural memory of the place. In addition, he wanted to re-establish the strong relationship between the mosque and all other relevant activities of everyday life.

The balance, in this case, between tradition and contemporaneity, is achieved in his decision to offset the sacred-secular equation by tempering the monumental aspect of the mosque and making the Palace of Justice seem less imposing. Harmony and equilibrium are skilfully and deliberately rendered. In the case of the mosque he achieved a more approachable image by breaking the stranglehold of thoughtless conventions. As he describes this decision:

The traditional vocabulary, which has now become visible on most mosques, such as high minarets and domes, does not really play a significant role in the importance of the mosque and its value in the fabric of the city. By way of contrast, I sought to achieve a modest architectural elegance that is more in harmony with the urban character of Riyadh.

This instinct, of striving for modesty rather than monumentality, is in harmony with popular sentiment in the region and can be said to be a faithful representation of contemporary values.

Morphology

Badran's extensive series of investigative sketches show his objective search for the essence of the local Najdi style, and of the appropriate expression for a mosque in particular, with special attention given to the proper proportions of the *sahn*, the *riwaq* and the prayer hall. He studied these proportions in rare images of the previous mosque built on the same site, and adopted the hypostyle model, because its venerable heritage can be traced back to the House of the Prophet. It also has metaphorical associations with the groves of tall palm trees that once thrived in various parts of Riyadh and were used as columns in hypostyle prayer halls. However, the balance with contemporary needs, in this case, was to utilize the columns as air-handling units, and to prefabricate them in concrete to allow for the wider spans called for by the number of people using the prayer hall. Badran extended this balance to detailed expression adapting Najdi decorative elements to the modern material.

The contemporary translation of a traditional morphology continues in the clusters of houses and shops connected to the mosque to re-establish a pre-existing pattern. He scales these clusters to be in keeping with other buildings in the region and uses them to enhance the composition of pedestrian paths, public plazas and smaller courts. These were all to resemble the urban fabric of old Riyadh, but also to reflect and serve today's needs.

Ecology

Responding to environmental considerations is always an important part of Badran's design approach and he is refining it as time goes on, as he learns more from each project and the background analysis that accompanies it.

In the case of Qasar al-Hukm, both the scope of the endeavour and the climactic extremes of the region prompted a concerted environmental strategy. His studies of the region yielded three insights. Firstly, he saw that thermal mass, the sheer weight of an exterior wall, was used in the past as a shield against the heat, and this mass was mudbrick, since it was more easily worked than stone. Dar al-Omran helped to develop a 'mud-stone' material for use on the outer wall, incoporating Najdi-style triangular slits to allow natural ventilation into the interiors. Walls were also layered to keep an inner one, which acts as a second layer of protection, out of the sun. The size of openings was restricted because of the heat.

Secondly, Badran noticed that in the Najd, ventilation towers were used to complete the convection cycle. His contemporary translation of these elements is very pragmatic. As he describes it:

The combination of wall openings to allow natural ventilation and light to enter a building, and towers to allow the convective cycle to operate were clear in all building types including religious and residential uses. In the Grand Mosque, I implemented these towers over the column, combining both their traditional function with modern lighting and ventilation systems. Their location allowed them to perform their functions directly, eliminating the need for horizontal air-conditioning ducts and the suspended ceiling systems that accompanies them.

People have responded very positively to the Qasr al-Hukm project, especially its attractive and evocative public spaces.

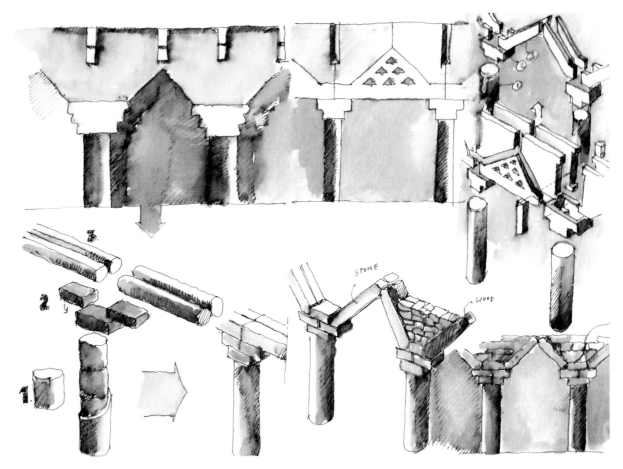

Qasr al-Hukm Complex, Riyadh, Saudi Arabia. Structural analysis of the mosque's constsruction systems, based on inherited techniques. In a dialogue between traditional and modern technology, environmental controls were integrated into the hypostyle structural system making the uniform delivery of air possible.

Qasr al-Hukm Complex, Riyadh, Saudi Arabia. The climatic treatment and its impact on the architectural environment of the interior space. Triangular openings, typical of the Najdi style, were incorporated wherever feasible, in keeping with the overall structural framework.

This point-specific decentralized air-conditioning system made up of simple components, was inexpensive to lay out and install and is easy to operate. It is also sized according to the various requirements of each zone, as determined by the number of people praying there. This system also fits in with the other traditionally based components in the mosque, in memory of the old building methods.

In the Palace of Justice, vertical air-conditioning ducts were placed inside the cavity walls, once again to avoid the use of suspended ceilings.

Qasr al-Hukm Complex, Riyadh,
Saudi Arabia.In some cases,
square, rather than triangular,
penetrates in certain walls
seemed more appropriate.

Technology

Badran discovered a 'framework of knowledge' at work in the traditional Najdi architecture he studied, especially legible in the old mosques. He saw pre-casting techniques as being the contemporary equivalent of this framework, since it is also the most up-to-date technology of the time. Badran used this system in the prayer hall to open it up by increasing the spans.

In addition to these four main areas of translation, Badran also focused on craft and landscaping at both the *Jumah* mosque and the Palace of Justice. Badran sees craft as culture made legible, with accumulated change manifested in the techniques that differentiate one culture, region or nation from another.

Landscaping, or the way in which nature is intentionally used to interact with architecture, is also related to memory and culture. The American architect Charles Moore made the point that gardens are actually the most accurate way of re-creating the past, since if we know the types of plants that were used and where they were planted, we can truly restore what had existed before, no matter how long ago. Badran did not go to the extent of archaeologically examining what plants had been on the site and where they were located; he tried instead to create 'unconscious, semiologically comparable images that provide continuity through time', to 'complete the poetic value of the open spaces'.

The Aga Khan Award

The Qasr al-Hukm Complex won Rasem Badran and Dar al-Omran an Aga Khan Award for Architecture in 1995, reaffirming all the hard work that had gone into its design, including the extensive research and analysis Badran had done to determine the regional precedents that were to be reinterpreted.

Qasr al-Hukm Complex, Riyadh, Saudi Arabia. The comparison between final spatial expression and the desired effect shown in early sketches shows a great deal of visual mastery, based on ecological needs.

The King Abdul Aziz Mosque in Al-Kharj, Saudi Arabia

Many of the concepts derived from the Najdi tradition and employed in the Qasr al-Hukm Complex were also utilized in the King Abdul Aziz Mosque in Al-Kharj, north of Riyadh. The programme reflects many of the same elements, but on a much smaller scale. A mosque already existed on the site but it was demolished along with several other buildings to create a new centre, which includes a new mosque, a public plaza, a justice square and a vegetable market. Interconnected open spaces were also incorporated at Al-Kharj to enhance its vitality, creating places for people to gather in and relax. Palm trees were planted to give shade, and arcades provide cool transitional zones between open and closed spaces. The auxiliary elements in the programme are attached to the side of the mosque, as at

The hypostyle system that was finally chosen for the King Abdul Aziz Mosque has its own characteristic rhythm, reinforced by natural light features in the roof and the beams, which accommodate the light fixtures, audio-visual and climatic elements.

King Abdul Aziz Mosque, Al-Kharj, Saudi Arabia. Exterior planting serves as a reminder that the original columns of early mosques were made from the trunks of palm trees.

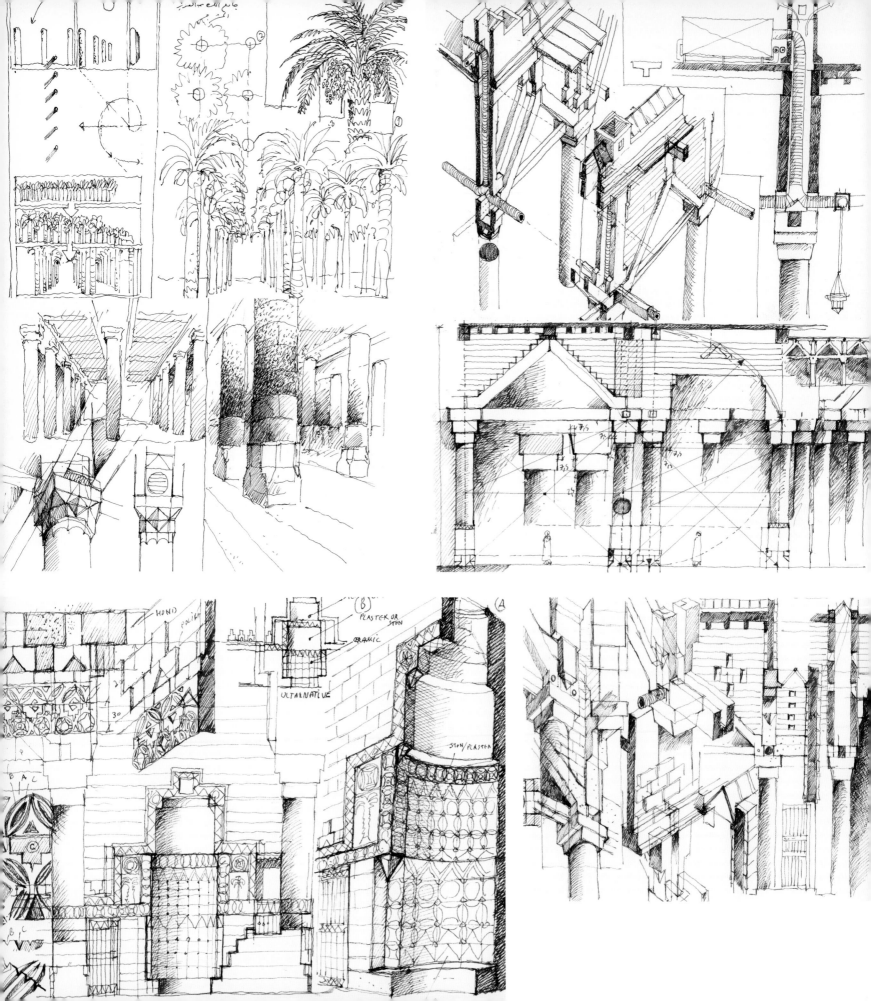

Qasr al-Hukm, establishing the same relationship of interdependency. Badran's lyrical sketches of palm trees, which were intended to augment those already on the site, shows his understanding of the link between the tree and the column; of the hypostyle hall as the architectonic equivalent of the palm grove or oasis. Sketches of the air-conditioning system, related to each twin column, show that it is meant to act as a tie-beam, a further development in the technology first implemented in the Riyadh Great Mosque. It extends the evolution of the hypostyle hall into a composite building system of structure and cooling. Al-Kharj also has a much more refined profile of the minaret than that at Qasr al-Hukm, created by squinched edges and pairing.

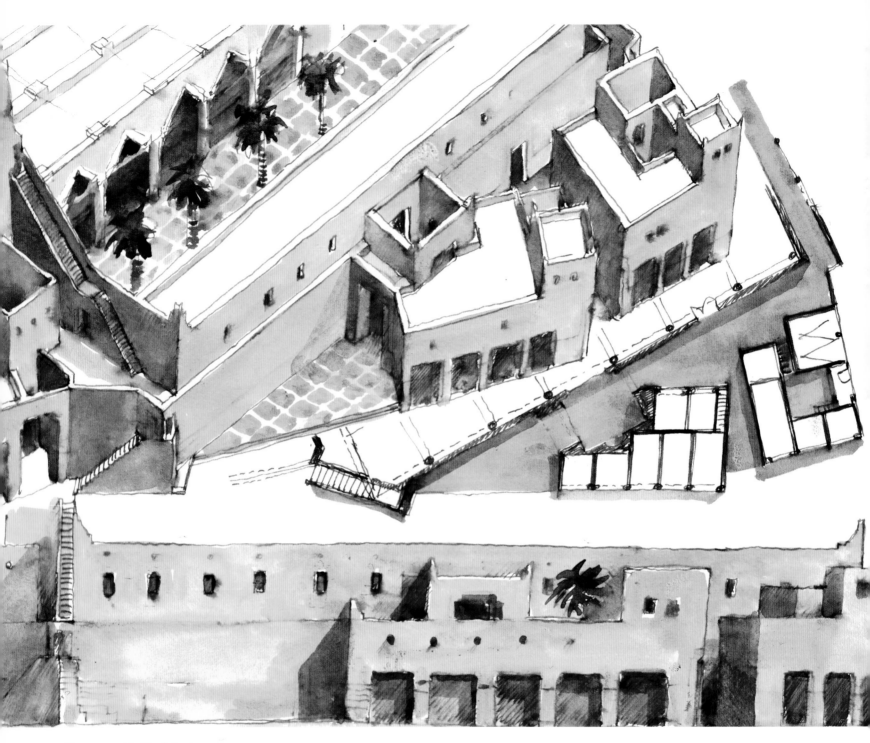

The success of the Riyadh Great
Mosque project led to others, in
which the reinterpretation of the
traditional Najdi style was
expanded.

The urban infill enhances
the physical approach of the
surroundings. The connection
between sacred and secular
space has also been continued,
making a valuable contribution
to this topic.

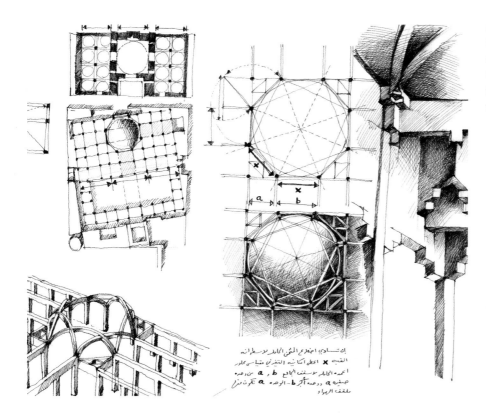

Ali Bin Abi Taleb Mosque, Qatar.
Morphology of the interior. The
squinch has been refined in
Islamic architecture, and Badran
finds the challenge of exploration
to be of great interest.

The Ali Bin Abi Taleb Mosque, Qatar

As they were built to replace pre-existing buildings, the Riyadh and Al-Kharj mosques are not particularly constrained on their respective sites. The *qibla* direction is, however, often at odds with the orthogonal, urban street grid, creating tension with it. There is speculation that Shari Al' Muizz, the main thoroughfare in medieval Cairo, was also orientated to cause the least dislocation with the various mosques along its length, and laid out to use the buildings on either side to cast shadow on the street to keep it cool.

If a mosque is added to a compact urban context, rather than being there first and having the community grow up around it, the architect has to be even more ingenious in finding ways in which to reconcile the entry sequence, washing requirements and prayer hall orientation with the orthogonal site lines and, if done well, another layer of exceptional richness is added to the plan. Historical examples are rare, but the Mosque of Shaykh Lutfallah in Isfahan, Iran, comes to mind in the way in which the *pishtaq*, or monumental portal, is used as a hinge to connect the mosque to the orthogonal *midan* and provide the designer with a device to make the mosque adapt to the opposing *qibla*.

The Ali Bin Abi Taleb Mosque in Qatar and, to some extent, the Al-Khore Mosque, each display this rotation. In the former mosque, Badran used an outer boundary or precinct to effect this reconciliation by intentionally violating the site boundaries of the client's brief, creating an inner enclave that mitigates between the mosque and the street. The twisting of the mosque plan causes tension, and the addition of the auxiliary elements between it and the boundary wall gives the impression of a small, walled city inside an existing neighbourhood. This recalls Badran's similar strategy in the State Mosque in Baghdad, where there were no site constraints.

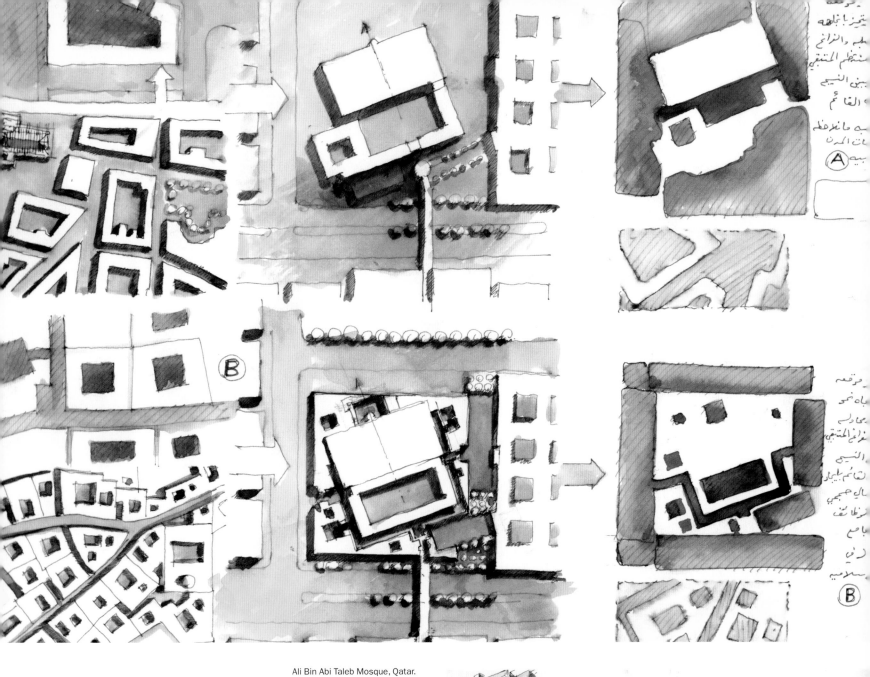

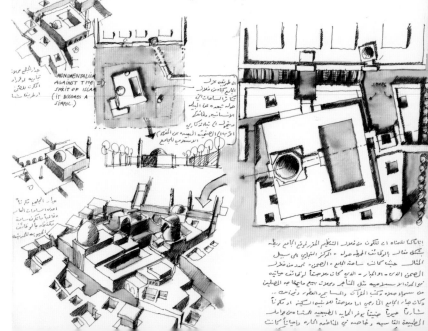

Ali Bin Abi Taleb Mosque, Qatar. The mosque, respecting the qibla direction and surrounded by orthogonal adjacencies that conform to the street grid, is a consistent element of Islamic urbanism. Shown above is the contextual approach (the building as an interactive fabric) and, right, the cultural approach (how the relationship between the mosque and the prevailing activity enhances the social aspect).

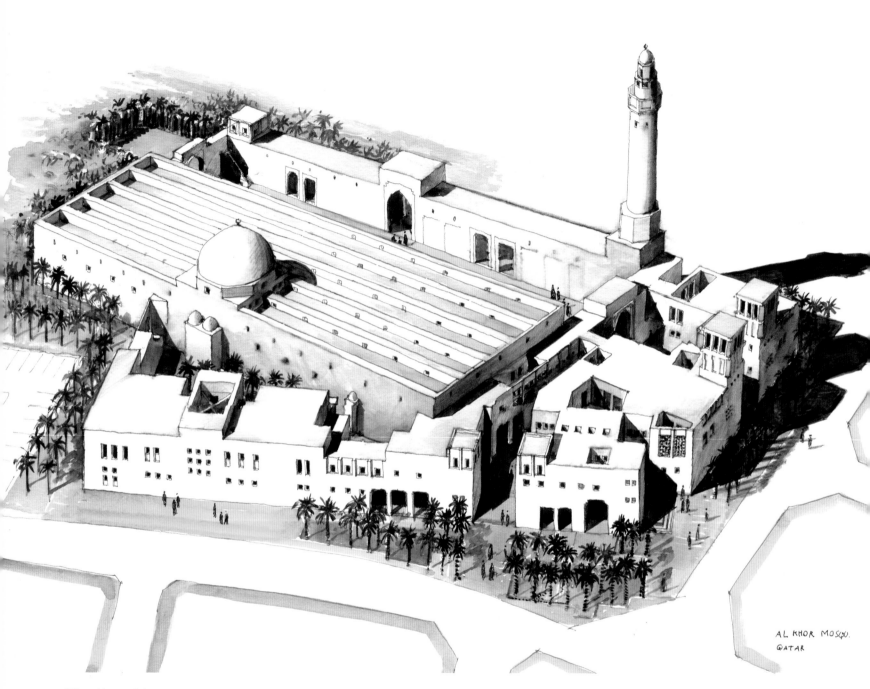

Al-Khore Mosque, Qatar.
The discrepancy between the
requirements of prayer and those
of urban street frontage provide
creative friction.

AL KHOR MOSQO.
QATAR

Al-Khore Mosque, Qatar.
The entrances and approach to
the mosque area.

Ceiling beams provide an order
inside the prayer hall just as
sequential openings do on the
way into it, allowing continuity
to be established using
different materials.

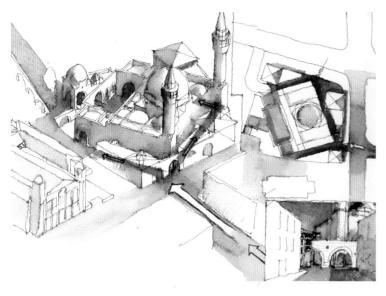
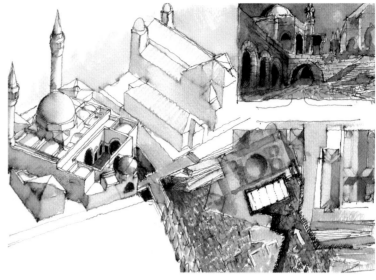

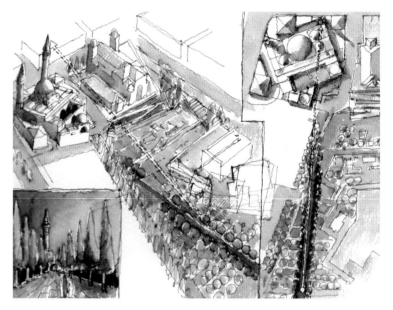

The Al-Amin Mosque, Beirut, Lebanon

In 2000, Badran had to respond to an existing context of a complex and sensitive nature because of the economical and socio-cultural history of Beirut. He had the opportunity to interrelate the Al-Amin Mosque he was asked to design and a pre-existing church on a trapezoidal plot next to it. As in the Ali Bin Abi Taleb and Al-Khore mosques, the *qibla* direction differed from both the street grid and the alignment of the church, calling for even more than the architect's characteristic inventiveness to establish an appropriate narrative between the two buildings and two beliefs. His sketches clearly tell the story of the strategies he has employed to do this: to form a continuous boundary wall that matches the height of a wall around the church, and to use two minarets of a thinner, Turkish profile, that echo the dual bell towers of the neighbouring church.

Badran's sketches also reveal that the interrelationship is even even more subtle than at first appears, since he has also used the space between the two

Badran's respect for context extends to other religious structures. In this case, as these studies for the Al-Amin Mosque show, the mosque he is designing takes certain cues from an existing church, resulting in two minarets.

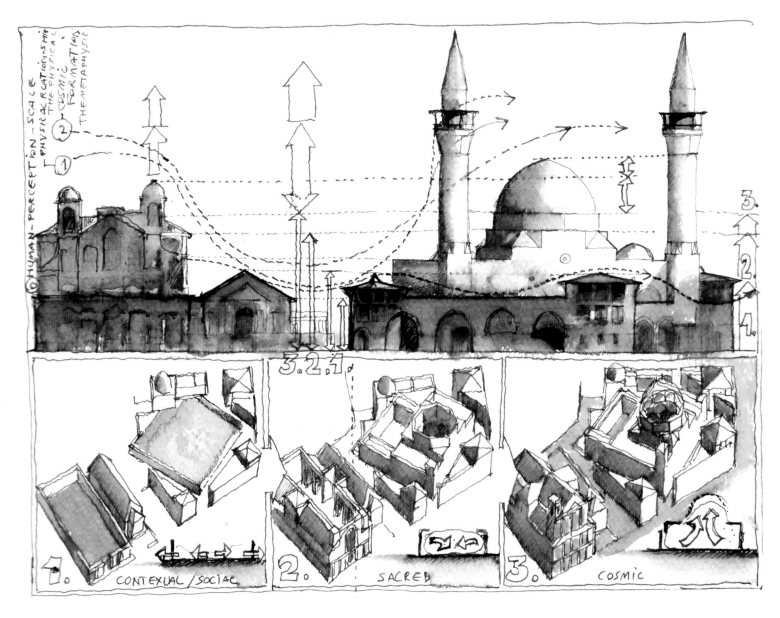

HUMAN - PERCEPTION - SCALE
PHYSICAL RELATIONSHIP
THE PHYSICAL
COSMIC
FORMATION
THE METAPHYSIC

1. CONTEXUAL/SOCIAL
2. SACRED
3. COSMIC

Al-Amin Mosque, Beirut, Lebanon. The cues extend to scale and proportion as well as the space between, which the architect views as one of interaction rather than confrontation. Badran identifies the relationship between the urban infill (the evocative mass), the hybrid skin walls (the social and physical) and the cosmological skin (the roofs). On the right is an overall view of the mosque.

Al-Amin Mosque, Beirut, Lebanon. Using a different sketching technique from his usual one, Badran conveys the importance of shade in a hot climate. All people, regardless of their religion and origin, can make of use of the public space.

In the final model for the Al-Amin Mosque, Beirut, mosque and church seem to coexist perfectly well, to the extent of seeming to have been built at the same time, which they were not.

buildings as a convective courtyard, to draw the prevailing breezes towards the mosque, which is scaled to accelerate this airflow. Peaked squinches, which are used to resolve the circumference of the mosque's dome with the rectilinear prayer hall that it covers, are another subtle gesture and establish another level of dialogue with the pediments across the street.

Lessons learned

Badran's intensive involvement in the issues behind the design of the contemporary mosque, which has been a crucial, but not the only aspect of his practice since he won the Baghdad State Mosque competition in the early 1980s, has nurtured many constructive ideas, which can benefit others investigating the same area. Two of the most significant of these relate to semiotics and context, which have each been contentious subjects in the recent past.

Semiotics and context

The fixation on domes and minarets as essential parts of any mosque design has been challenged in each of Badran's projects presented here. His position has been shown to be far more reflective and less dogmatic, specifically responding to each condition and context. While he has used these elements in appropriate ways related to circumstances, he has also transformed them to adapt to particular requirements and the collective cultural impact of the different societies involved. The Qasr al-Hukm project is the most obvious instance of this kind of transformation, since his in-depth analysis of local precedents led to the conclusion that these forms would have to be reconsidered there. The process he went through in making that determination is very instructive.

At an even more fundamental, urban planning level, Badran has provided a viable, historically accurate alternative to the prevailing model of a single monument isolated in the middle of a large lot, to be found throughout the world today. In each of his mosque designs, regardless of its scale, he has reinstituted the critical connection between the sacred and secular uses that characterized this building type in the past. This is no small achievement and bears close examination.

5 | Preserving a Living History

Opposite

Shade and shadow are intentionally implemented to great effect in many projects. Entrance approach, Al-Dara Complex.

The Aga Khan Trust for Culture invited Rasem Badran to participate in a star-studded international competition to design a Museum of Islamic Arts in Doha, Qatar, in April 1997. His radical winning scheme involved a different approach to the museum concept. A brief look at the origins of the museum will reveal how Badran managed in his projects to change the institution itself.

It could be argued that the origins of the modern museum are a product of the Enlightenment, and as such, the museum is a relatively recent institution with Western roots. By the 18th century the craze to collect, describe and display natural objects was fuelled by the idea of creating comprehensive systems of clarifying natural phenomena. Leading French intellectuals of the Enlightenment saw it as an attempt to rid society of superstition and promote a rationalist mindset. This included undermining the royal claim to God-given authority and challenging Catholic dogma by questioning its role as the sole source of knowledge. The *Encyclopédie* (1751–72) by the French writer and philosopher Denis Diderot is a famous example of these endeavours. An additional attempt to categorize nature was launched by Carl Linneaus (1707–78), a Swedish biologist who became a model of scientific enquiry for French intellectuals. Linneaus gave us our present structure of biology, based on Aristotelian precedents of genus, phylum and species. The attempt to classify and categorize was extended to architecture first by the Abbé Laugier (1713–69), who wrote his *Essai sur l'architecture* in 1753, in which he classified the basic elements of buildings such as columns, doors, windows and roof. This was further extended by Jean-Nicolas Durand, who in the early 19th century put forward the idea of architectural typology which became the basis for French rationalism. One of these typologies was the museum.

The museum typology was originally based on the concept of the scientific preservation and protection of anthropological, historical or artistic artefacts. It is also a fundamentally urban phenomenon, like the cathedral, inexorably tied to the transformation of the metropolis in the industrial age.[1] The forerunner of the museum, then, as a primary civic building type, was the small, private cabinet of curiosities (*Kunstkammer* or *Wunderkammer*, literally 'art' or 'wonder chamber') of the 16th and 17th centuries, which were given over to the private pleasure of viewing an individual collection. Its potential as an instrument of cultural and ideological dissemination was soon recognized.

123

The Louvre, Paris

The Louvre was arguably one of the first instances of this critical transformation. Previously only partially opened to the public on a limited basis by its royal occupants, who sensed the growing public animosity towards its exclusivity, the Louvre became the Musée central des arts in 1793. In 1803 it was expanded by Napoleon to reflect the egalitarian shift that had occurred and renamed the Musée Napoléon in 1803. It was used to house the growing spoils of war by Napoleon's acquisitive director, Dominique Vivant Denon, which were displayed as symbols of the expanding power and prestige of France. It is important to remember that the Louvre was not originally intended to become a museum. The *salle des antiques* that Henri VI set up on the ground floor of the Grande Galerie was not accessible to the general public, nor was the king's cabinet of drawings, created in 1671, or the king's cabinet of paintings, to which access was reserved for a privileged few. When Louis XIV moved his court to Versailles, the Louvre's new role as a 'palace of the arts' seemed a natural progression in the eyes of its resident artists and the academies.[2]

The Alte Nationalgalerie, Berlin

The Alte Nationalgalerie in Berlin, designed by Karl Friedrich von Schinkel, extended this 'geography of power'.[3] Deliberately located near the palace, cathedral and university, it is based on classical forms, but is of a far more monumental nature. The building marked the beginning of a pattern that many now mistakenly believe is recent, of the structure itself taking on as much, if not more importance than the collections it houses. The empty Alte Nationalgalerie was opened to the public soon after it was finished, before the various collections were put in place, to emphasize its symbolic architectural importance.[4] Karl Friedrich von Schinkel was the foremost museum architect at this time and used the language of French Classicism because of its roots in the Enlightenment. Parts of the Ottoman Empire had begun to open up in the early 18th century, including the classical world of Asia Minor. The Germans were avid archaeologists, and German archaeological teams pioneered many digs in these areas including Olympia (1875–81), Pergamon (1878–86) and Magnesia (1891–93).

The Altes Museum in Berlin and the Pergamon Museum are full of the artefacts of the German archaeological expeditions and it is possible to see a system emerging in the formation of museum collections: colonial powers remove ethnographic artefacts from colonized countries or from those too weak to resist and transport them back to their own country as symbols of what they see as the power and superiority of Western culture.

Sir John Soane's Museum, London

Sir John Soane's house, museum and library at No. 13 Lincoln's Inn Fields, is another example of such appropriation. On his appointment as Professor of Architecture at the Royal Academy in 1806, Soane began to arrange the books, casts and models in his house so students might have the benefit of easy access to them, and proposed opening his house for the use of the Royal Academy students the day before and after each of his lectures. By 1827, when John Britton published the first description of the museum, Soane's collection was being referred to as an 'Academy of Architecture'. In 1833 Soane negotiated an Act of Parliament to preserve the house and collection for the benefit of the 'amateurs and students' in architecture, painting and sculpture.

On Soane's death in 1837 the Act came into force. This vested the museum in a board of trustees who were to continue to uphold Soane's own aims and objectives, which are to allow free access for students and the public to 'consult, inspect and benefit' from the collections. This collection reinforces the idea of assimilating other cultures because it is filled with artefacts appropriated from Egypt, Greece and Turkey.

'Orientalism' and its aftermath

In its initial evolutionary path, the museum as a Western, primarily civic institution, exhibited what one critical theorist has perceptively described as 'the materials and symbolic embodiments of a power to show and tell in open, public space, and rhetorically included people in the processes of the state'.[5] This interpretation sounds remarkably similar to that used by the American critic Edward Said in his book *Orientalism*, published in 1977, in which he attributes similar motives to that field of scholarship, because it uses devices that also attempt to exert power. This is germane to the discussion of Badran's museums because it is important to grasp the roots of this institution in order fully to understand how he has changed it.

The original term Orientalism, or the study of Near- and Far-Eastern societies and cultures by the West, has been redefined by Said, who rejects the set of biased beliefs that have led to false and romanticized images of Asia and the Middle East in Western culture. Said's *Orientalism* posits that Western, and primarily colonizing, powers used knowledge as a tool to achieve power over the people they studied and eventually colonized. It reveals that there were twelve overt techniques which these powers used to that end:

1. Exteriority
Taking a superficial rather than a substantive view that becomes evident through 'style, figures of speech, setting narratives devices, historical and social circumstances.'

2. Second order knowledge
A reliance on fabricated mythology rather than fact, presented in such constructs as the history, the fable, the stereotype or the polemical confrontation.

3. Didacticism
The tendency to impose order on certain representations and then to present this ordering as the result of learned, systematic judgment in order to imbue it with more power and make it more transferable and teachable.

4. Generalization
Social, religious and geographical differences, cultural nuances, and all other forms of human variety are disregarded, replaced by a uniform *schema* because this is less threatening, and is easier to comprehend and propagate.

5. Reducing truth to text
A reliance on text as the quantifying mechanism used to contain something perceived to be different, strange or threatening.

6. Typology
The use of taxonomy to categorize or classify the natural world as an intellectual process expanded during the Enlightenment, and extended into the Orientalist canon to include cultural and racial generalizations.

7. Synchronic essentialism
An extension of typology, the tendency to be ahistorical, to view the racial characteristics Orientalists identify as typological, to be also timeless.

8. Science and pseudoscience
Scientific method, including classification, used to support a growing body of generalizations in a discipline.

9. The traveller
Part of the second order knowledge, the device of the traveller relates to non-fiction books and journals written by those who felt compelled to experience the object first-hand.

10. Proprietary condescension
An attitude that stems from the belief in comprehensive knowledge.

11. Collective self-consistency
Similar to generalization, in which differences like religion and geography are subverted to uniformity; this device differs in the extent of reductivism.

12. Duality
The shift from the beginning of Orientalism as an academic pursuit to its final function as an instrumental attitude that paved the way for colonial expansion[6].

The relevance of Orientalism to the early mission of the museum
These primary characteristics of Orientalism are relevant to the way in which the museum grew as a social institution in the West because its self-defined purpose has been described as being 'to collect, preserve, study, exhibit, and interpret collections'.[7] Public perception has focused on scientific aspects, in keeping with the functions of collection and preservation mentioned in this definition, but since the 1980s there has been an equal and opposite focus on its interpretive function. Up until recently, science was believed to be, or was promoted as being, value-free, a process in subjective judgment played no role. Consistent with its rational beginnings, the museum was equally perceived as an objective instrument. In the early 1980s, theorists such as Karl Popper began to chip away at the value-free principles of scientific enquiry, noting that logical induction itself, which is integral to the scientific method, requires judgment, which may be subjective. This has important implications for the museum, because it also claimed to be objective as an instrument of science.

Neutrality in question
The institutional history of the museum can be characterized as a shift from the more technical aspects of the preservation and protection of artefacts, or the technical means of transmitting cultural heritage, towards the more basic question of

the social outcomes it can achieve. There is now a keen awareness that in the past values were inherent in information and that the museum therefore disseminated values.[8] In other words, the museum has always been an agent of social change and has implemented the devices integral to Orientalism as a system of power exercised through the calculated use of knowledge. Many of those affiliated with the institution throughout the world are only now beginning to understand this link. For example, consider one contention that 'the museum's voice is no longer seen as transcendent. Rather, it is implicated in the distribution of wealth, power, knowledge and taste shaped by a larger social order'.[9]

The devices of dissemination

One can argue that exhibitions in themselves are value-free and depend only on the interpretation of the viewer. However, the construction of the exhibition constitutes an intellectual framework through which the objects are perceived. The museum, in its role as an educational institution, promotes social and political views, which may colour identification and classification. Add to this all the minutiae of the exhibition process, such as didactic texts describing each object, the labels, handouts and catalogues, the audio-guides, as well as the lectures and symposia connected to the exhibitions, and one must agree with past New York Museum of Modern Art director René d'Harnoncourt that 'there is no such thing as a neutral installation'.[10]

In this fundamental shift from considering what a museum does, without self-reflection on its method or agenda, towards questioning why it does what it does, a seismic social change can be read; the institution is simply a reflection of the major social network that feeds it.

A mirror of social change

Those involved in directing and curating museums seem to be less concerned with their role as the guardians of aesthetic standards than they once were, and no longer as intent upon presenting the institution as the last bastion of the secrets of civilization. In a manifesto prepared by the Committee for a New Museology, passed in October 1987, this shift is expressed in a determination to 'react to changing social realities rather than being concerned with theories that must be forced upon populations. Our methodologies should be based on such realities and should aim for the liberation, development and transformation of society through that awareness and participation of such population'.[11]

Values made manifest

A central issue in museology today, then, seems to be the redefinition of the mission of the museum. First described in 1970 by Joseph Veach Noble, a past vice director of the Metropolitan Museum of Art, as the responsibility to 'collect, conserve, study, interpret and exhibit', and then refined a decade later by Peter van Mensch as the means to 'preserve, study and communicate' the best values of a society or civilization, that mission is now believed to be in need of expansion once again, to allow for the museum to become 'the median of extraordinary experience'.[12] Along with the recognition that it has transmitted values in the past and that those values were often ideologically loaded, there has been a surprising but unmistakable determination to use this inherent tendency towards political alignment to best effect.

Left

Badran has followed his father's lead in embracing the art of calligraphy, which is a traditional Islamic craft requiring great skill and patience. Shown here is a balanced combination of geometry (cosmic order), plant ornament (the scroll) and mind intervention (writing).

Below left

This exercise in calligraphy (Kufic writing) represents a synthesis between meaning, beauty and value.

Below right

A first attempt by Rasem Badran at learning Islamic art from his father.

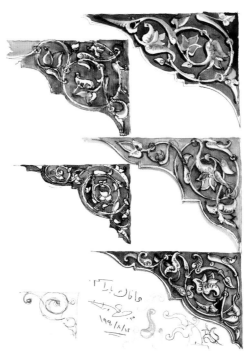

Above

Badran has also produced exceptional calligraphy for glass. This is especially difficult to produce, given the unique geometry of the container and the fact that the characters must seem effortlessly to fill the space intended for them. The skill lies in balancing the solid and the void.

By definition, exhibitions are biased, so it is now thought better to flaunt this bias than to deny it. This is the museological equivalent of defining brand recognition, part of the commodification process in which the institution is so obviously taking part, and the general awareness that selective bias has now become an undeniable part of the contemporary condition. This awareness has also led museum professionals to question the ways in which its 'communication' function can best be carried out. It recognizes that, like the media, it is not objective, but that bias is today seen as a good thing, since it is a device by which one museum can be differentiated from another. This enables it to establish more effectively its market niche in an increasing competitive field, but raises a question over what form the information should take and how the values can be made clear.

Rather then being the unquestionable source of historical interpretations, or the mediator of aesthetic judgment that it claimed to be in the past, the new museum seeks to communicate a specific, highly tailored, value-laden message driven by a particular purpose. It is no longer simply content to be an archive or a storehouse of artefacts, but feels the need to provide 'experience, stimulation and empowerment'.[13]

Fragmentation

This resolution to find a market niche may account for the remarkable fragmentation of the typology that we are now witnessing today, the shattering of what was once considered an emblem or symbol of the Western cultural tradition. It is reinventing itself to adapt to the diversity of social roles required of it today, moving, as Douglas David has said, 'beyond the expression of current social values and tastes toward the making of a cultural statement that can re-establish its place in history'.[14] That redefinition includes civic status symbols of a new order, tourist destination, repository of arcana, ethnic synonym, fun palace; the list is endless.

The Museum of Islamic Arts in Doha, Qatar: the fourth turning point

The brief given by the Aga Khan Trust for Culture for the new museum in Doha included making provision for four outstanding collections of paintings and engravings, rare books, manuscripts, maps and prints, numismatics and weapons and armaments, respectively, and envisioned the future expansion of each collection. The brief also specified the urban design of a large site with the particular requirement of a connection between the proposed museum and the National Museum across a main highway nearby. It encouraged a master plan that would allow for future growth and a design approach that would reflect the cultural heritage of Islam, as well as the regional climate, by landscaping as much of the site as possible with local species.

Design approach

Badran was struck by a comment in the brief which said that the design should emphasize 'the cultural, environmental and historical values emerging from the context' and that it should 'express these in architectural form'. The brief also emphasized that the museum should be viewed as a socio-educational and cultural event for the people of Qatar, especially intended as an educational resource for students at all levels, and should become a centre for 'cultural tourism', in the best sense of the term.

In the extensive report that accompanied his final submission, Badran responded that the intention of his design was 'to offer an understanding of Islam through the living event represented by the Museum', so that 'those experiencing its spaces would be able to comprehend them within the culture that produced them and read them through the lens of the values that contributed to their making'. The idea, Badran said, was that he was not restricted to the creation of a physical product that could be misinterpreted at a later date because of the use of unintentional symbolic references. Instead, he sought to provide 'metaphysical content that would offer symbolic references that would be unmistakable and would create a museum that had living value'. He sought to create 'an experience of the place through a design approach that would provide an understanding of

Right

Museum of Islamic Arts,
Doha, Qatar. The progressive
arrangement of individual galleries
along a spiralling internal 'street'
is the basic concept of the
design. The museum's urban
fabric acts as a fluid continuity of
the existing city's structure.

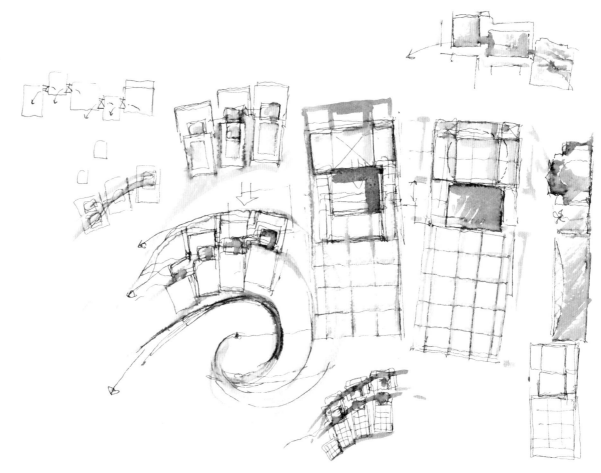

Below

Museum of Islamic Arts,
Doha, Qatar. The final model
shows that the 'street' was
then further punctuated with
wind towers.

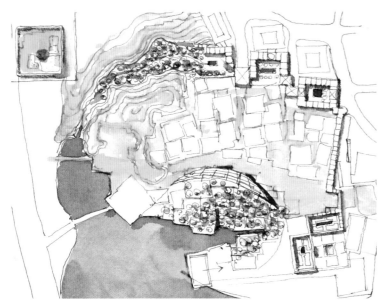

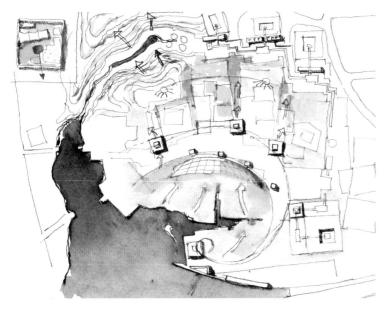

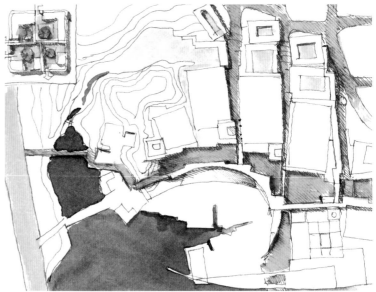

The evolution of the Doha design
describes Badran's intention to
utilize the rhythms of this
particular site near the water to
evoke physical, topographical and
cultural memories of this
seafaring community's past. It is
the process of incremental growth
– the narrative of the place – that
identifies the architectural
elements. Illustrated on the right
is the transformation from nomad
to civic, from mobility to stability.

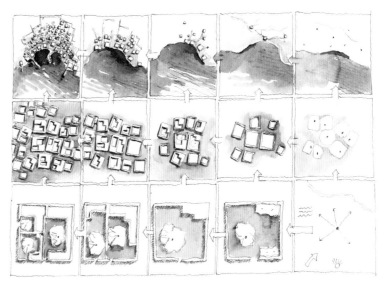

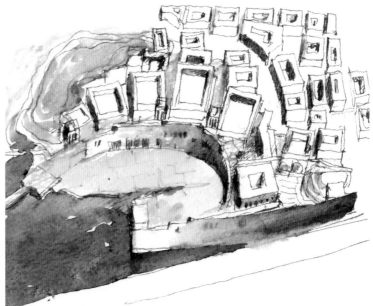

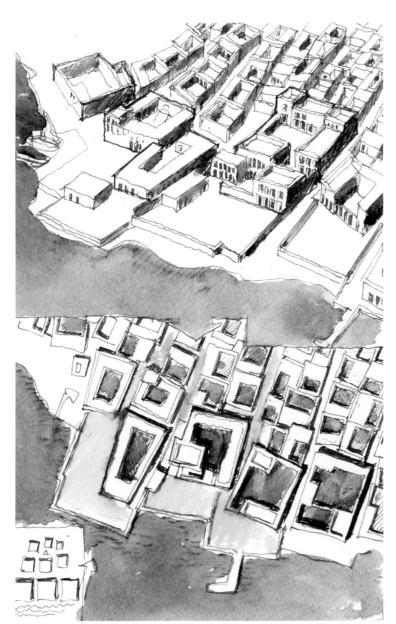

Museum of Islamic Arts, Doha, Qatar. The sweeping curve that characterizes the design continues the line of an existing bridge, visually uniting the new architecture with the water. Badran has a keen understanding of the narrative of inherited urban settings, and the dialogue between the past and the present on water as a source of life.

the living nature of art: what I call the demummification of knowledge. This museum will interact with the place itself, with Doha City, to the extent that it will be seen as the City of the Museum'.

An artist architect at work

It is significant, in this instance, that Rasem Badran, who is shown here to be a consummate artist as well as architect, began his design by synthesizing his life-long exploration of the meaning of the role of art in Islam, in order to express it appropriately in this particular context. He initially identified two general interpretations that he has observed over time: of an externalized form of Orientalist representation that predominated in the 19th and 20th centuries, which attempted to impose an independent methodological reading on the artistic production of another culture and to judge that product by Western aesthetic

standards, and the more internalized Muslim and primarily Sufi approach that projects symbolic interpretations on the artistic product from within the culture itself. In attempting to give precedence to the Islamic tradition from among the two directions he had experienced, he then identified two additional requirements within it. These were a need to explore thoroughly the substantial body of established knowledge on the historical and archaeological origins of Islamic art and the cultural basis of this art from within its own context, rather than from a superficial, external reading.

To identify that internal context, Badran started with the most basic original sources, the Prophet's Mosque in Madinah, the Umayyad mosque and the Dome of the Rock in Jerusalem, in which calligraphy, or inscriptions of Quranic verses in each instance, help to establish a human relationship with both the creator and the universe. Ornamentation, in each case, is used as an abstraction of infinity and a universal order, which transcends human reference alone.

Starting with a metaphysical matrix

The specific methodology that Badran used in designing the Doha Museum of Islamic Arts was a tripartite strategy of determining what he calls a 'metaphysical

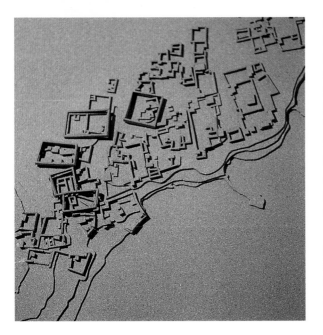

order' as well as conceptual precedents and a museological philosophy. To uncover a metaphysical order, along with a matrix, working upwards from human experience, through 'vital' (natural) and cosmological considerations on the x-axis, with Makkah, place, pattern and geometry used to filter each of those vast topics into a conceptual order for the project on the y-axis. Badran maintains that in the Islamic world human order is legible through worship, knowledge and craft. Vital, or natural order, in Doha, is most visible in the pattern produced by the sea, the rituals of survival on and by the water and the cyclical festivals related to it. Gardens, which Badran characterizes as 'connecting water with life', are also a crucial part of this link. Cosmological order for him consisted of finding those elements that tie Doha to universal aspects of the Islamic world, at a conceptual more than a physical level. These could then be used as a spatial basis for his scheme.

As it turns out, directionality (as the strand connecting the site to Makkah), the pattern of *tawaf* (the ritual circumambulation around the Ka'bah during the *Hajj*) and geometrical patterns of basic elements, are the organizational rules and limitations found throughout the Islamic world. These proved to be among the most critical factors in determining conceptual development and the presence of what might be called traces of the traditional city of Doha, uncovered in Badran's second strategy of conceptual precedents, and in reinforcing his commitment to make this a living, rather a static museum. This is a central guiding principle of the third aspect of the design, of his museological philosophy.

Conceptual precedents

As he did with his investigation of metaphysical order, Badran set up a matrix as a screen to further refine his previous findings, with a shorter x-axis related to historical reference, and a larger y-axis, of five categories in this case. Beginning at the axis intersection, the categories were: urban growth (the city), spines – which include the *suq* or market, the *khan*, or craft stall, and the *wekala*, or hotel, for craftspeople, as well as gardens and *madresas*, or educational buildings – and religious buildings (the mosques). His intention in creating this matrix was to determine how each of these five categories, once established, could be applied as design guidelines for the project, as a way of determining a 'fit'.

Settlement as a process of differentiation

In the first category, of the city, Badran defines the traditional process of settlement as being one of differentiation, set into motion by the establishment of boundaries and key points or gates in those boundaries. It is also a successive development evolving in layers that are added to, or subtracted from in various places over time.

In the second category, of spines of development, he conducted a thorough study of Islamic cities and found that such spines are the main element around which social, cultural and economic activities were located; he resolved to use these spheres as an organizational device in this project. To do so, he believed an effective method would be to uncover points of continuity between the surrounding context and his proposed design. He found, in his site survey, that people living in the area crossed it on their way to the existing mosque, especially on Fridays. Badran decided to make this a main pathway in his design, dimensionally amplifying it by adding upper walkways and bridges through his scheme to maintain the physical continuity of the existing, neighbouring urban tissue.

In the third category of open spaces, he studied the role that landscaping, and especially closed gardens, have played as initiators of urban growth. He also considered the different historical functions of such landscaping, in the forms of agricultural fields and orchards, or contemplative precincts such as the Mughal gardens or the Court of the Lions and the Court of the Myrtles at the Alhambra in Granada, in which water plays such an important role. He also looked at astronomical observatories, such as the Jantar Mantar Gardens in Delhi. Badran incorporated appropriate aspects of each of these types of gardens throughout the museum so that their morphological composition would allow visitors to experience the universal, vital and human order'.

Educational institutions, as the fourth category on the y-axis of his matrix, are relevant because of the substantial pedagogical component of the brief. The *madresa* is the archetypal spatial model for this aspect of urban growth in the Islamic city and is often combined with the fifth category of study, the mosque.

The mosque that exists on the site is of the traditional hypostyle type, with a minimal formal vocabulary that follows the precedent of the Prophet's Mosque, being partially enclosed. Badran wanted all of the elements of the mosque to be clearly legible as a fulcrum for the future development of the site, with a new larger mosque to be built nearby. The most pressing reason for this would be the increased number of people that the museum would bring to the area.

Before turning to Badran's museological philosophy, his structural approach to the project, and his phasing strategy, the environmental strategy he employed must be appreciated to bring his final submission into perspective.

The natural envelope

Just as Badran had investigated general ordering systems and conceptual precedents in preparation for this design, he also analyzed traditional environmental systems that might be relevant. This is consistent with his longstanding commitment to the issue, as well as the client's requirement that environmental considerations play an important part in the design of this museum. By early inclination and by professional training, he has been drawn to technology, because of the potential that it has to improve lives.

This attraction to technology, and his realization that it is not the antithesis of tradition but an extension and by-product of it, is what sets Badran apart from others claiming to be dedicated to the search for authentic cultural expression in architecture. Once understood, this insight offers a key to understanding this facet of his work.

His environmental strategy for the Doha Museum of Islamic Arts reflects the duality of utilizing traditional systems that have existed in this region for centuries in combination with technological advancements that augment their performance. The *badgir* is a good example of this: a wind tower with diagonal fins inside that cross through its centre like an x, it allows a breeze coming in any direction to be funnelled into its throat and then into the building below. Badran has modified this venerable device, which used to be prevalent throughout the Gulf region prior to the massive post-war development that began to take place there. He has added glass panels to convert it into a solar chimney, and to accelerate the air flow into and out of the tower. Dust, a major concern expressed by clients about the current implementation of the *badgir*, is dealt with by sophisticated filtration techniques, making this model much cleaner than it was in the past.

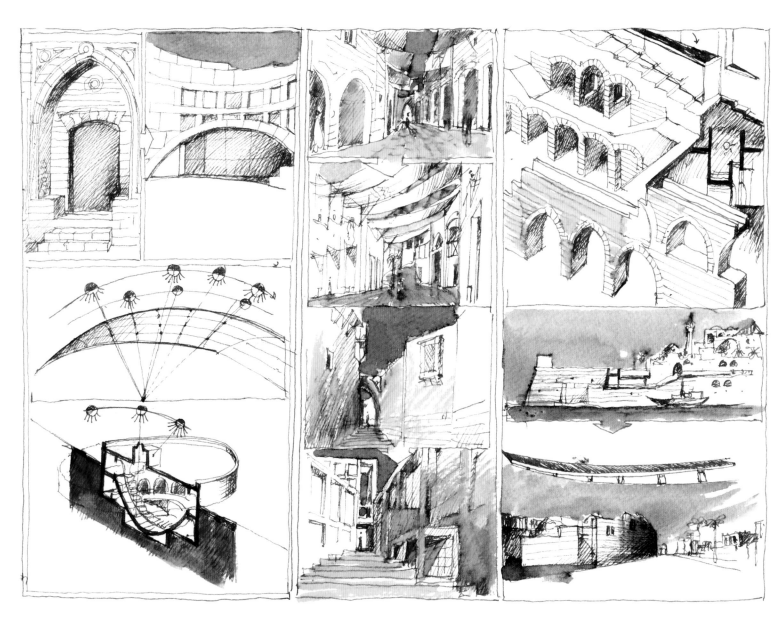

Above and right

Museum of Islamic Arts, Doha, Qatar. The subject of the passage of time, which is of obvious importance in a community which has witnessed so much change, is once again introduced and expressed in architectural form. The importance of the position of the sun and its track through the sky echoes Badran's use of a sundial in the design for Amman City Hall, Jordan.

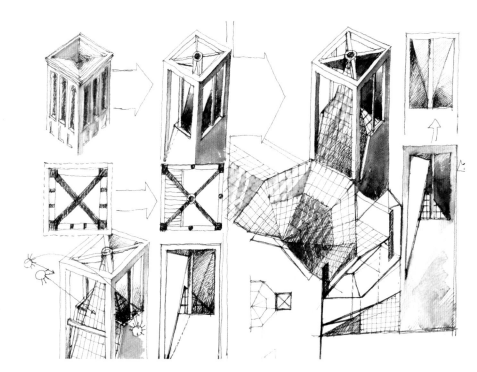

In the Doha Museum, Badran followed the client requirement for extensive landscaping to best environmental advantage, by using gardens as a natural cooling and filtration system – as they were in the past – in conjunction with the upgraded *badgirs*. By locating palm-filled, oasis-like greenscapes on the windward side of the site, to take advantage of the constant sea breeze and then ranking the *badgirs* behind them, Badran guaranteed a steady flow of natural ventilation into the main circulation spine of the museum, which could then be

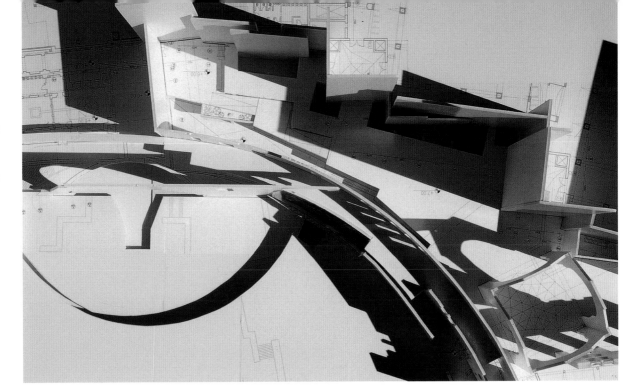

Right and below

Museum of Islamic Arts, Doha, Qatar. New structural solutions, related to the tent as the oldest enclosure of all in this area, allow clear-span spaces for exhibition. The sketch below shows the passive cooling technology within the buildings.

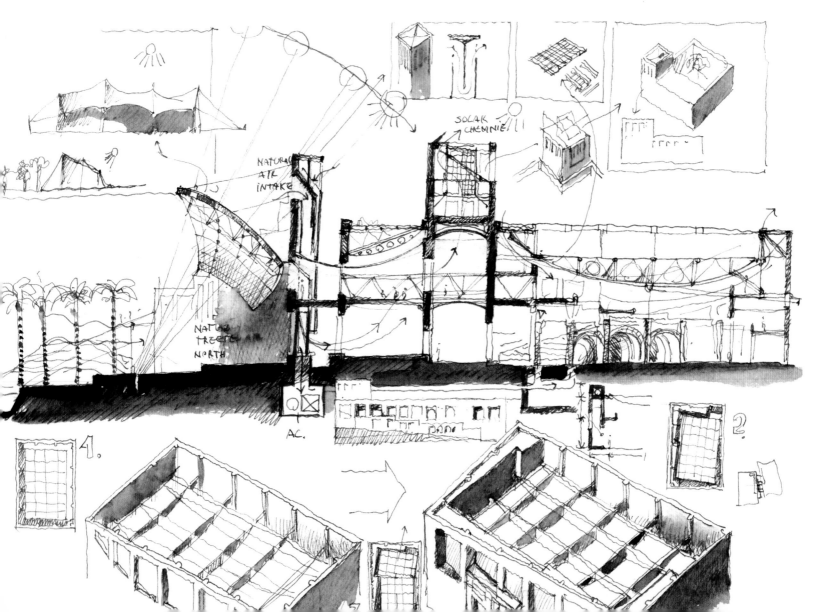

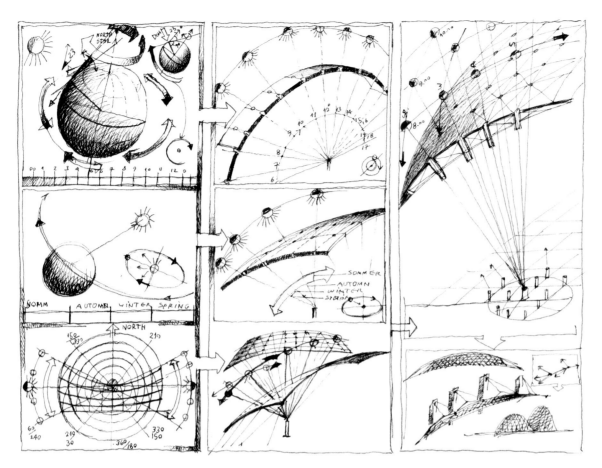

Left and below

Museum of Islamic Arts,
Doha, Qatar. The buildings
as a cosmological device, a
structure based on solar time
measurement. Perforations in the
vaulted ceiling allow sunlight to
penetrate in a controlled way, with
buffers introduced to prevent heat
build-up and glare.

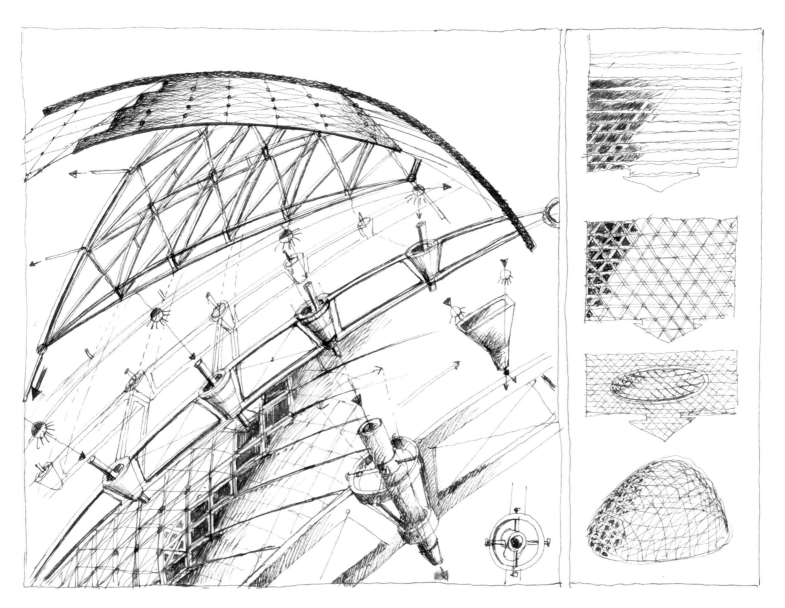

conditioned and distributed to the remainder of the complex. The *badgirs*, which can be classified as an active system when converted to solar chimneys to complement conditioned internal air, are augmented by passive and composite systems, also derived from traditional models. The cavity wall, previously found throughout the Gulf, is one of the most effective of these, in which vents placed in an external skin allow air to filter in through a gap between a second inner wall, which also has a vent, lower than the one outside, to trap dust. Badran has reinterpreted this double, cavity wall system by shifting the inner wall slightly, creating a layered effect of an inner and outer shell. Practical requirements are satisfied in this way, and tradition respected.

Each of these specific tactics takes place inside what the architect has called a 'natural envelope' around the entire site, which connotes a green perimeter but is much more than that. It is a holistic notion of the entire site as a differentiated, contemplative place in which social and cultural re-awakening and environmental rehabilitation can take place together.

As previously discussed, the worldwide trend in museums today is to move away from being a sacrosanct temple of aesthetic values to be preserved against the depredations of popular culture towards an institution of universal accessibility to the public, regardless of age, economic level or educational background. Museums are becoming more inclusive. This inclusiveness takes on more urgency in social conditions in which highly identifiable cultural values are perceived to be under threat from alien alternatives.

In this context, it should come as no surprise that in addition to a conventional request for a permanent exhibition gallery, the client, through the competition organizers, decided to add temporary thematic exhibitions in what they referred to as 'treasuries' and 'studies' to their list of requirements, with a specific directive for various types, or categories of interactive exhibits. These 'Integrated Experiences', built around historical environments that the architect has re-created, are 'Interpretive Exhibits', involving collections presented with labels and graphics, 'Affective Exhibits', intended to create an emotional impact, and 'Discovery Learning', to reinforce a specific educational purpose using interactive techniques.

Badran's approach, in terms of such experiential techniques, was spelled out in detail in his report, which accompanied his winning scheme, and bears repeating at length here for the insights it offers about the ways in which exhibition design has changed. The report states that:

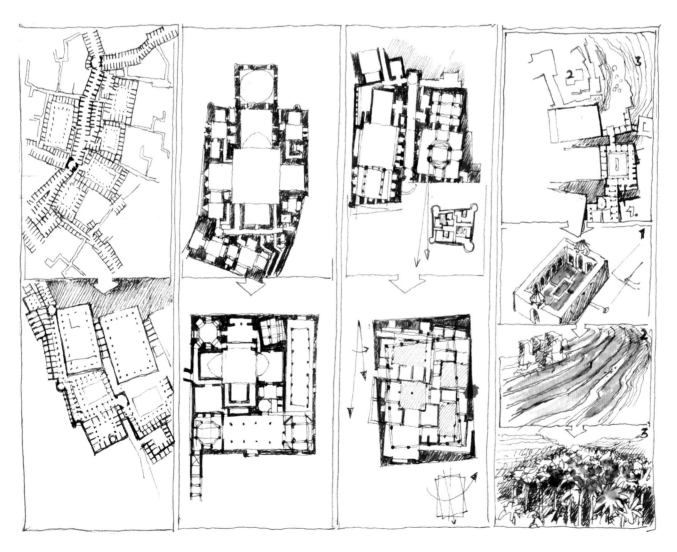

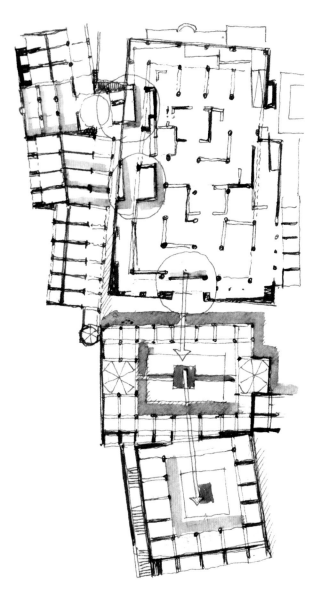

Above

Museum of Islamic Arts, Doha, Qatar. *Suk*-like spatial sequences, using *iwans*, connecting to courtyards, forming arcades.

There are many things an individual or a family can choose to do with their leisure time and a museum must ensure that visitors feel that their visit is worthy of their investment of time and effort. Today we have sophisticated technologies for ensuring that museum education also has an element of entertainment. This style has come to be called 'edutainment'. We all learn more when we are predisposed to learn and when the communication and tools used to communicate have been designed to help us learn. All contemporary museums ensure that the messages they wish to communicate, whether they are about the connoisseurship of a collection, the history of an object or the importance of a concept, are structured to be learned and remembered. Every museum gallery and exhibit makes a statement, and the goal is to ensure that the message, which a display makes, is the one the curators and museum want communicated. This is not an easy task recognizing the range of people who walk through the front doors of our museums and cultural institutions.

There is far more in a museum than can be assimilated and understood in a single visit. It is well understood that the average museum visit for an adult is about 100 minutes and for a family about 80 minutes. At about this point, museum fatigue sets in and the visitors want to leave or rest and refresh themselves. Our goal as museum designers and planners is to try to extend the visit and then to ensure the quality of the visit is such that the visitor wants to return soon. One of the methods we use is called pacing, where different display techniques appeal to different portions of the brain or human sense. It is well understood that museums that vary the visitor experience using all the techniques including dioramas, high-touch interactive exhibits, 'treasuries', 'high-tech' displays, smell, sound and other display tools are the ones that succeed. This is evident in the Louvre, which even in an old building found ways of varying the light levels and the ambience to change the visitor's environment.

One of the hardest things to do in a museum is to stop visitors long enough to teach them something. We have all seen people wandering through museums or charging through galleries of important artefacts because they are tired or overloaded by what they feel is only more of what they have seen. What we have to do is create 'stoppers', for once the visitor slows down we can begin to communicate at a deeper level. Alternating or rotating display techniques extend a visit and significantly improve memory.

In general, our approach to the galleries and displays is to use a paced programme of environmental reconstructions, interpretative displays, interactives (and here we speak not only of computer interactives, but also other techniques for engaging the visitor's mind), connoisseur displays and reflection spaces. While all displays will speak to the average visitor, targeted programmes and exhibits will be developed to address the special needs of children, young minds, and the knowledgeable visitor looking for more than the average experience.

We contemplate placing scholarship in the middle of every major gallery space. In addition to the specified study rooms which will be segregated to provide maximum security, discovery and study zones will be provided for each gallery with digital database and study collection cabinets so that the average visitor may share some of the discovery experience that visiting scholars and others enjoy.

The collections in the museum, of manuscripts, numismatics, arms and armour and the arts of Islam are designed with thematic exhibits and have a 'treasury', as mentioned; this has the character of a special room that conveys the impression of exclusivity, but also facilitates security, as well as a 'Cabinet Study Room' with a separate controlled entrance.

The rebirth of urbanity

In a larger sense, this 'experimental' sensibility and approach is in keeping with a more general concern for the health and vibrancy of the city, which may be read in each of Badran's projects, from the Al-Beit Foundation at the beginning of his career up through the remarkable urban proposals presented in Chapter 7. The Baghdad State Mosque, like many of his other buildings, was conceived as a city in microcosm, and the concept for the Doha Museum expands on that strategy; not just to emphasize Doha as 'the city of the museum', but to make the entire complex of the museum as a city. He envisioned a museum in this place, part of which was once a thriving neighbourhood, of the old city fabric, that 'functions

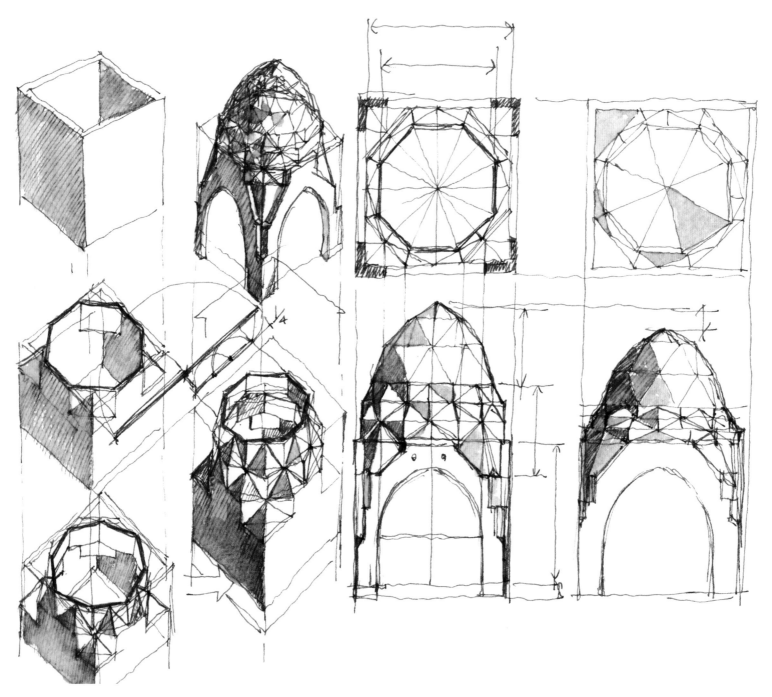

Above

Museum of Islamic Arts, Doha, Qatar. The *muqarnas* is an Islamic squinch, much refined. In this sketch of the entrance structure the *muqarnas* is transformed into the dome itself.

Above

Museum of Islamic Arts,
Doha, Qatar. The exhibition hall,
Al-khan (the traditional market).
The effective contrast here is the
use of an advanced technology
for the roofing system, over a
historically based columnar hall.

Above
Museum of Islamic Arts, Doha,
Qatar. The sweeping arc of an
internal 'street' reveals a trace of
the old city, and updates it into a
contemporary lobby.

as a reborn urban space, complete with plazas, streets and alleys, public buildings and private homes, courtyards, gardens (the remaining trees on site are evidence of the demolished living quarters), workshops, *suqs* and shops. In this context, the collections can be seen in a renewed context suited to their original meaning'.

A pervasive feature of many coastal cities in the Gulf States is the corniche, a raised multi-lane highway that runs along the seafront. The provenance of this type of highway is unknown but the French name is a possible clue that it has its roots in Le Corbusier's Plan for Tunis, in which a long ribbon of roadway with housing underneath, stretches along the coast. Whatever its source, the corniche has effectively cut off many cities from their seafront, making their coastline a wide strip of concrete. The shape of the Doha shoreline is no exception. Between 1953 and 1976, when a corniche was built on landfill or reclaimed land, there has been a progressive separation from the sea, which originally sustained the city and gave it meaning as a source of survival. Badran's re-creation of a 'harbour' turns back the collective mental clock (even though the corniche obviously cannot be moved), subliminally making the point that this imported European typology is divorcing cities in this region from their original source of life. But the curve of the corniche also has its blessings as it contributes towards establishing a high profile for the museum, giving it sufficient stature to stand as an equal partner with the National Museum, the Museum of State nearby and restores to a certain extent, the traces of the original shoreline of the old city of Doha and its sea frontage.

A record of life
As discussed previously, Badran expands on the rationalist view that the city is a logical entity to study because it is a repository of typologies, incrementally produced and adjusted over time. The Eastern tradition to which he belongs infuses this objective opinion with subjective memories, viewing the city not just as a collection of typologies, but an accretion of successive generations of *Iman*, or life, the record of the duality of the sacred and the secular, acting together. He believes that the Doha Museum can be understood as a virtual model of the narrative of place, and that by understanding the place's hidden values and the collective behaviour of its people, accumulated over time, he can unveil the *genus loci* of the place. As he describes this process:

I found the narrative ability manifested in Islamic texts translated through, but also beyond the limitations of place and time, and very evident in the understanding of the relationships between concepts of the 'fixed' (static) and the 'changeable', enabling place to be sustainable into future generations. This is exactly what I strive for in several of my architectural projects.

The galleries in this museum are viewed as an extension of that layering of life, in which visitors, according to Badran, 'can find something that helps them identify who they are, regardless of age, social background, gender, educational level, or place in the community'. They are far more than mere repositories of art.

Al-Ain Museum, United Arab Emirates
A transformation of another sort is described in the Al-Ain Museum, in which Badran, with his design team at Dar al-Omran, responded to an existing Ottoman fort that rises in a series of stacked drums at one end of an L-shaped site; a park

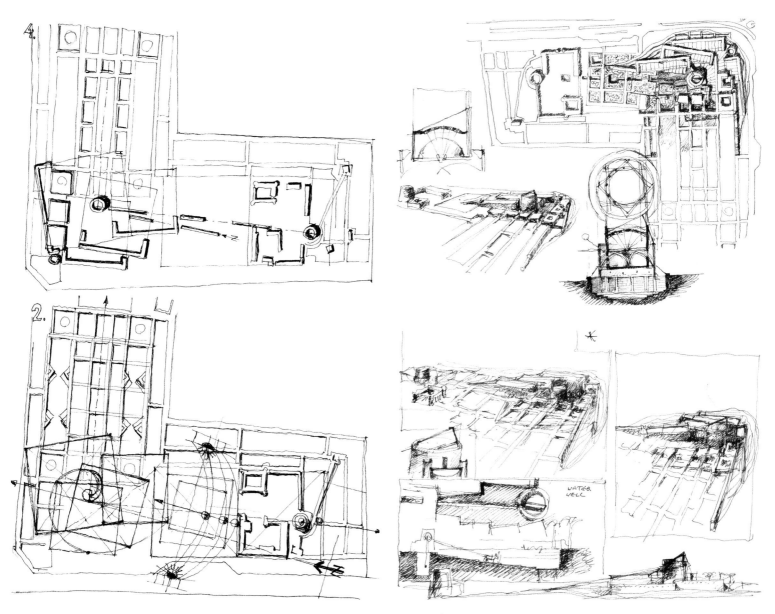

Above

The concept behind the Al-Ain Museum was to respect an existing Ottoman monument on the site by going underground, creating a series of subterranean gardens to which the galleries could relate. Shown above left is the force of the hard landscape elements and the old ruins of the site. The impact of the remaining ruins forms the overall morphological order.

Preserving a Living History **149**

inspired him to continue the idea of the oasis, which is such a prevalent, if subliminal metaphor in this arid region. Badran chose to respect the fort by placing the
various exhibition galleries and other functional elements of the museum eight
metres below grade to act as an ecological 'sink'. However, he also had the
museum clad in stone, to differentiate it from the mudbrick garrison, and used a
steel and glass canopy to allow light to penetrate down into the core of the new
subterranean world he has created. This core is on an axis with and diametrically
opposite the mudbrick fort, a glistening multi-faceted contemporary rendering of
this remnant of the past, which acts as an ordering device by which visitors can ori-
entate themselves. The galleries cascade away from it, overlapping in places to
make a graceful transition from the central core to the edge of the oasis-like site.
They are placed inside the protective U-shaped, stone-clad arms, which are glazed
on one side. Al-Ain demonstrates Rasem Badran's ability to translate the past into
a meaningful and aesthetically elegant contemporary language and is one of the
clearest examples of the narrative he describes. The axial alignment of the fort and
his crystalline, technologically expressive translation set up a dialogue between the
past and the present within a literal representation of an earthly paradise.

Curatorial spaces are not forgotten in this elegiac encounter, but are placed on
the other side of the core, along with the additional public functions now usually
found in a museum, such as an auditorium, restaurants and shops.

Below

The final model of the Al-Ain
Museum shows the
interrelationship between
landscape and architecture.

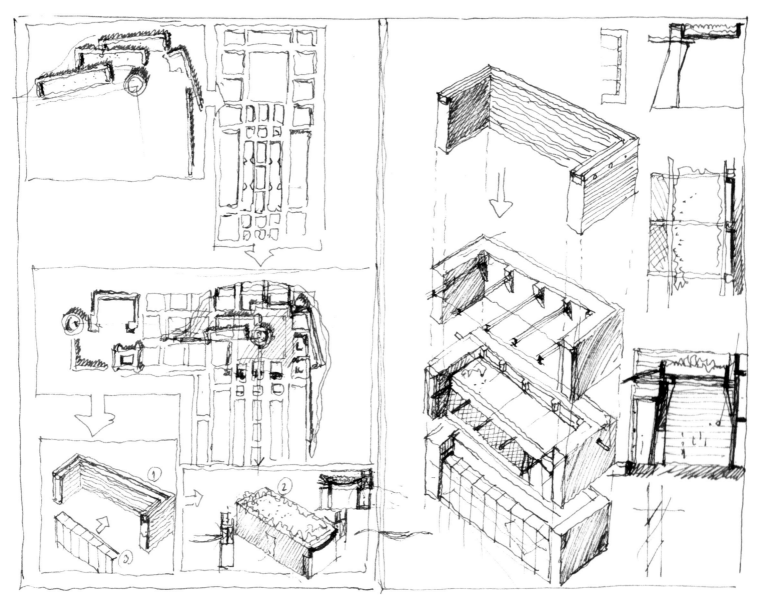

Above and right

Al-Ain Museum, United Arab Emirates. This sequence shows how an enclosure is created A series of 'U'- shaped retaining walls hold back the earth to create long linear galleries as well as an internal circulation spine that serves them. These galleries are slightly offset and see to cascade down the slope they replace. The suggested scheme blends with the exising site components, in a contextual approach.

Above

The enclosure contains the
cosmic roof device. The consistent
theme of the internal sundial as
cosmic connection is a focal point
once again in the Al-Ain design.

Above

Al-Ain Museum, United Arab Emirates. The bowstring trusses in this instance project past the wall line to allow the structure to be expressed on the outside.

Al-Ain Museum, United Arab
Emirates. Shown here is the
oasis morphology, in the
garden's ecological approach.
The cylindrical tower, which acts as a
hub for the galleries that fan out from
it, is a dominant presence.

Al-Ain Museum, United Arab
Emirates. The lobby. Light
articulates the circular tower from
the internal circulation spine and
the galleries it serves.

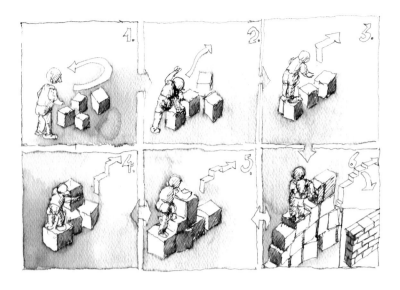

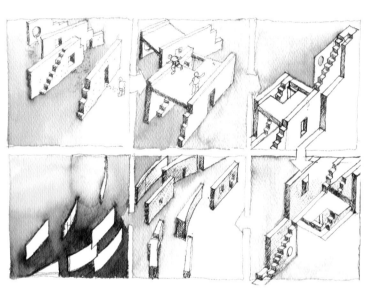
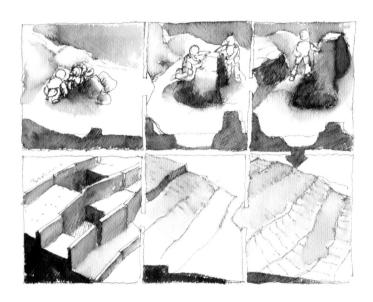

A museum for children in Amman

Badran also chose to bury most of another museum in Amman, but for a very different reason. This project, intended for children, is also located in a park, and is as much a playground as it is a place to accommodate exhibitions. The park in this case has a steeply sloped edge, which prompted the architect to make another attempt at what he calls 'zero architecture', following Al-Ain. In a series of wonderful sketches, he visually describes how children actually play, as opposed to the artificial ways that the manufacturers of playground equipment mistakenly believe that they do. This description led to enclosed spaces stepping down the slope of the park in terraces, terminating in a curved retaining wall that brings the series of terraces visually down to grade. Badran saw this as 'an experimental field for spatial creation which encourages childlike fantasy'.

Unfortunately, the attempt to create a 'zero architecture' succeeded too well as far as the client was concerned and this museum was not built because they believed it lacked a definitive visual image.

Above

In a delightful series of sketches Badran investigates how children really play, showing how they love to climb, slide and tunnel through spaces, and then how these natural inclinations can be converted into a playground of which they will never tire.

Right and below

Museum for Children,
Amman, Jordan. The landform
with which he had to work also
instructed how best to adapt the
site into the kinds of spaces he
felt children would like to explore.
Right: defining the domain
(the child's field of activity).
Below: the complexity of the
enclosure enables the child
to discover nature's logic.

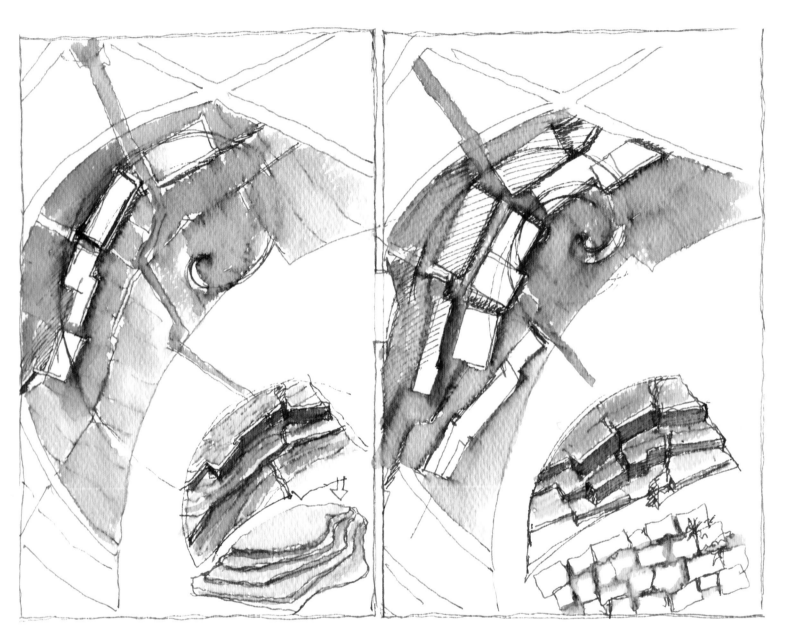

Above

Museum for Children, Amman,
Jordan. Traces of the domain
(the field of activity). The final
design begins to evolve into a long
series of terraces that follow the
contours of the hill.

Above

Museum for Children, Amman,
Jordan. Retaining walls and a
small tower to anchor them, as
well as perpendicular light wells
and a small outdoor enclosure,
complete the scheme.

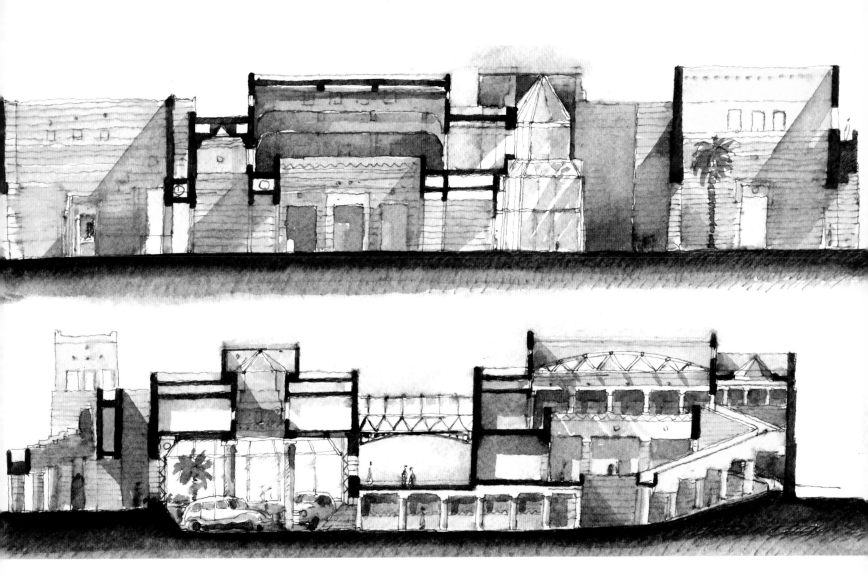

Above and opposite

The museum's structure resembles the overall fabric of the city. The unspoken mandate for the Al-Dara Complex was to present the idea of the past still being a part of contemporary life, and of progress, of continuity rather than disjunction.

The King Abdul Aziz Historic Centre, Riyadh: the Al-Dara Complex – The Living Cultural Museum

Preservation and restoration can qualify as museology if the latter is viewed in terms of the protection of heritage; with this in mind, the King Abdul Aziz Historic Centre in Riyadh could fit into the museum category. The project consists of three parts: the Al-Dara Complex (The Living Cultural Museum), the Folk Museum and the Historical Museum. These are intended to safeguard the characteristics of several historic buildings, intricately woven into the traditional urban fabric of the courtyards and narrow alleys of the old city. The Al-Dara Complex is considered to be an open living national museum reflecting the socio-cultural and political aspects of Saudi Arabia, which makes it an educational experience for school students, university researchers, tourists and families. It consists of an administration building and a museum of 13,000 square metres distributed on two floors. Al-Murabaa Palace, the second part of the complex, also houses a conservation department. The King Abdul Aziz Mosque is the third part of the centre and has been almost entirely reconstructed. Perpetuating the architectural craft of the Najd region was an essential part of this effort, so that a 'living museum' would enclose an actual one here.

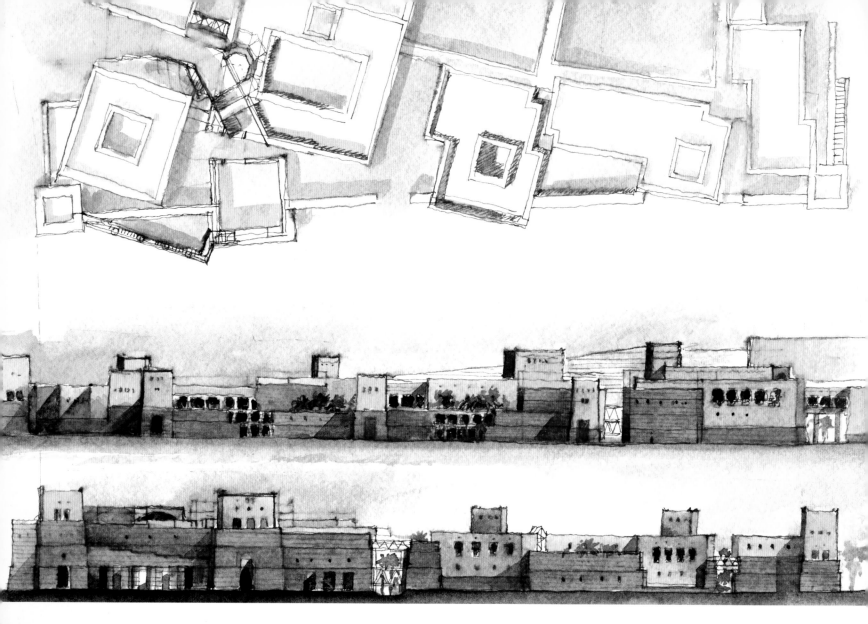

Above, left and opposite

The elevation of the Al-Dara
Complex is punctuated by vertical
towers and horizontal bridges,
which give it definition and a
feeling of strength appropriate
to its function. Top and above:
an active boundary wall works
as a source of knowledge through
its entertainment approach.
Opposite: The entrance to the
Al-Dara Complex.

Opposite

The exhibition hall as a traditional market (Al-khan).

Above

Orientation is an important consideration in any museum. In Al-Dara this is addressed by providing a clear sequential diagram to follow and many visual clues to make the path legible. These clues include being able to see the next level from the entry hall (above left), and the way up to it, without confusion.

Left and opposite

Interpretation of exterior spaces
has been a consistent technique
used in each of the urban projects
with which Badran has been
involved. In the Al-Dara project,
it adds a sense of expectation
and depth to the way in which
people experience the spaces.
The balance between light and
shade, between darkness and
brightness, increases wind
movement. The shape of the
man-made column complements
and echoes the naturally produced
beauty of the palm tree trunks.

Left
Al-Dara Complex, Riyadh,
Saudi Arabia. Whenever possible,
natural, local landscape forms
and plants found in the region are
used in open spaces. This makes
it easier for people to relate to
and interact with these spaces.

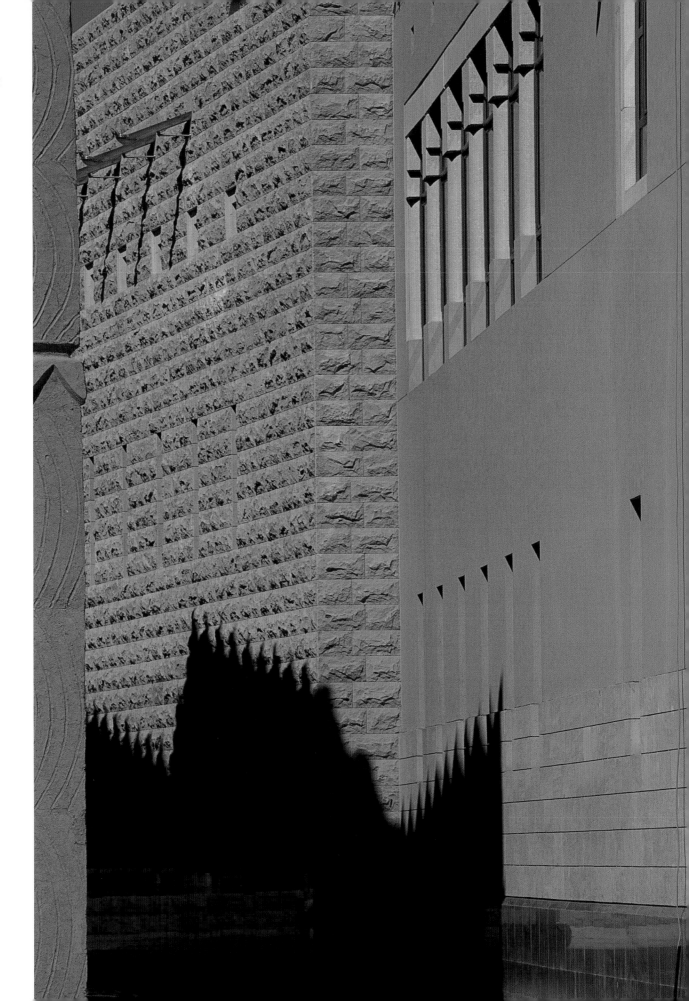

Right

Al-Dara Complex, Riyadh, Saudi Arabia. This image shows the strength of the ecological wall. Placed in the intense climate of Saudi Arabia, with a design punctuated by vertical and horizontal motifs as lighting fixtures, the dramatic shadows on different textures are far from coincidental.

Left

Al-Dara Complex, Riyadh, Saudi Arabia. The extensive use of glass on skylights over internal spaces makes little sense in a hot climate, but does work as an eye-catching canopy outside, with light penetrations.

Right

Al-Dara Complex, Riyadh, Saudi Arabia. Although many people do not realize it, Saudi Arabia has a rainy season, so glass to steel connections must be watertight.

Above and right

Al-Dara Complex, Riyadh, Saudi
Arabia.
Making a large canopy, however
skilfully structured, appear to
hover in air is difficult. Badran's
successful articulation of both the
aesthetic and engineering aspects
achieves this feat, and dramatizes
the entrance experience.

Right
Al-Dara Complex, Riyadh, Saudi Arabia. Juxtaposing linear and segmented forms contributes to an impression of visual complexity.

A divergent range but similar intent

The museums described in this chapter vary widely in function and stature, but share a similar connection to their respective locations which conveys Badran's commitment to the idea of wedding architecture to its individual place. In some cases, this has required a modest design approach that is far different from the egocentric museum architecture now typical in other parts of the world. The Al-Ain Museum, for example, respects and reinterprets the past and does not seek to upstage it. Each of the projects included here may be considered as being illustrative of a divergent direction in museum design, since they all defer to a cultural tradition and the people who have created it, as well as the environmental relationships that have formed them.

Above, left and right

A light fixture based on traditional forms designed by Badran.

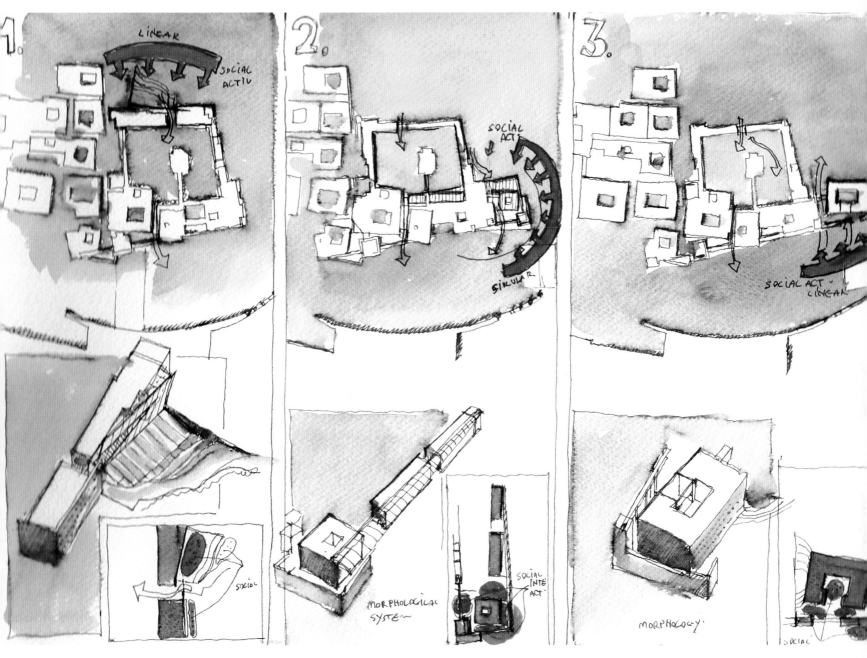

1. LINEAR
SOCIAL ACTIV
social

2. SOCIAL ACT
CIRCULAR
MORPHOLOGICAL SYSTEM
SOCIAL INTE ACT

3. SOCIAL ACT LINEAR
MORPHOLOGY
SOCIAL

Above

Studies for the extension to the
Al-Dara Complex, Riyadh,
Saudi Arabia. Often a series of
diagrams helps to reveal the
permutations affecting a specific
design solution. These drawings
explore a potential open-air
interaction with the buildings,
through a flexible process
of future development
and expansion.

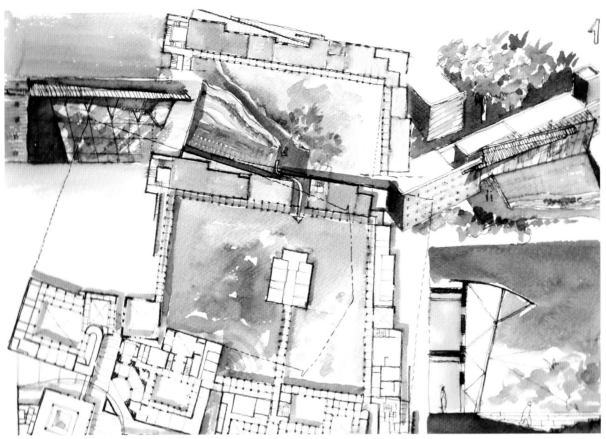

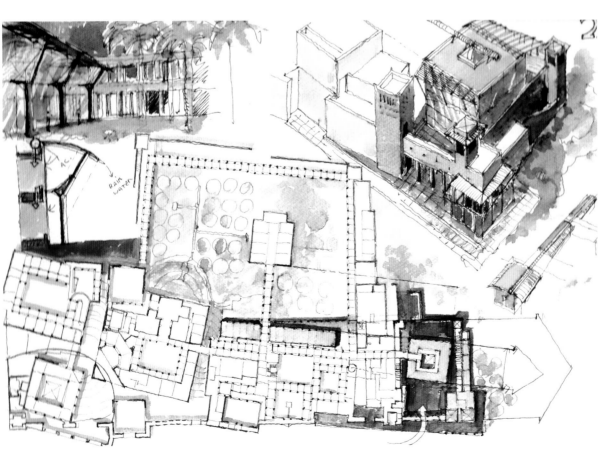

Left and opposite above
Studies for the extension to the
Al-Dara Complex, Riyadh, Saudi
Arabia. Badran is rigorous in his
approach to all of his sketches
and watercolours – once all the
conflicting criteria are resolved,
the evolution of the design
proceeds to the next stage.
These drawings suggest further
alternative future expansions of
the project with (opposite below)
a view of the organic growth of
the structure through time.

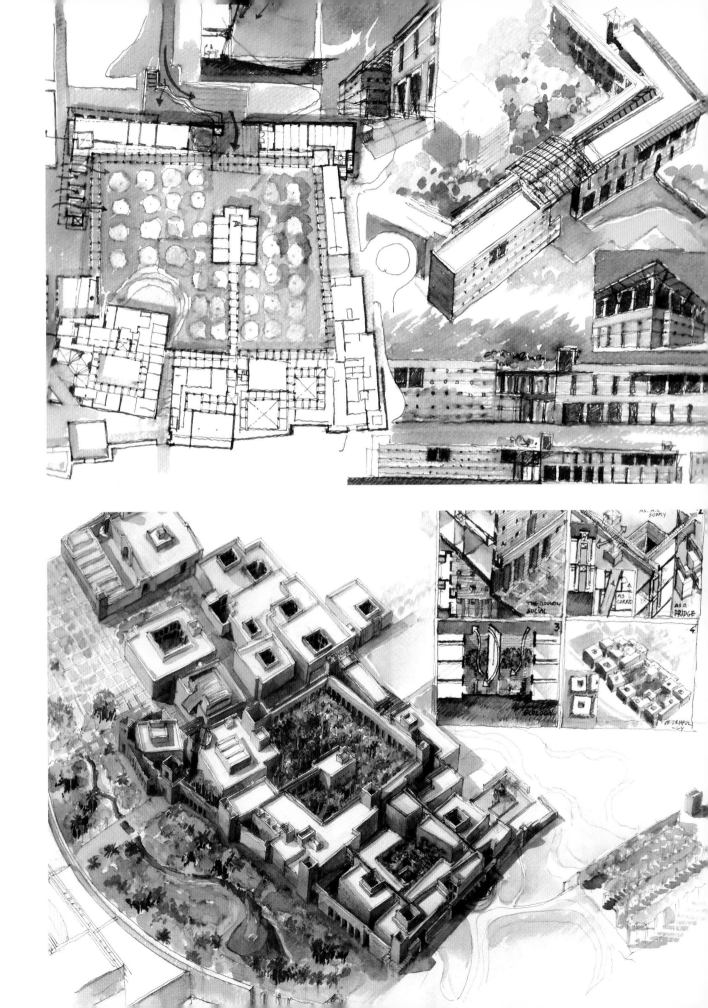

An Earthly Paradise

The garden has a special place in Islamic culture. As most of the region in which Islam was born is arid, any green area with water, like the oasis, is more than just a respite from the heat. It represents life and death, or survival. It stands to reason that the garden is also a symbol of paradise, or *al-firdos*, which may be attained by the righteous after death. Water is especially precious and its use in the garden is carefully prescribed. Historic examples of Islamic gardens clearly demonstrate the guiding principles, which are perhaps even clearer than in the case of architecture. The Alhambra in Granada, Spain, has two classic gardens that define the type, the Court of the Lions and the Court of the Myrtles. In each case there is a clear sequential progression from public to private space, leading up to layered containment by dematerialized surfaces and the judicious use of greenery and water.

Al-Azhar Garden, Cairo

Rasem Badran had the opportunity to contribute to this tradition when he was invited by the Aga Khan Trust for Culture to participate in an international competition to design a park near the Al-Azhar Mosque in the medieval quarter of Cairo. The design brief for the Al-Azhar Park Project called for a five-star restaurant with an outdoor dining area, a pavilion/gallery and a larger landscaped area with parking. Others may have considered this brief to be straightforward to the point of allowing little latitude for creativity. In his characteristically systematic and thorough way, however, Badran saw this as an opportunity to engage in a narrative with the rich history of Cairo, which has one of the largest concentrations of historically significant Islamic architecture in the world. To understand his design approach and competition submission it is necessary briefly to describe Cairo's history, which so thoroughly informed his scheme.

Al-Qahira, the victorious

When Islam burst out of the Arabian Peninsula it was inevitable that Egypt, then held by the Byzantine Empire, would be one of the first to come into the orbit of the nascent empire. The forces of General Amir Ibn al-As besieged the fortress of Babylon on the Nile, and despite reinforcements from Alexandria, it fell to the Muslim army in 641. The mosque that Amir built, now much changed, reflects

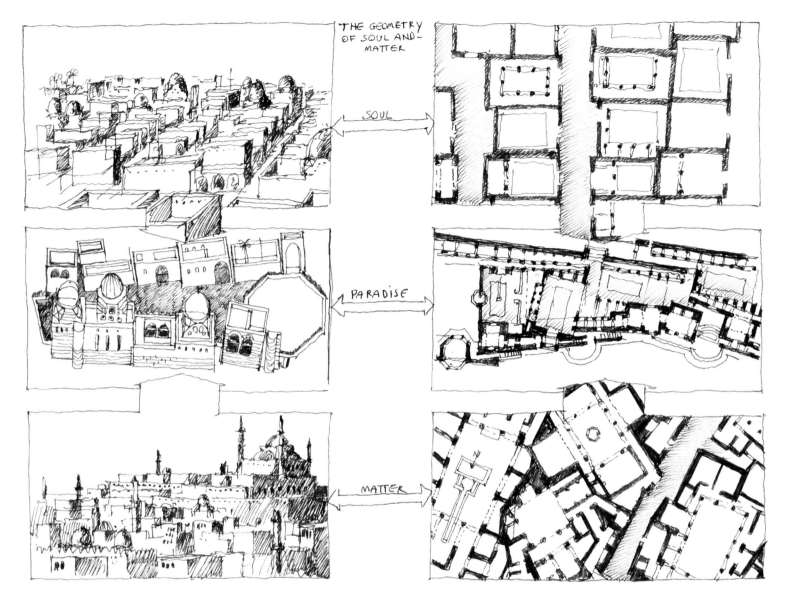

THE GEOMETRY OF SOUL AND MATTER

SOUL

PARADISE

MATTER

the hypostyle structures with central open courtyards first built in Makkah and Madinah. The surrounding settlement, named Al-Fustat, was not architecturally impressive. Successive expansions moved north-east between the Nile and the Muqattam Hills. Al-Fustat, near the fortress of Babylon, remained the Islamic capital until the end of Umayyad rule in AD 750, eventually stretching more than five kilometres along the riverbank. It was supplanted by Al-Askar in AD 752 and Al-Qatai, founded by the powerful Ibn Tulun in AD 870. All of these settlements have now largely disappeared, with only the mosques of Amr and Ahmad ibn Tulun remaining as major landmarks. The impressive Ibn Tulun mosque is noteworthy as an architectural masterpiece. The following century saw the arrival of the Fatimid General Gawhar Al-Siqelli, who laid out 'Al-Qahira' ('the victorious') in AD 969, north-east of the warren of mudbrick houses that his predecessors had built in the marshy lowlands near the bank of the Nile. This new city, a fortified rectangle, established an urban polarity in which Al-Qahira was the privileged enclave of the ruling class and Al-Fustat and its extensions

Above

The geometry of soul and matter. In preparation for the Al-Azhar garden design, Badran identified appropriate precedents in Cairo.

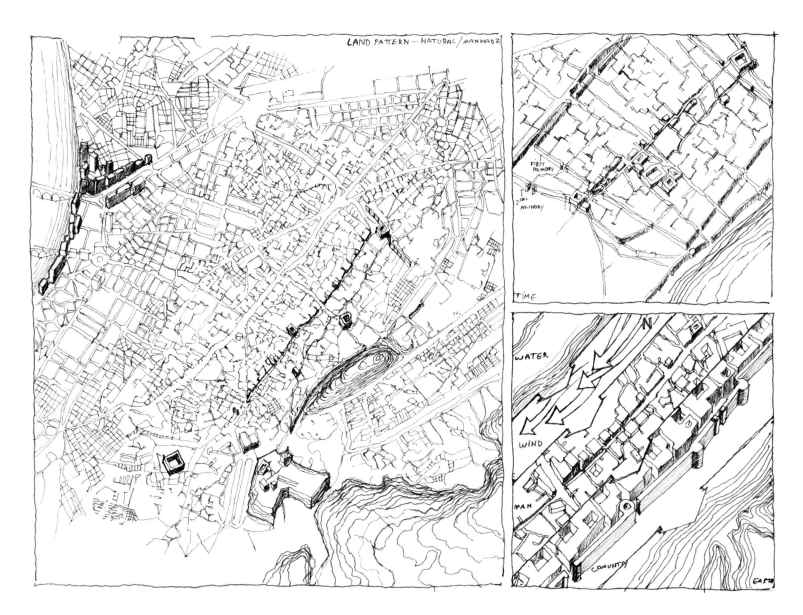

LAND PATTERN – NATURAL/MANMADE

Above

The natural versus the man-made land pattern. As part of his research, Badran also identified the overriding importance of Shari Al'Muizz, the north-south spine running through the medieval part of Cairo.

were the *colloga magna* as a crowded commercial port. The Fatimid city has been succinctly described by Victoria Meinecke-Berg:

The plan of Al-Qahira shows a roughly regular rectangle encircled by fortification walls, and divided (...) by a great thoroughfare, the main street or qasaba. *In the centre two gradually enlarged palace complexes faced each other on either side of the* qasaba *which here opened into a large square, the Maidan Bain al-Qasrain. South of the great Eastern Palace the Friday Mosque, Al-Azhar, was erected. Around this central complex of palaces, which contained all the government dependants and stores, the great mosque, exercise fields and gardens were located and, in accordance with the usual practice of Arab settlement, the city was divided into various quarters to house the (...) caliph's military entourage.*[1]

The 3.7-square-kilometre area Meinecke-Berg describes has one of the greatest concentrations of historic Islamic architecture in the world. It is bounded by the

Left

Al-Azhar Garden, Cairo.
A series of diagrams makes
parallels between the medieval
city and the site for the garden,
a city in microcosm, with each
described as being made up of
the whole as a sum of its parts.
Here is a poetic dialogue between
the changing behaviour of the old
city through time and the way in
which the site's condition has
responded to this.

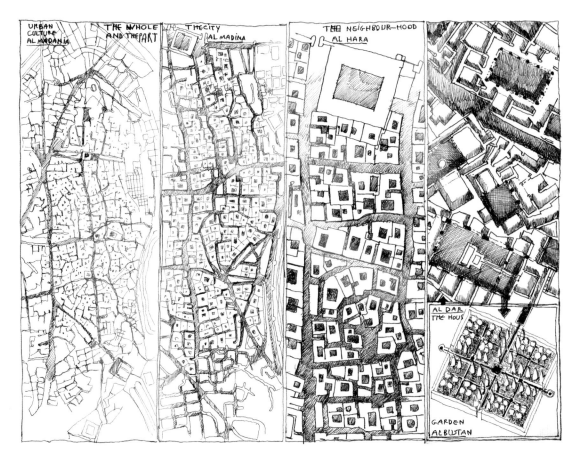

The acknowledgment of the urban
tissue's cosmic skin creates a
dialogue between the whole and
the part.

Bab al-Futuh and Bab al-Nasr to the north, the Mosque of Ahmad ibn Tulun to the south, Sharia Port Said to the west and the Salah Salem Road to the east. The mosques alone constitute a veritable catalogue of the cultures that, in their turn, supplanted the Fatimid's, and which are begging to be studied while still under threat of destruction. Few Fatimid examples remain, but those that do, with their characteristic keel-arches and ingeniously adaptive plans, such as the Al-Aqmar Mosque, are all the more precious for their scarcity. Such adjustment to the street line, caused by the necessity of observing the *qibla*, continued in other stylistic periods in the city, but there are few other examples that demonstrate such finesse. Intricate detailing is also a characteristic of Fatimid architecture, as the finely wrought sunbursts, *muqarnas* and calligraphy on the single exposed exterior façade of Al-Aqmar shows. A Cairene tradition that may be seen to begin with these mosques is their function not only as a place of prayer, but also as interrelated landmarks along established routes of travel. These devices establish a 'human-scale intermediary' between outside and inside, act as cooling devices in a hot arid climate, and provide interior public spaces for quiet meditation between the five established times of formal prayer during the day.[2]

Walking along the Shari Al'Muizz (which Meinecke-Berg refers to as the Bain al-Qasrain in the description previously cited), one must recall that this north-south thoroughfare, which begins at the Bab al-Futuh and runs to the Bab Zuwaila, was once more linear than it is today. Variations in that linearity began to occur only after the Ayyubid ruler Salah ad-Din (the Saladin of medieval legend, scourge of the Crusaders), opened the previously inaccessible Fatimid city to public habitation and use in 1175. Beginning with the Mosque of Al-Hakim, a sequence of similar structures was placed at intervals along the main street to act

Below

Al-Azhar Garden, Cairo.
The garden design begins to become more clarified, inside its own segmental walled enclosure intended to reveal as well as conceal. There is a dialogue between the micro and the macro and its impact in shaping the overall order of the garden.

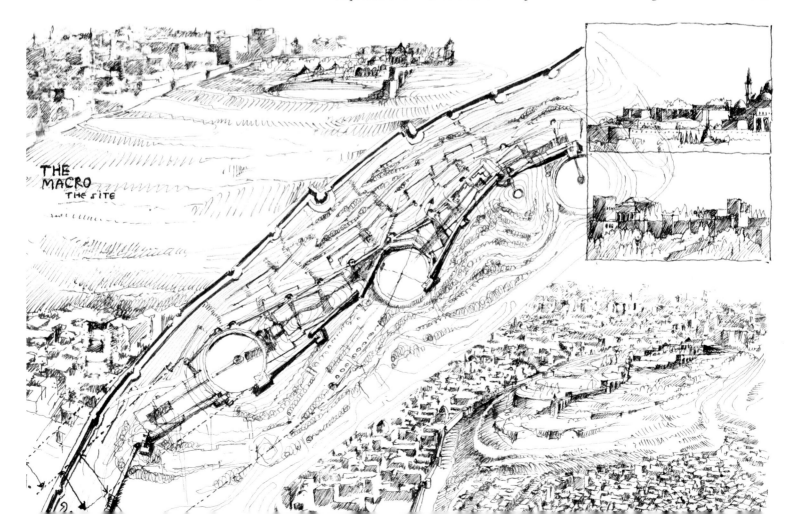

THE MACRO
THE SITE

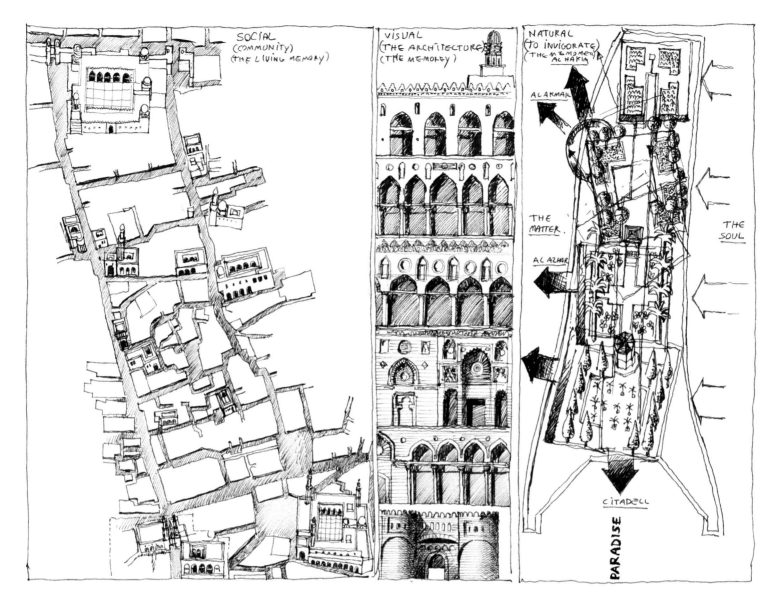

The medieval core of Cairo has several layers of historical influence from Fatimid to Ayyubid, Mamluk and Ottoman, which are cross-referenced to the Al-Azhar Garden as a representation of paradise. The garden is a balance between the social (community), the visual (memory) and the natural (meditation).

as landmarks. Al-Aqmar Mosque can be found halfway down the main street, with the Al-Salih Talai Mosque – which is now outside the Ayyubid wall but nevertheless a more obvious part of this string – opposite the Bab Zuwaila.[3] These marking points, placed according to their visibility, also served as devices for gradually increasing or decreasing architectural scale as pedestrians moved from one end of the city to the other. Standing at the top of one of the minarets of the Mosque of Shaykh al-Mu'ayyad – incorporated into the wall above the Bab Zuwaila – it is possible to look back along the length of the Shari Al'Muizz and see the open, green areas in the midst of the remaining mosques. A team from the Architectural Association in London produced a report based on recorded temperatures taken at sunrise, noon and sunset at various times of the year, which shows that these green areas, now becoming increasingly rare in the city, acted as natural cooling and filtration devices not just for each mosque but for surrounding buildings as well. Extending their studies to houses and open squares, the team found that a deliberate tactic of interlocking spaces had been employed,

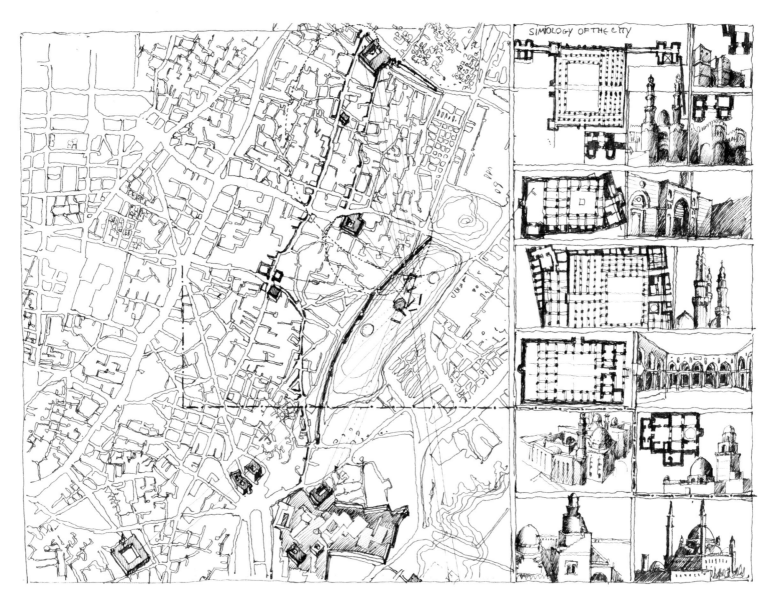

SIMIOLOGY OF THE CITY

The semiological elements of the city as matrix pattern of reference. Various monuments in medieval Cairo are identified as resources, including Bab Zuwaila, the Mosque and *madrasa* of Sultan Hasan, Al- Guyushi Mosque, the Mosque of Ahmad ibn Tulun Mosque, and the Citadel.

each with two courtyards – one with plants on the windward side and the other paved. As the sun and hot air generated by the paved area rises, the simple principle of convection pulls the cooler air, trapped by the vegetation in the planted court from the previous evening, through the open space. Since the planted courts were located to intercept the desert breeze first, the higher palm trees acted much like the cilia in the lungs to clean it. This process turned the entire pattern of solids and voids into an effective combination of air-conditioning systems. Air filter gardens and courts were not only the earthly manifestation of *al-firdos* in microcosm, but also served the very real and practical purpose of keeping the city cool and clean.[4]

The Mamluk monuments, begun in 1262 with the Mosque of Sultan Baybars, continued such traditions, albeit in a different stylistic direction. One of the most renowned and visible of these is the *maristan* (hospital), *madresa* and mausoleum of Sultan Qala'un, begun in 1284 and completed in the following year, which combines many of the elements that are now recognized as distinctly Mamluk.

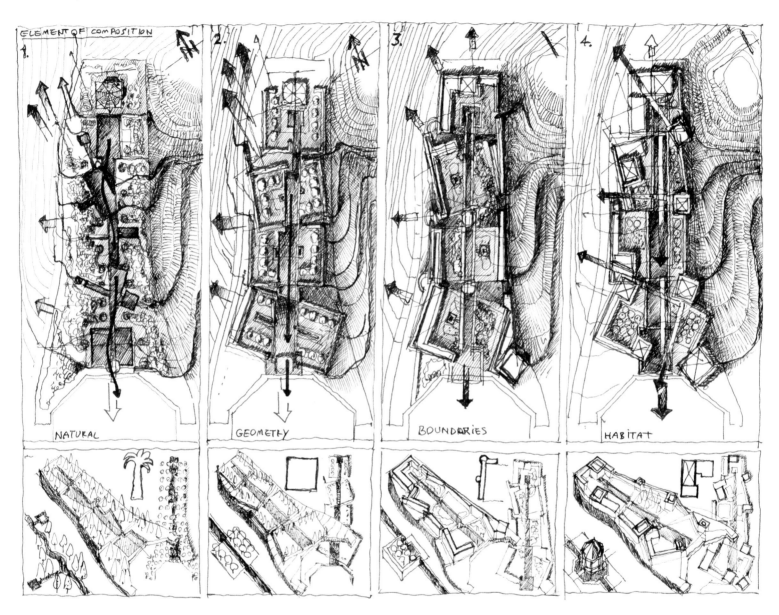

A sequence of diagrams of the Al-Azhar Garden focusing from left to right on the natural surroundings, geometry, boundaries and habitat.

It contains a breathtaking array of coloured glass windows and soaring interior spaces equal to many Gothic structures of Western Europe.

The Mamluk period (1250–1517), which saw Cairo as the capital of their powerful empire, has left many of the monuments that define the city's Islamic character. Most of those monuments are mosques or complexes containing mosques.

The dome and minarets of the mosques are particularly individual, built of stone instead of brick and featuring intricate ribbing and chevrons as motifs. The cruciform-plan *madresa*, best exemplified by the Sultan Hasan Mosque of 1356–62, was a great accomplishment of this period and remains one of the most significant historical monuments in Islamic architecture, because of the originality of its solution to a difficult functional problem. The 38-metre-high main entrance is a masterpiece of metalwork and stone carving with an intricate stalactite composition capping the doorway.

The next historical period is that of Ottoman rule in Egypt from 1517 to 1805, which coincided with a military victory over the Mamluks by Sultan Selim. The Mosques of Sulaiman Pasha on the Citadel and Sinan at Bulaq reflect this style, which is characterized by a broader, flatter dome with more pronounced minarets. While generally considered to be less vibrant than the Mamluk period (any effort would by comparison be considered so), the final Ottoman phase is now being re-evaluated and is beginning to yield valuable insights as a rich era in its own right.

As modern Egypt emerged in the 1840s under Muhammad 'Ali, a mosque was built at the Citadel, which still dominates the skyline of Cairo today. It is a typical Ottoman-style mosque of exceptional elegance, especially in its pencil-point minarets.

These many layers of historical influence inform and define contemporary mosque design in Egypt generally, and in Cairo specifically. The extent of this reliance on historical styles is the result of the country's role as an aesthetic crucible during a critical period for Islam, which was then facing the Mongol threat. No contemporary mosque designed in Egypt has been able to rival this legacy, though many current efforts are illustrated here, including the truly outstanding and modest work of Hassan Fathy at New Gourna Village, which dates from the late 1940s and 1950s. Perhaps all the vernacular examples may be traceable to one or several of these historical influences; the intellectual challenge lies in an accurate determination of the mixture used.

The design approach to the Al-Azhar Garden

The unique topography of Cairo was one of the first things that attracted Badran's attention, in particular what he refers to as the predominance of a number of 'valleys' or 'cracks'. The most elemental of these, of course, is the Nile Valley itself, which for millennia was the source of annual renewal until it was contained by the Aswan High Dam in the 1960s. The inundation caused by the Nile deposited fertile silt on a thin band of farmland on either side, which was covered by water for nearly six months a year. This annual cycle of renewal was the origin of the Pharaonic cult of death, the idea of resurrection, and the elaborate burial monuments, such as the pyramids, that are a significant image of early Egyptian history.

The first Muslim settlement was supported by the port city of Al-Fustat, located on the Nile and the Fatimid city of Al-Qahira, or Cairo, and it took advantage of a

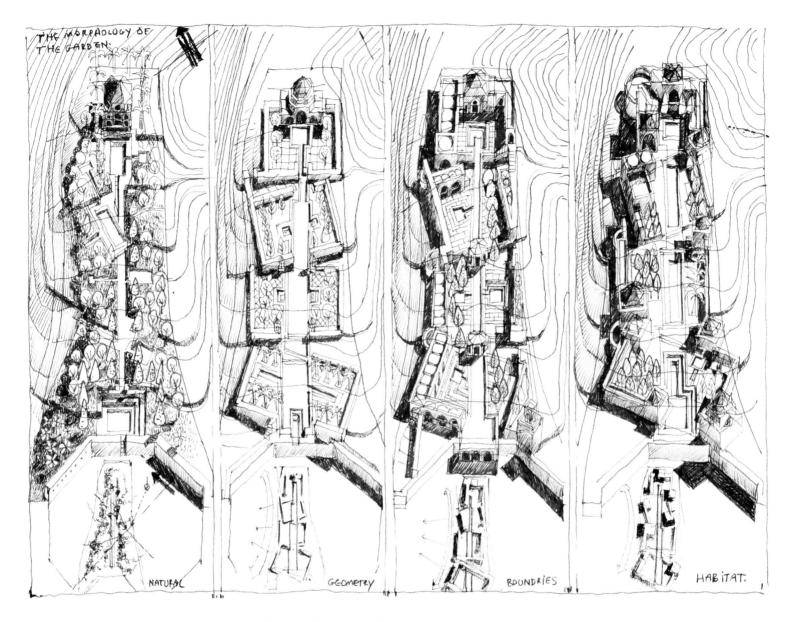

The morphology of the garden.
The four considerations are
further refined, with walls and
architectural features defined
more clearly.

depression or valley below the Muqattam Hills for military and climactic protection. Badran also interpreted Shari Al'Muizz, the main north-south thoroughfare through the city , named after the first Fatimid ruler, as a 'valley' or 'crack' as well. There is speculation among some historians that the Fatimids were influenced by the Roman cities they had seen on their trek across North Africa on their way to Egypt, and adopted the idea of a *cardo maximus* from them; others argue that Shari Al'Muizz runs north-south for environmental reasons, so that alternating halves of the street would be cool for half of each day.

Whatever the reason for its orientation, Shari Al'Muizz became the main conduit or connection between the Sahara trade routes to the south-west and major cities like Damascus to the north; it was the source of the phenomenal prosperity experienced by Cairo during a period equivalent to the Middle Ages in Europe. This prosperity was augmented by two additional historical events, the Mamluk victory over the Mongols at the Battle of Ain Jalut in Syria (1260) and the fall of Constan-

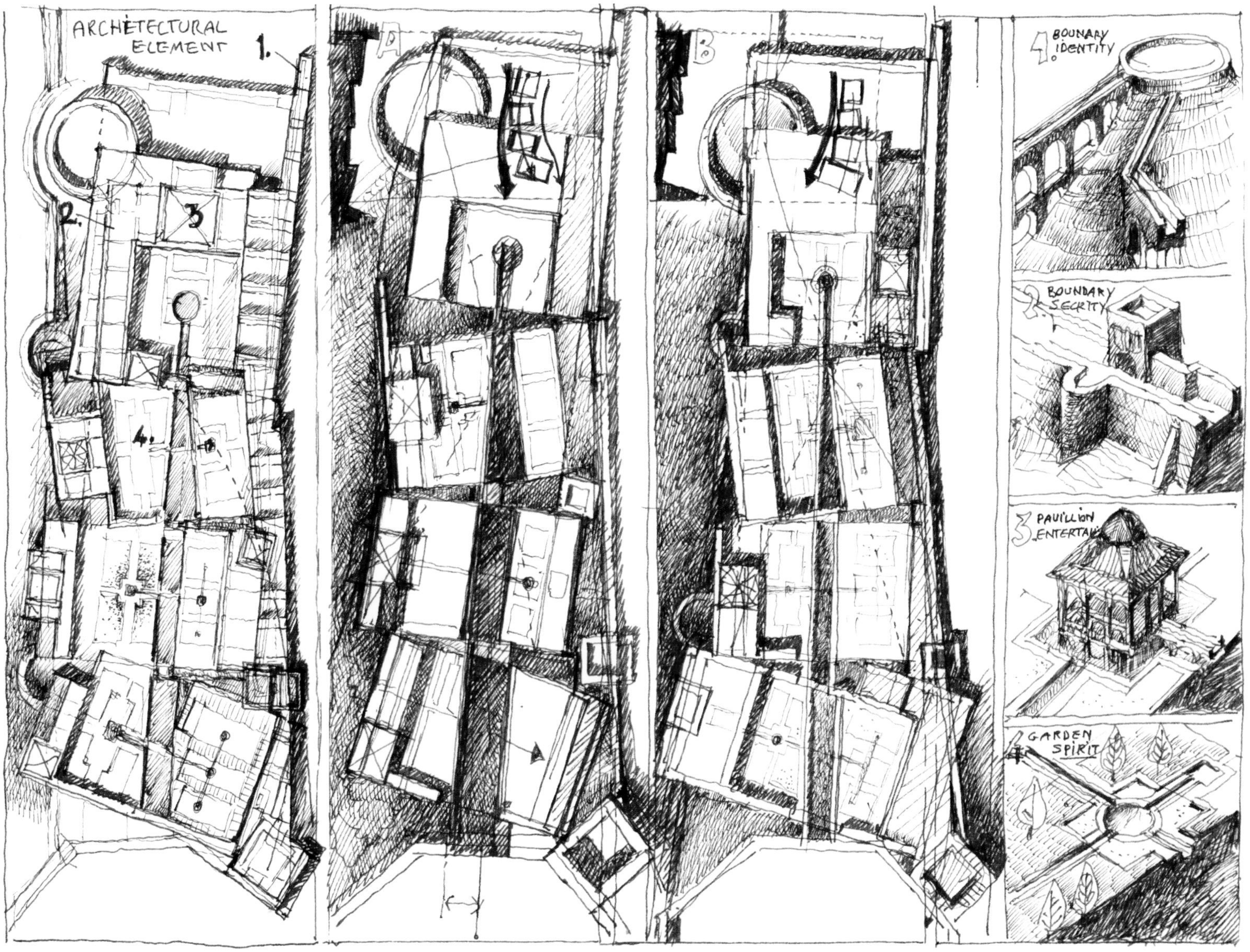

Al-Azhar Garden, Cairo. The boundary, partially recalling the aqueducts that once served Mamluk Cairo, as well as a water line as a liquid spine through the entire garden, emerge. The architectural elements enhance the identity of the garden, the sense of security and entertainment, all within its spiritual needs.

tinople to the Ottoman Turks in 1453. Both these events made the city of Cairo a safe haven for refugees and the most cosmopolitan urban centre in the entire region.

Valleys

Badran commemorates the significance of these 'valleys' in determining the urban morphology of the medieval quarter, the concept relative to the garden he designed, by creating a valley in its midst. He describes the importance of this factor in this way:

I saw the site as one part of the overall topography of the city, including both the natural and the built environment, the high and the low, the hill and the valley (or 'crack'); the positive and the negative. This topography is a product of human interaction with the context of Cairo over time. On the one hand the site must be seen in relationship to the high rises of modern Cairo along the banks of the Nile,

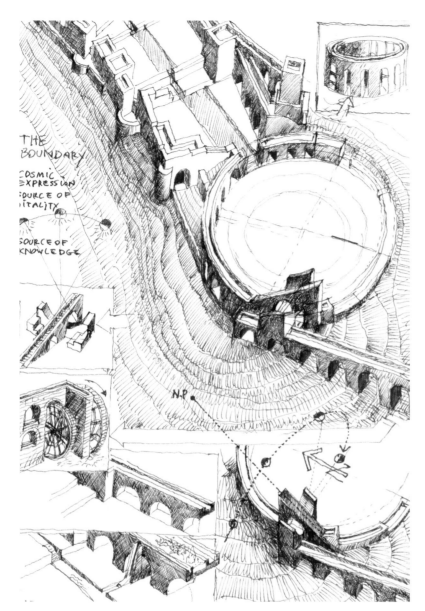

mirrored by the natural hill on which the Citadel is built and the Muqattam Hills behind it. On the other hand, these high rises and the opposing platform on which the citadel sits contrast with the "cracks" of the city, including the Nile as a water crack; a vital source of life, and Shari Al'Muizz as an urban crack, a vital source of social interaction.

His conceptual design approach takes into consideration the important historic urban and architectural context of the site, and its physical and visual characteristics, as well as the client's interest in making specific references to Fatimid architecture and to the philosophy that produced such artistic creations. Badran's vision of this project, which takes into account both historical background and symbolism, is an overall one. His sketches intended to convey the main ideas and forces influencing the design in this sensitive location, including issues of historical continuity and symbolism. Badran explains his approach:

Al-Azhar Garden, Cairo. The balance between the vertical and the horizontal skin. The boundary curls up to become both an outdoor amphitheatre and an overlook, terminating one end of the garden and adapting the sundial concept.

Various kinds of trees, reflecting Pharaonic wall paintings, are shown in partial elevations.

THE·BOUNDARIES

AQUA DUCKT·

THE
WALL

Al-Azhar Garden, Cairo.
Axonometric sketches begin to
explain the layering of the edge
condition that is an important part
of the boundary concept.

As stated in Al-Isra; (The Night Journey), 14:44: 'The seven heavens, the earth, and all who dwell in them give glory to Him.' This is a relationship that joins man and the universe to be united in front of God. Accordingly the Muslim sees the power of Allah in every event, and every existing being draws its existence from Allah. Therefore, the divine approach in this understanding of the philosophy of life works in every time and place. It is a methodology of life that respects Man's instinct, capabilities, strengths, and weaknesses, and enables him to ascend towards perfection.

Life is a symbol of sacredness because it is a divine gift. It therefore, through its relationship to God, prepares Man to establish a faithful relation with all aspects of God's creation including place, time and universe.

The translation of this understanding into a way of life within the social and environmental context, reflects in turn on Man's artistic products which are not considered a mere symbolic reference related to this understanding, but part of it.

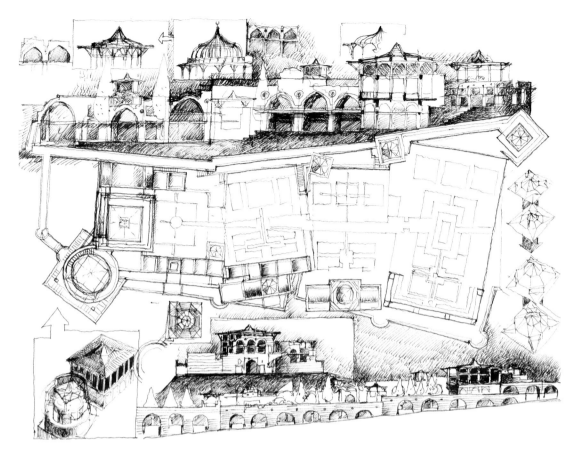

Al-Azhar Garden, Cairo.
Various configurations of the
pavilion are explored. Because
architectural elements are
minimal in the scheme they take
on heightened significance.

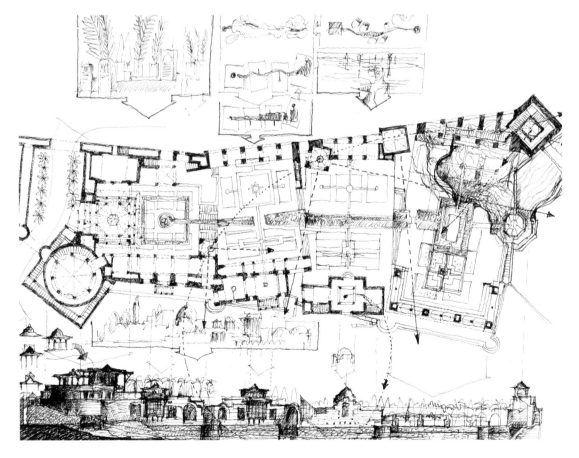

The spatial composition of the
boundary. The section through the
site shows how massing
accentuates topographical
changes.

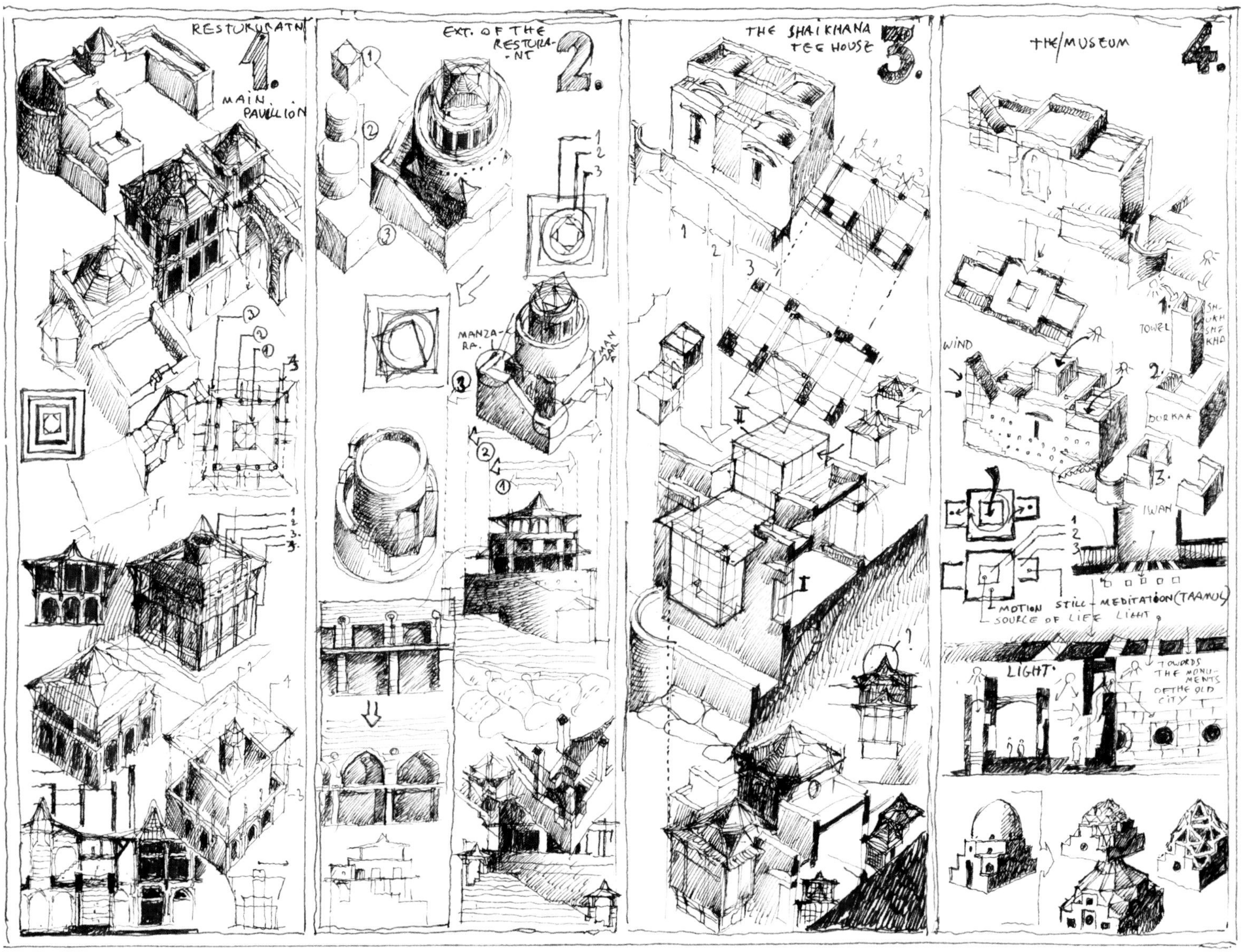
1.
MAIN PAVILLION
EXT. OF THE RESTURA-NT
2.
THE SHAIKHANA TEE HOUSE
3.
THE/MUSEUM
4.
MANZA-RA.
WIND
DURKAA
IWAN
MOTION STILL MEDITATION (TAAMUL)
SOURCE OF LIFE LIGHT
LIGHT

Studies of the various architectural elements to be used in the garden.

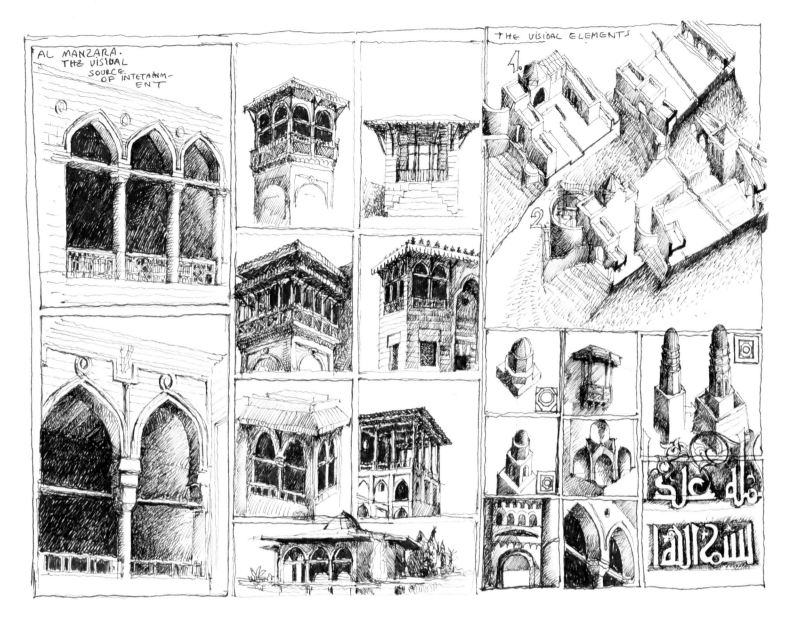

This is a philosophy that is not independent from the reality of life; but represents an understanding of such reality based on an actual experience of it. Therefore the Muslim realizes the value of his existence within place, time, society, environment, and universe. Accordingly, architecture and the city with its patterns, spaces, morphology, and socio-economic aspects not only represent this understanding, but also become catalysts in developing new dimensions to it.

This Islamic view of the relationship between Iman and life and between man and the universe provides a highly transparent understanding which defines frameworks, but does not define modes of thinking, and leaves horizons and doors open for interpretation. It is a transparency that transcends time and place so that history does not turn into a frozen part of the past, and place is not fossilized as a piece of archaeology in order to become a living reality in transparent contemporaneity; a reality that is deeply rooted in the past, and is the basis for a future that is a natural extension to it.

Understanding the historical layers and elements in the old city of Cairo. Sketches of various maqa'ad from Mamluk homes in old Cairo, and Sabil-Khuttub, as well as the minaret of the Mosque of Al-Hakim.

Boundaries

Some of the most distinctive features of Islamic Cairo are the long stretches of its defensive wall that are still intact. The points at which the north-south thoroughfare Shari Al'Muizz punctures this massive masonry circuit are marked by gates, called Bab al Futuh on the north and Bab Zuwaila on the south, which have also survived relatively unscathed. The construction quality of the masonry of the surviving stretches of wall is outstanding, and large buildings, such as the Mosque of Al-Hakim, engage with it in certain places. The wall, gates and buildings attached to it all informed Badran's design.

Aqueducts are another defining element of the urban layering of Cairo. Although they seem unnecessary in a city that is now so close to the Nile, the course of the river has shifted significantly since the founding of Al-Qahira (Cairo) by the Fatimids and its subsequent occupation by the Ayyubids, Mamluks and Ottomans. The Mamluks were keen builders and installed a large aqueduct to supply the walled city with fresh water from the river, as well as a Nilometer to better predict the extent and duration of the annual flood. Badran has used an aqueduct along the eastern windward perimeter of the garden to provide a feeling

Further historical references are provided by mosque entrances in the old city of Cairo.

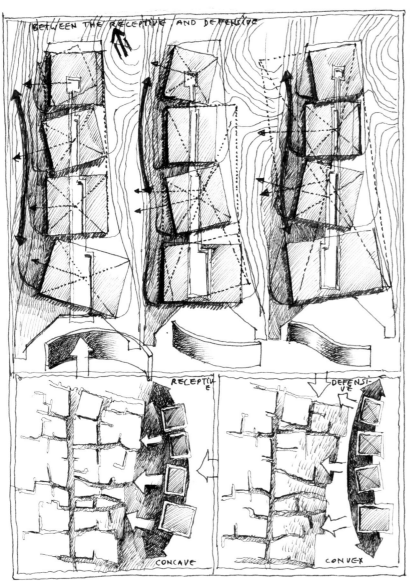

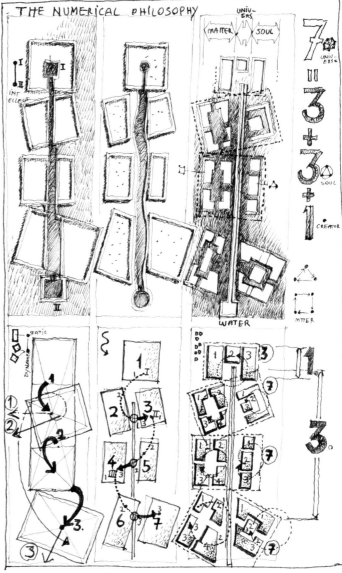

Numerological variations configure the various segments of the Al-Azhar garden plan.

of enclosure without blocking natural ventilation. It is filtered further by a band of palm trees that runs the entire length of this semi-permeable arched edge. The aqueduct turns along the northern entrance edge of the terraced enclosure and acts as a screen and gate at that end. It almost touches the pavilion near the main portal, creating a certain degree of tension between this upper edge and the bastion-like tower that holds the key position on the corner.

Numerology

Sufism, which can be described as a mystical and scholarly variant within Islam, is prevalent in Cairo and has also played a role in Badran's design:

One important stream of the Islamic view of life and artistic creation comes through Sufism, which is the inner dimension of Islam, expressing hidden archetypes in concrete symbols. Sufi philosophical principle includes the concept of

The final model of the Al-Azhar Mosque Garden competition submission, showing its integration with the topography of the site.

unity in multiplicity, and the symbolism of numbers and geometry. According to Sufism each number has its symbolic reference. For example, 1 is symbolic of the Creator; 2 of the intellect; 3 of the soul; 4 of the matter, and so on. The gathering of opposites is another important element, transparency is contrasted with solidity, barren with fertile, dry with wet, life with death. Also, cosmological symbols constitute another element of this philosophy. For example, a mountain symbolizes the divine, while water is symbolic of life. According to Sufism, everything in creation is a symbol; for everything perceived by the outer senses may be conceived through the inner senses as a sign of a higher state of reality. These principles have been interpreted in the past through the art and architecture of Muslim gardens and pavilions. In our design approach, a number of Sufi beliefs have been found informative and inspirational, for their relevance in the particular context of designing a public garden at the edge of Fatimid Cairo.

Cumulative order

Another determining factor in Badran's garden design was cumulative order, or the layering of historical influence over time, which has taken place in Cairo to an extent not found in other Islamic cities. The city that the Fatimids founded was a royal enclave from which the general populace was excluded. Possibly because of the influence of Roman city plans mentioned earlier, the Fatimid city was also organized on a grid, with major monuments located at intersections, much as the theatre, temple and bath-house are in the Roman city. After the Sunni Ayyubid forces, under Salah ad-Din, took over the city, it was opened up to the public, and the texture changed from orthogonal blocks to the more organic twisting warren of streets seen there today. Salah ad-Din also moved his palace outside the city wall to the Citadel, allowing for change to take place more freely inside the old Fatimid enclave. The social and economic pressures and constraints are only now becoming more clearly understood, thanks to the work of researchers such as Dr Jamel Akbar and Besim Hakim.

The Ayyubids brought in mercenary soldiers called Mamluks, or slaves, from various places in central Asia. They were mostly recruited from Turkic tribes and some were brought from Circassia. The Mamluks eventually usurped power from the Ayyubids and subsequently embarked on a building programme of unprecedented scope in the Muslim world, perhaps only rivalled by the Mughals in India, which paralleled their military success. They were eventually replaced by the Ottomans after they were weakened by the Napoleonic invasion in the late 18th century. Each of these various waves of occupation borrowed from the previous polity in power, and introduced its own social and cultural processes and the architectural expression that resulted from them. This syncretism is difficult to interpret, but Rasem Badran attempted to do so and to translate his interpretation into the design of the Al-Azhar Garden. He determined that this process of historical integration is linear as much as cumulative, a factor of 'the arrow of time' and layering.

Typologies

Numerous typologies remain from these successive waves of rule, which have been exhaustively identified and catalogued by Badran in preparation for his design, a natural practice in each of his projects. Cairo is unusually rich in such typologies, making it a treasure trove of legibility and a rich source of material for the kind of narrative in which Badran engages. One of the most interesting of

The labels visible in the drawing include:

NORTH WIND

HOT AIR

THE RESTURANT: AL MANZAR STUDY

ROOF STRUCTURE. AL MODARNAS

GEOMETRACA

CURVE

ROOF-CIELING IMAGE

these typologies is the *qa'a*, which was also of particular interest to Hassan Fathy. Serving a function that is best described as the main hall in a medieval Cairene house, the *qa'a* has been traced by Fathy to the Ukhaidir Palace in Kabala, Iraq, where it began as two *iwans* flanking a small central courtyard. This grouping of *iwans* straddling an open space occurred repetitively on either side of a larger court in the palace. This configuration emerged again in Al-Fustat during the Tulunid period hen transferred to Cairo as a fully enclosed, composite typology.

Rasem Badran demonstrated a thorough awareness and understanding of this and other uniquely Cairene typologies, which span the Fatimid, Ayyubid, Mamluk and Ottoman period. Their historical layering in the medieval city also made it possible for him to juxtapose them with impunity in the Al-Azhar Garden. Additions to the wall and the gates mentioned earlier include the *wikala* or combination stable, storage facility and hotel commonly used by the caravans travelling along the Shari Al'Muizz. They also feature the minaret, stacked one

Al-Azhar Garden, Cairo. Plan, section, elevation and roof plan of the restaurant (Al Manzarah).

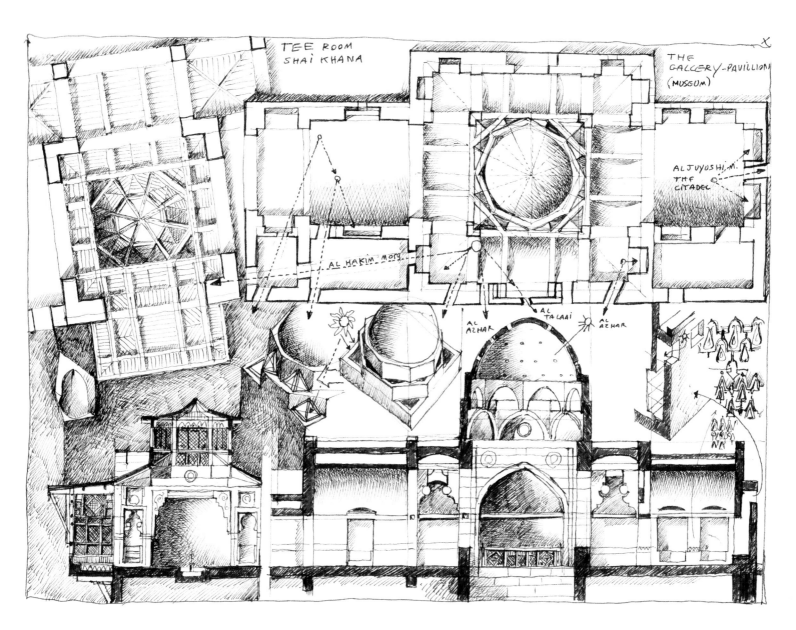

Al-Azhar Garden, Cairo.
The museum (the living school).

on top of the other above the Bab Zuwaila, dominating the urban corner of the Sultan Hasan Mosque, and spiralling upwards in imitation of the famous replication of the tower of Babel in the Mosque of Ahmad ibn Tulun in Cairo. The pavilion is reminiscent of an elegant pergola overlooking Istanbul, in the most private zone of the Topkapi Palace built by Mehmet (the Conqueror), the first Ottoman Sultan. The selection of this feature, called a *manzarah* from the last period of Muslim rule, prior to the British occupation of Egypt and its emergence as a modern state, completes Badran's utilization of typologies from each of the significant periods of Muslim occupation of Cairo.

The morphology of the garden

The garden, protected by the aqueduct and wall, steps down its valley slope in four distinctly angled terraces, bisected by a widening line of water that culminates in a waterfall at the end. The different angles of each terrace recall the

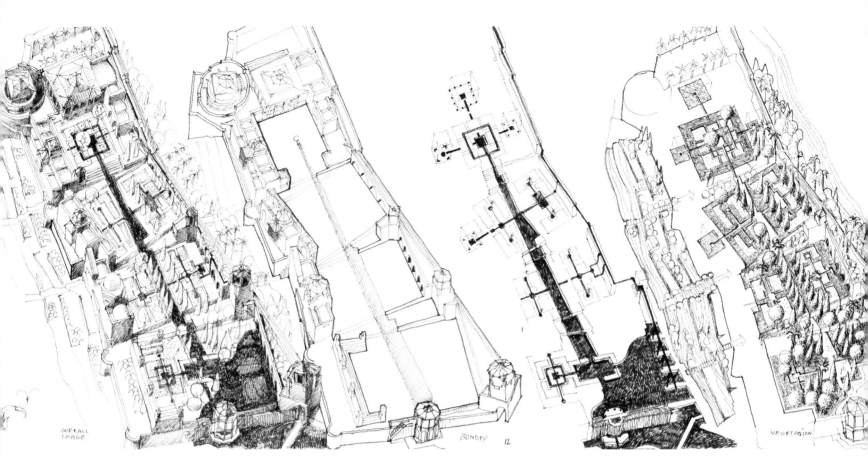

OVERALL
IMAGE

BONDEV 12

VEGETATION

tightly compressed building footprints in the old city, caused by owners taking advantage of every inch of street frontage along Shari Al'Muizz. In reference to the garden, which is the heart of the scheme, Badran says:

The garden and the courtyard are important forms of paradise. The garden is traditionally an enclosure planted with trees surrounding a central pavilion providing both a centrifugal movement outwards into the paradise of nature and a centripetal movement inwards through its four openings to the water. Water is the most spiritual element of all, according to Sufi Philosophy.

A dialectic of life and death

Water, as the ultimate symbol of life, especially in Egypt, is the appropriate liquid spine of Badran's design, and is a delicate foil for the massive boundary walls that surround it. It is an appropriate conclusion to the carefully choreographed entry sequence that has been established here, as the final gesture after being admitted into an earthly paradise.

Above and opposite

Sketch (above) and final watercolour rendering (opposite) of the Al-Azhar Garden, Cairo, showing the water line spine, and its perpendicular tributaries, with the planting that it supports, in a poetic reading of the garden's morphological and natural compositions.

7 | Rediscovering the Islamic City

Cities in the Islamic world were once the perfect grist for the Orientalists' mill. All the tendencies listed in Chapter 5 in relation to museums are even more evident in the Orientalists' attempt to come to terms with and represent the city in whatever medium they selected. Among these tendencies, the most prevalent were didacticism – the desire to impose order on representations – along with the generalization of social and geographical differences, and the 'synchronic essentialism' inherent in second order knowledge, which is best expressed through the device of the travelogue.

Islamic cities were invariably represented as exotic, mysterious, cacophonic, voluptuous, redolent, confusing and dangerous. They were presented formally, but it wasn't until their historic remnant was threatened with destruction in the 1980s, when development fuelled by oil revenue reached its first crescendo, that a concerted effort was made to go beyond such simplistic formal representations in order to understand how the Islamic city really worked.

Two of the most ambitious and groundbreaking studies came from a Saudi and an Iraqi, both published in the mid-1980s. Dr Jamel Akbar looked at the city as the product of reciprocal arrangements made between people, the incremental establishment of such social interrelationships acting as the invisible glue joining the urban fabric together. Besim Hakim, on the other hand, specifically examined religious, legal and economic factors as the unseen hands that shaped the city in the past, detailing the complex daily process of give-and-take that created the city's form over time.

Several other important studies have been conducted since then, but the important point for the work of Rasem Badran is that it is now well understood and taken for granted that the formal difference described by the Orientalist, between cities in the 'East' and the 'West', was not stylistically driven, as they claimed; a deeper look at social, cultural, religious, economic, legal and environmental issues was required to understand how they came to look the way they did. Islamic cities are not accidental in structure, evolving as they do as part of an overall, time-honoured philosophy and way of life. Rather than being a descriptive process, urban analysis demands an understanding of the convergence of each of the factors mentioned above, making it a sociological as well as a geographical endeavour.

A growing awareness

For Rasem Badran, this process may be considered to be in a state of change. In his early involvement in urbanism, he demonstrates some of the same formalistic tendencies as those looking at the Arab city from the outside. He seems to follow the pattern of Hassan Fathy before him in fastening on typologies or the use of taxonomies to categorize or classify, rather than on the social processes and inter-actions that have created them. This is because the bulk of the information we have about the Islamic city has, paradoxically, been written by Orientalists and has been the only source available until Jamel Akbar and Besim Hakim added new insights in the 1980s. Cairo sums up this situation well, since it was the research field that Badran's philosophical if not actual mentor, Hassan Fathy, chose as a tool for understanding how his own culture built in the past. The only archive open to him was the Institut Français Archéologique et Oriental, founded by Napoleon Bonaparte. The majority of those writing about Cairo were French and only a few sources existed in Arabic.

It is hardly surprising then that Fathy's initial attempt to create an authentic language for his culture was biased from the beginning by the limited sources available. And it is just as understandable that Badran at the beginning followed a similar path. In his unbuilt Al-Beit Foundation project, intended for Amman, he concentrated on pan-Islamic models of gates, courtyard walls, houses and other typologies, utilized in a scheme closely attached to its topography. His housing complex for the Jordan Cement Factory Employees Housing in Fuhais near Amman is similarly based on models he had uncovered, and this is the critical point about such discovery: it had not been made before. Hassan Fathy and Rasem Badran have each been able to extrapolate typologies, such as the *qa'a*, *maqa'ad*, and *maqaz* from literary sources and from field research and observa-tion – a substantial achievement because they were the first within their own culture to do so. This is exhilarating for an architect intent on finding an alterna-tive to what are felt to be socially inappropriate configurations, and who takes a great deal of pride in his heritage.

Badran, like Fathy, also looks to his own city (or cities, if Jerusalem is also con-sidered to be a part of his purview) as a source of inspiration and investigation, and Amman is far removed from Cairo. Archaeologists have established that a prehistoric settlement had existed there, and that it was a wealthy economic centre under Roman rule, thanks to its strategic location on a north-south trade route. Jerash (Gerasa), north of Amman, began to be restored in the early 1920s, and presents a vivid picture of what Philadelphia, as Amman was known, must have looked like. Although each Roman city contained a fixed set of institutions, such as the theatre, the bath-house and the temple, they were all carefully adapted to their location. The forum in Gerasa, for example, is deformed from a circle to an ellipse, because of a change of direction in the *cardo maximus*; it is this defor-mation, along with other peculiarities such as a steep stairway leading to the main temple, that gives the city its identity and charm.

Amman was conquered by a Muslim army in AD 635 and, being close to the capital Damascus, it thrived during Ummayyad rule. This period of prosperity ended when the capital of the caliphate moved to Baghdad as the Abbasids came to power. A long period of steady decline followed and by 1921, when it was des-ignated as the capital of the new state of Transjordan, it was no more than a small town. Over the next twenty years its population rose to about 40,000 people, and

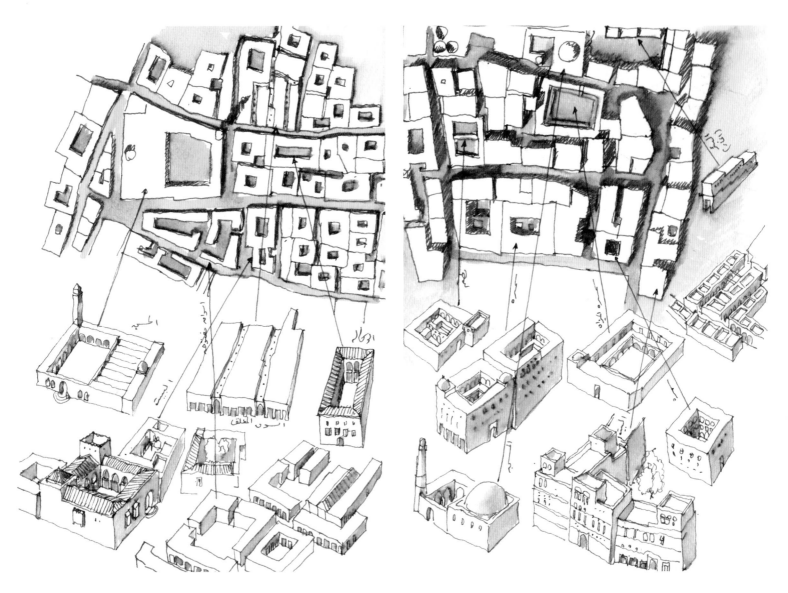

Above

The socio-cultural elements of the
housing project in Sana'a, Yemen.
Badran's Western education has
resulted in an awareness of many
different typologies.

after the Second World War the population swelled again, due to dislocations
nearby. Amman, like Jerusalem and Cairo, is a product of its own layered history,
though the layers are quite different in each of them. Like Jerusalem, Amman was
initially built of local stone, which has its own tectonic rules, creating a homoge-
neous appearance and fusing each city to its site. None of these lessons has been
lost on the extremely observant Badran and his photographic memory: Roman
and Islamic typologies adapted to different topographical conditions, the memories inherent in historical layering, the visual power of a city unified by the
material from which it is made, and the way it is built.

Since the 1980s, Rasem Badran has contributed to many projects that have
involved urban planning to some degree. The works selected for discussion here
have been chosen because they raise issues that are relevant to the evolution of his
ideas. At the risk of generalization, Badran's approach to urban situations has
shifted towards more place-specific investigation since his first foray at the acrop-
olis of the Al-Beit Foundation. His systematically considered design for a housing
project in Sana'a, Yemen, for example, involves general comparisons with other

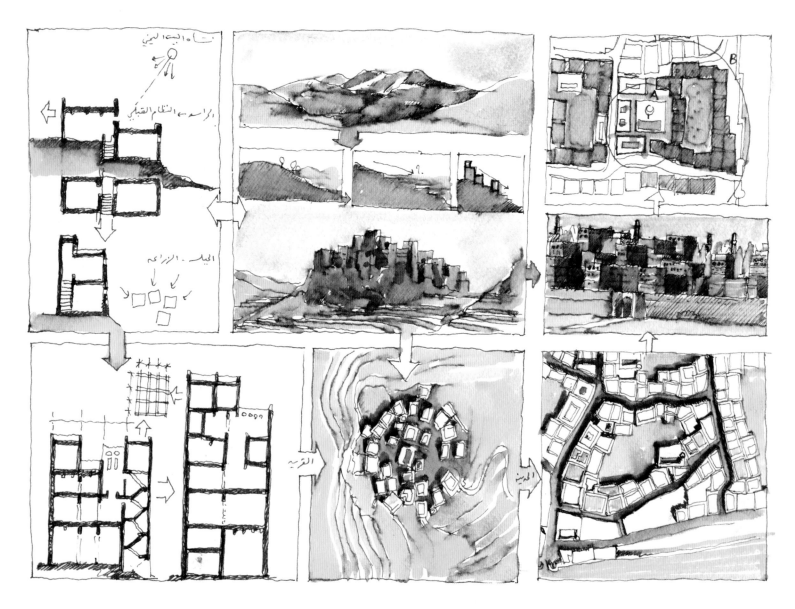

Islamic cities such as Cairo, Qairawan, Baghdad and Tangiers, but finally revolves around place-specific considerations. His competition entry for the design of another, much larger housing complex in the Jabal Omar district of Makkah, relies much less on such comparisons, and concentrates intently on the history of the city and the religious implications of intervening in such a delicate and sensitive context.

A mixed commercial and residential complex for Dubai Creek, underway at the time of writing, intends to address the issue of rapid development to explore the implications of juxtaposition – of mixing the old and the new. In it, Badran allows himself free aesthetic rein, demonstrating a level of technological virtuosity he has hinted at previously in such projects as the Al-Ain Museum in the United Arab Emirates. In a Sea Front Development in Sidon, Lebanon, he continues this dialogue about change in an even more extensive way, since growth has been legislated there and is taking place on a wider scale after a protracted period of destruction. In Kuwait, the question of place and culturally specific investiga-

The cultural references and the origin of building behaviour from rural to urban. To prepare for the design of a housing complex in Sana'a, Yemen, Badran studied Yemeni villages in detail.

As a result of his studies of Yemeni villages, Badran became aware of vertical stacking for defence and view, air and privacy.

tion emerges again in a 'Heritage Village' designed in 2003 and submitted as a proposal by his team. Badran demonstrates his ability for regional master planning, using geographical, ecological and economic constraints to best advantage to create a model of sustainable development in this developing country.

Al-Beit Al-Kamal, Sana'a, Yemen

In 1991 Rasem Badran won a competition to design a housing and office complex in Sana'a, Yemen. At the southern end of the Arabian Peninsula, Yemen's distinctive climate and topography have created a highly individualized vernacular architecture. Badran went through a systematic process in a three-stage design methodology that set the standard for projects to follow; it offers a clear example to those wrestling with the question of how to intervene in a highly defined architectural environment. The three stages consisted of the analysis and evaluation of the local culture, the setting up of design guidelines based on that analysis, and the implementation of those guidelines in the design.

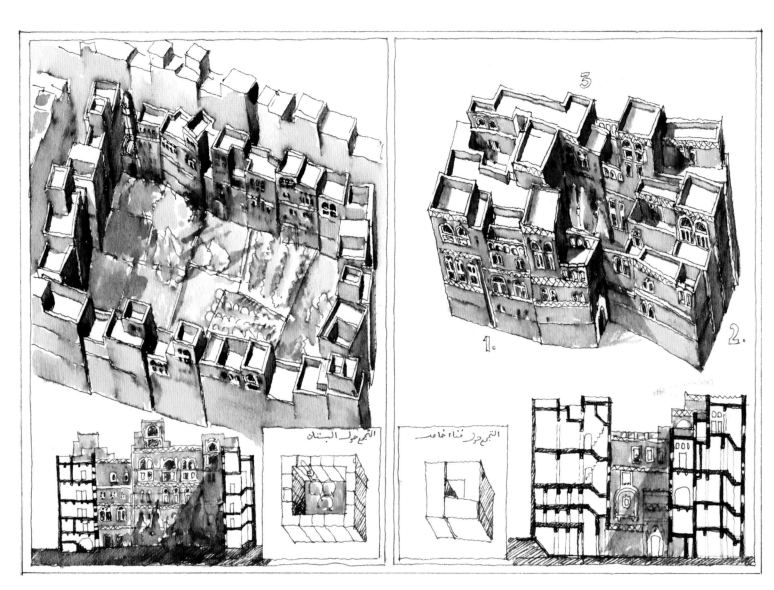

Above

Al-Beit al-Kamal, Sana'a, Yemen.
The living wall (towers) create a
sense of the communal within a
sustained social structure.
Transferred to his site, these
discoveries of an existing set
of typologies and vertical
stacking led him to enclosed
common courtyards.

Right and below right

Al-Beit Al-Kamal, Sana'a, Yemen. The logical order behind the vertical accumulation of the living space (the cosmic order). Badran's studies also showed elevational details to be far from random, serving environmental and social functions.

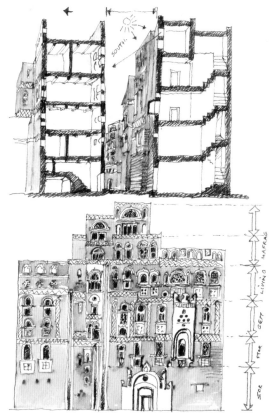

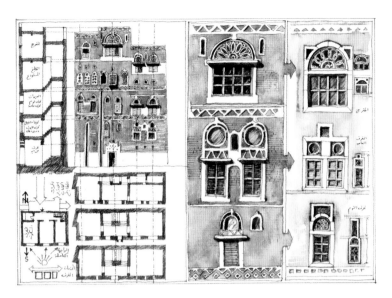

Analysis and evaluation

A key insight that guided the beginning of the study was that Sana'a was an aggregation of elements found in villages throughout the rugged terrain of this frontier nation; these elements both mirrored and adapted characteristics throughout the Islamic world. The balance in this project tips noticeably towards the particular and the unique within Dar al-Islam, rather than leaning towards the reaffirmation of general similarities that Badran noticed prior to this study. The elements discovered in the early part of the exercise revolved around the verticality of the individual house, generated by familial, climatic and defensive considerations. Stacking levels allows for a hierarchical separation and increasing degrees of privacy. Badran recorded this segregation saying:

The houses in Yemen are usually five to six floors in height with vertical separation of the floors according to the function and the users of the space. Usually the ground floor is used for small commercial purposes or to keep the livestock – traditionally it is called a mesam *– while the first floor is used for storage. The second and the third floors are the male areas with guest rooms while the fourth and the fifth are for the women, with the kitchen and the family living areas: the traditional name is the* marawh. *On the top floor, there is the* mafraj *or the lookout point, which is a combination of a covered and open space.*

The tower also allows the top floors to receive the cool breezes that flow through the high mountain passes and elevated desert regions, which are typical features of the Yemeni landscape. Such tower houses are found elsewhere in the Arabian Peninsula, most notably in the port city of Jeddah and in the Hijaz, as the analysis of the Jabal Omar competition design that Badran submitted for housing in Makkah demonstrates. While the social determinants for vertical stacking are the same in Jeddah and Makkah as they are in Yemen, Badran found that climatic variation, as well as the availability of local materials, has resulted in different external expressions.

In Yemen, the prevalence of stone makes it a logical building material, while wood has been used in the north-western part of the Arabian Peninsula. Wood is

The patterned elements of the cosmic order (light, vision and atmosphere). In the Yemeni villages, the almost infinite variety of details Badran found, within prescribed guidelines, inspired him to be equally creative.

scarce in Saudi Arabia, but as a port city, Jeddah has access to it through trade, primarily with India, and nearby Makkah shares in this supply. The defensive component is also unique to Yemen, since it has historically been a tribal society with settlements primarily identified with one family or group; incursions between settlements are a frequent fact of life. Agricultural land is scarce in Yemen because of the large amount of rocky soil, and so the tower form allows it to be maximized and protected. Jeddah was originally a walled city until the mid-1940s, when the walls were removed and replaced with a ring road; the tower house form helped to conserve land, but the defensive aspect lost its purpose.

Further investigation into the environmental implications of the tower house in Yemen revealed interesting and surprising implications related to the size, location and ornamentation of the window openings, which turned out to be far from random. Badran discovered that the placement of internal spaces and the openings to the outside in each are directly related to the daily seen path, 'to the extent', he recorded, 'that people themselves classify houses according to the amount of light they receive'.

Al-Beit Al-Kamal, Sana'a, Yemen. Badran began to apply the lessons learned in his research to his design. Shown here is the methodology of the urban elements (the vertical, the vital, the social and the cosmic).

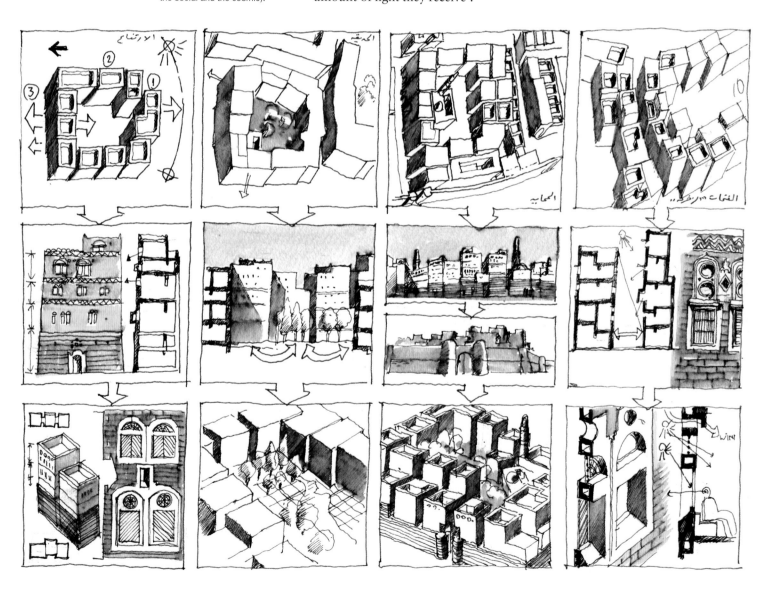

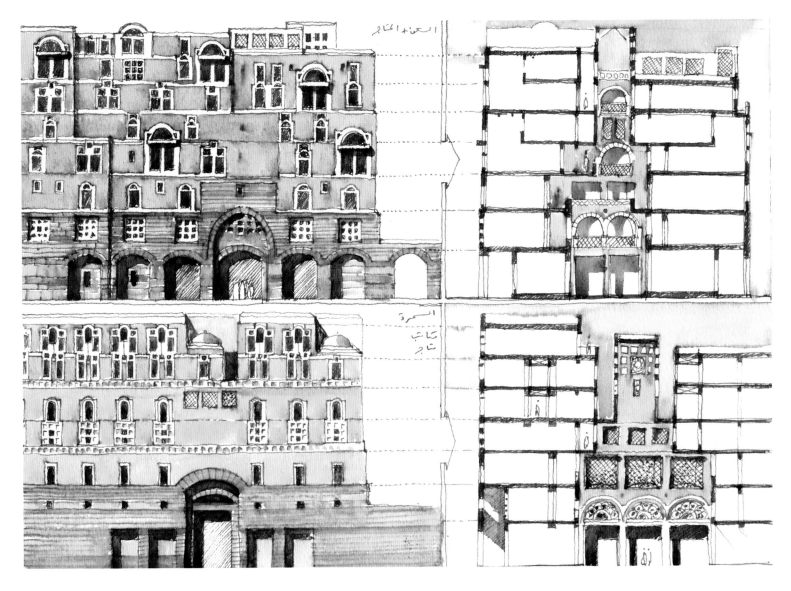

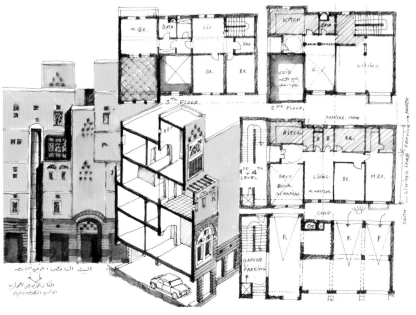

Al-Beit Al-Kamal, Sana'a, Yemen.
Various elevational treatments
related to vertical stacking, as
they are in traditional Yemeni
houses. The complexity of the
cluster, and the special elements
pertaining to it, are best
appreciated through an
understanding of tradition and
lifestyle.

The character of the outdoor skin of commercial and residential buildings provides a dialogue between traditional and contemporary approaches, and a degree of unity within diversity.

Comparisons

Badran began the Yemen study by looking at similar urban situations in Cairo, Tunisia and Morocco. This comparative analysis led him to conclude that the city centre, with its large mosque, the Masjid al-Tami'i, and its commercial activities, was a constant, but that Sana'a had developed very differently from cities in the two other countries, since, 'in other cities, the residential neighbourhoods have spread out horizontally and are based on the internal courtyard, which creates a private space for each house'. In Sana'a, the verticality of the houses, which developed because of the need of an agricultural society to protect its land, crops and herds, creates a more direct interface with nature, since sunlight and natural ventilation are more prevalent at the higher levels of the house. Traditional Arab houses in other countries are typically found to be modest and plain on the outside, while having a rich series of spatial arrangements within. In Yemen, however, the exterior elevations of all the traditional houses are richly decorated and this ornamentation – which looks like icing on gingerbread – serves several important functions. First of all, it provides a means of social differentiation,

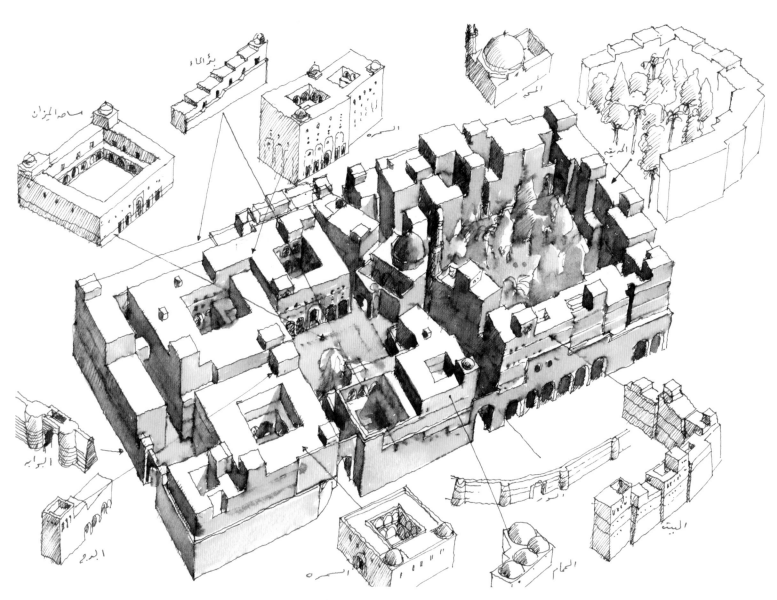

Opposite, top and bottom

Ala-Beit Al-Kamal, Sana'a, Yemen.
The final massing model
(shown bottom) is startling in its
modernity, before the exterior
wrapper is applied. this is a
successful dialogue between the
value of inheritance and the
contemporary.

Above

The precedents (cultural
references) of the overall urban
fabric. Each entry into the project
is visually described, as is
customary in Badran's
design methodology.

sending key clues to everyone in the neighbourhood about the status of each family. Secondly, the ornamentation contributes to environmental mitigation, since it reflects the sunlight away from the windows and thus reduces both the heat and the glare.

The tower versus the party wall typology perpetuates an individual, or family mentality rather than a group or communal one, and this ornamentation underscores that individuality. The *mafraj*, similar to a *majlis* or reception room, is the highest and most prestigious space in a traditional Yemeni house, and its scale and magnificence is also broadcast by external decoration. Because of the isolation of families into tower houses, this *mafraj* serves the function of a courtyard in the sky, as open as possible to light and air. Light is augmented and controlled by *kamriya* (the use of coloured glass) similar in appearance to large panels of stained glass, which visually enhances the house interior.

Part of the prestige value of any house in Yemeni culture depends on its orientation. Since the best direction, environmentally, is towards the south, the Yemeni's call a 'complete house' one facing in that direction. A house facing east or west is 'semi-complete' and one facing north is 'deficient'. The allocation of functions inside the house changes in each case.

The house's vertical growth is a gradual process, and it happens according to the family's means. In order for a house to look finished at each phase, it is capped with a wide white band that serves as a horizontal marker on the elevation. Vertical growth of the house also requires an efficient drainage system, which the Yemenis have developed as external channels incorporated into the ornamental system.

Translating the analysis

Badran translated his investigations into the formation of rural villages and towns and residential districts in Sana'a into a list of generational aspects that are responsible for form. He found that each residential neighbourhood is a result of the following constants:

(1) Water, and a well, or *abiyar* to reach it, are the most important factors in establishing a community.

(2) A green area called a *bustan* (equivalent to a common) formed around the well.

(3) Houses, built vertically, were placed around the edge of the *bustan*, to act as a fortress wall to protect the *abiyar*. Sometimes there is a building on top.

(4) The *bustan* is supervised by the same family that takes care of the mosque.

(5) The mosque, *Al-Jami*, is located on or close to the *bustan*.

(6) There are specific commercial districts, called *samsara*, in which the *suqs* are located. The number of *samsara* in a city reflects its culture status, because trade requires interaction with other towns, cities and districts; this exchange brings a transfer of knowledge with it. The *samsara* include places for traders to stay, similar to the *caravanserai* or *khans* in other cities.

One major environmental advantage of the Yemeni way of building that Badran recorded, in addition to the extensive use of local materials, is that the vertical house has a very small footprint and thus occupies a minimum of the already scarce agricultural land. He also noted that this organizational system and the ornamental additions that result from it, create neighbourhoods on a human scale.

A detail perspective of the Sana'a housing project. The flexibillity of the vertical maintains the indigenous character of the traditional fabric.

The final result

These findings were used to formulate the Sana'a housing project on a site in the historical part of the city that has the same proportions as the older neighbourhoods around it. This was an important factor in the design because it allowed Badran to maintain similar relationships to those used in the past. Public activities in the brief, such as shops and offices, were located close to the street, while the residential complex was grouped into towers that surrounded a *bustan* or garden, away from the busiest edge of the site. The mosque and its associated activities were situated midway between each of these, to fulfil both the public and residential aims of the project.

The spatial concept was modulated to fit individual parts of the project. The apartments were designed to have two or three levels, to make them similar to the traditional Yemeni tower houses and to accommodate an extended family. The bath-house was reconfigured as a swimming pool and sports centre. The traditional *samsara* reappeared as a community centre, in which the lower floors were allocated to shops and the upper floor to offices. The *khan* portion of the *samsara* became a hotel and the translation extended to details as well: the drainage system was exposed, making it easier to maintain, the window openings were framed in pre-cast concrete to allow for flexibility of construction and to provide the façades with horizontal bands to delineate the portion of each apartment.

'The lesson we learned, in producing this proposal,' Badran recalls, 'is the extent to which social and economic factors affect the architecture character of the city'. Those lessons have been assimilated and expanded upon in his later projects, most notably in the Jabal Omar competition project in Makkah and a mega development scheme in the same city called Jabal al Shamia.

The epicentre of Islam

Makkah is the most important city in the Islamic world, the location of the Haram al-Sharif and the Ka'bah. It is in the north-western Hijaz region of Saudi Arabia, an area characterized by barren mountain ranges that gradually drop in elevation as they encircle the city. Since it contains the most sacred sites in Islam, it is the goal of the annual pilgrimage or *Hajj* which millions of Muslims from all over the world undertake. Many more come to Makkah at other times to perform *Umrah*, which is observed outside of the proscribed pilgrimage time. As transportation became safer and more reliable at the beginning of the 20th century, the number of pilgrims began to grow. Jeddah's large port was the main point of entry into Arabia prior to that and still remains the primary gateway because of its proximity to Makkah, and the large air terminal built there in the late 1970s. It is a well conceived holding facility that accommodates pilgrims during the several days that it takes for their documents to be processed and medical checks to be completed.

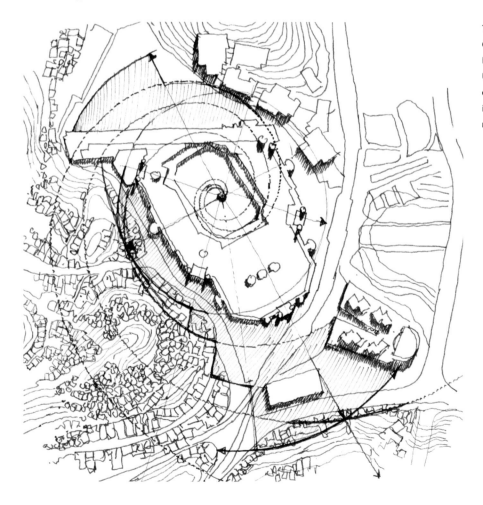

The first inspiration for the Jabal Omar project was the epicentre of Haram Al-Sharif, the Ka'bah. Understanding the power of the entire site shows the spiritual impact of the holy mosque in relation to its surroundings.

The Ka'bah became the central reference point for all the design decisions that followed in the Jabal Omar project, a morphological response to the radial rotation structure.

Pressure on the historic core

As might be expected, this cyclical wave of humanity has put a great deal of pressure on the historic core, changing its character in the process. Interestingly, the old houses there share many of the Yemeni features, but for different reasons. The pilgrimage has always promoted commerce and trade, so many of the old houses had shops on the lower level and residences above. A smaller footprint also made sense here because, clearly, land was so valuable and scarce the closer it got to the Haram al-Sharif.

Using past lessons to best advantage

His work in Yemen made Rasem Badran even more aware of the extent to which social constraints affect architectural form and expression. The Jabal Omar competition, sponsored by Millennium, a well-known Lebanese planning and

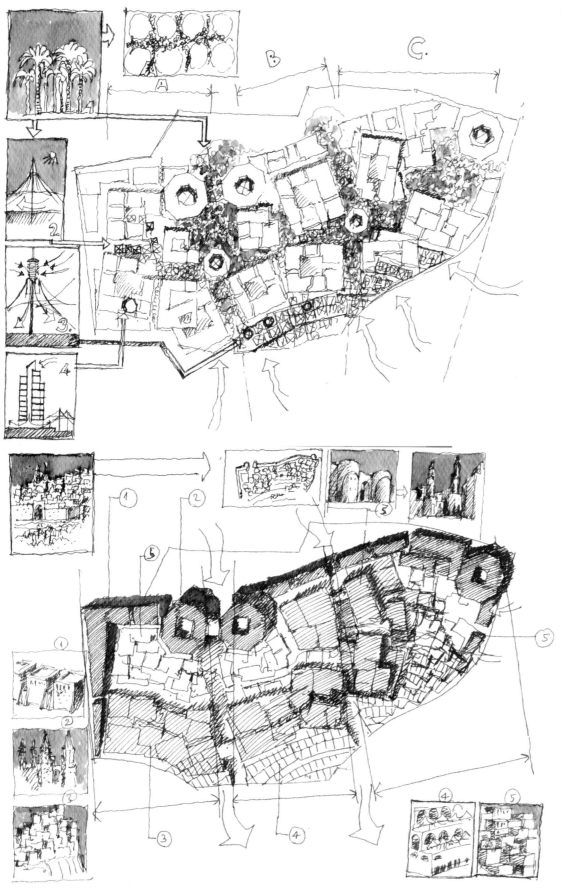

Jabal Omar housing development, Makkah. Allowing views from all the components of the scheme, towers with gateways became integral to the concept. This study shows a first response to the reading of the site through its physical order in accordance with its constsraints and the hidden qualities in the macro scale.

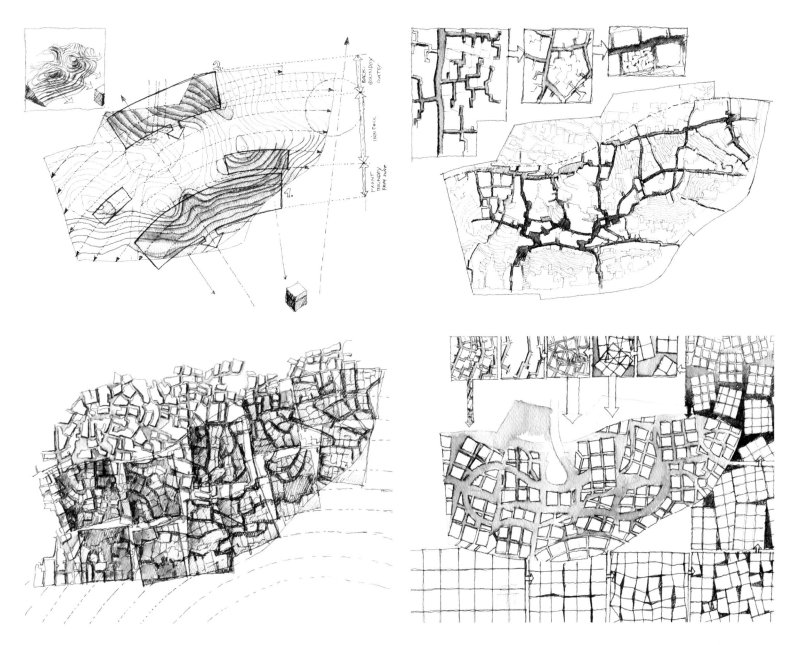

The Jabal Omar project ties in closely to the site contours, which are steep in this part of Makkah. It was important to identify the impact of the different elements and forces that shape the hidden factors of the site (the topography, the spiritual power, and the social pattern).

investment organization, allowed him to apply the knowledge acquired in Sana'a on a much larger scale. The competition brief required urban planning and infrastructure design in the southern part of the historic core in an area called Jabal Omar. In addition, it asked for six- to twelve-storey apartment buildings, with more than 9,000 underground parking spaces.

Stage one

Following the pattern he had established in Yemen, Badran started the project with an intensive period of research, assisted in this instance by a book of site information supplied by the competition organizers. This research led to a two-stage design strategy that moved from general to specific requirements.

Badran's first reaction to the planning questions posed by the competition was spiritual and intuitive, based on cosmological significance, and this led him to

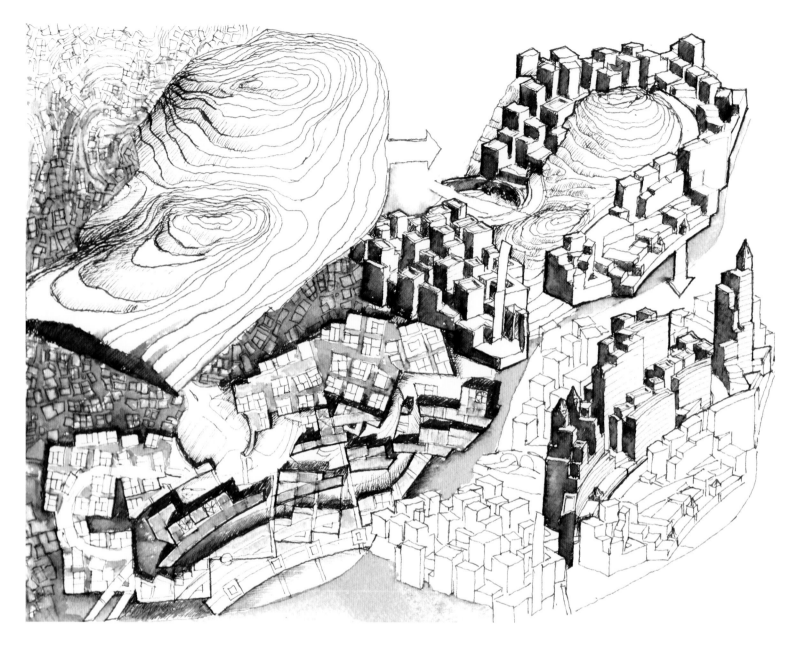

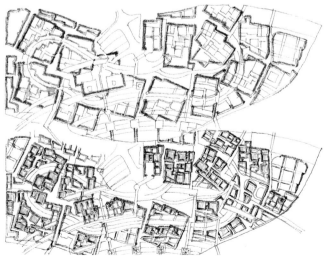

Jabal Omar housing development, Makkah. An axonometric drawing showing how the slopes were used to best advantage to ensure views towards the Haram al-Sharif and the Ka'bah. Rasem Badran identified the social diversity of the overall structure. Shown on the left is the living cluster.

Jabal Omar housing development, Makkah. The vertical accumulation of urban behaviour. Views of the spaces between the units as well as tents near the Haram al-Sharif to protect spectators from the sun. The tents are temporary facilities, erected on terraces around the Haram al-Sharif.

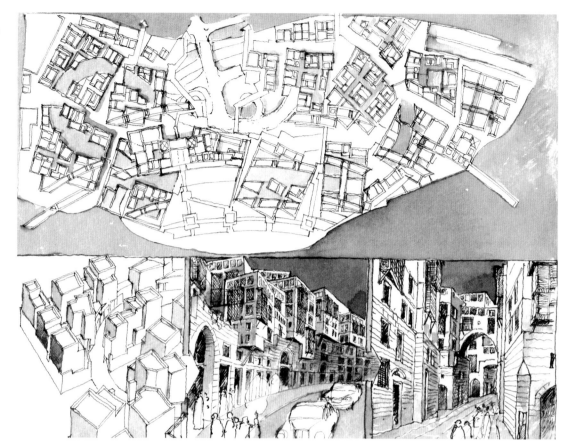

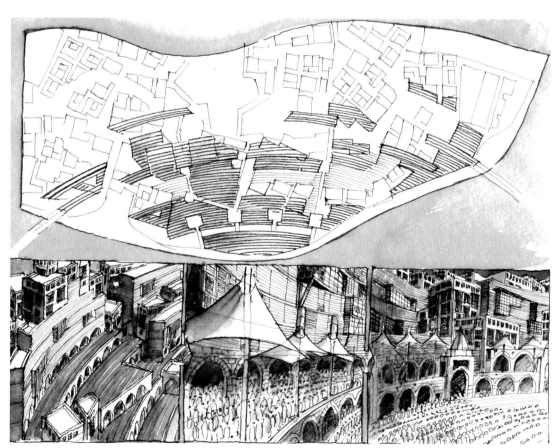

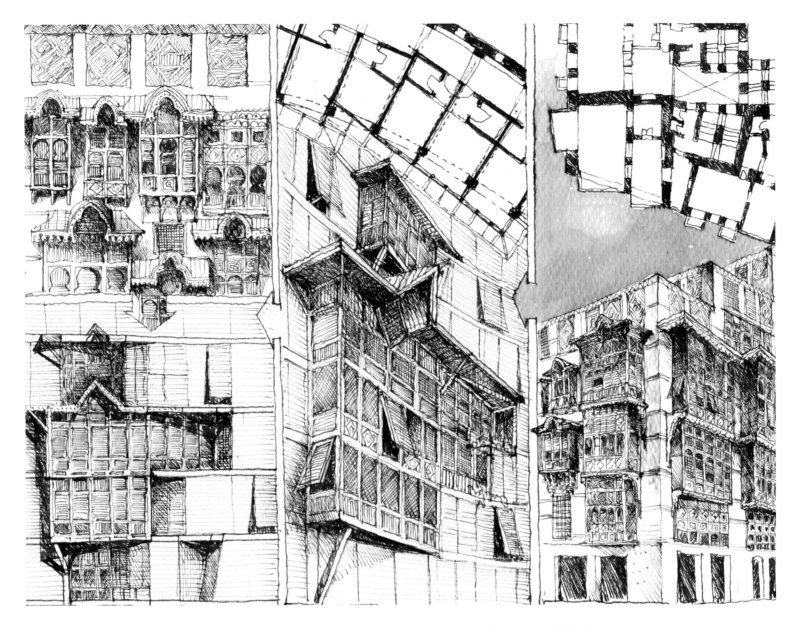

prioritize his ideas. He believed that growth in and around the core had compromised its historical integrity, which needed to be restored. His first step towards this was to establish defined boundaries for the district, complete with specific entrances or gates. Next, he worked out the optimum size of the sectors and the neighbourhoods that were required, in order to reverse the anonymity that had begun to typify the core, due to more modern architecture being built there. He also saw the potential for prototypes that could be used by others in the future, to help counter this trend.

View corridors

In creating more human-scaled neighbourhoods, Badran was guided by his belief that paramount consideration should be given to providing views towards the Haram al-Sharif and the Ka'bah. This subsequently led him to establish view corridors and to focus once again on the tower typology for housing, which was also

Jabal Omar housing development, Makkah. The social and climatic impact on the outer skin. Projecting wooden windows, called *rawashawn*, are traditional and are replicated on the new towers.

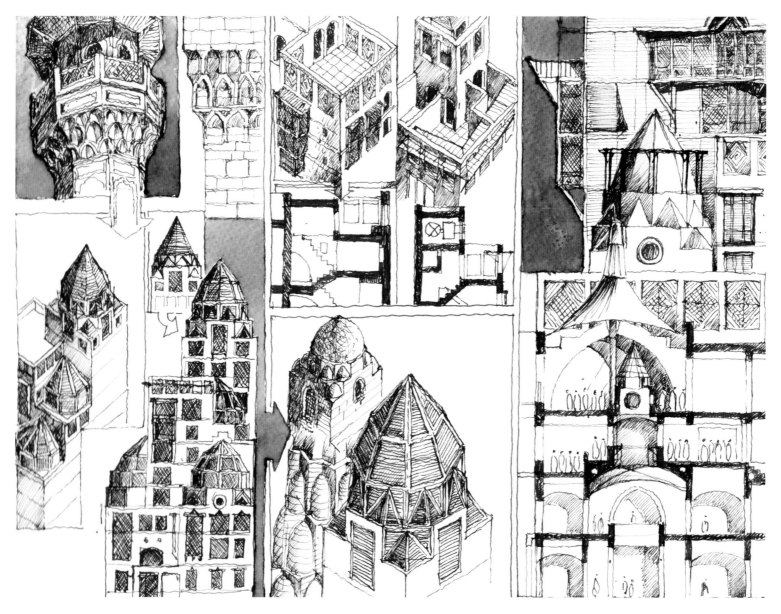

Jabal Omar housing development,
Makkah. The architectural
elements, and their pattern.
Due to the verticality required,
Badran explored innovative ways
of getting light into interior atria.

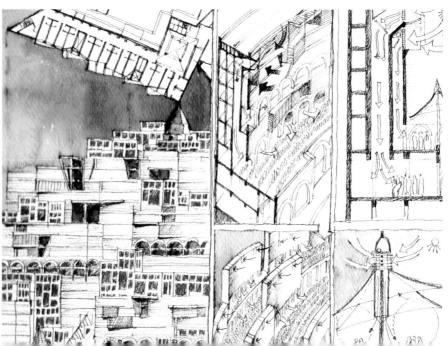

consistent with previous historical solutions. Once again, Badran balanced practical considerations with a respect for tradition. In describing his approach to this singular set of circumstances, he said:

Jabal Omar housing development, Makkah. An elevation of the project showing vertical layering to allow views.

I conceived Jabal Omar as an organic whole. At both the planning and design level, I saw the spatial module I was proposing to use on this mountain as a prototype or model for the future development of the entire city of Makkah. The building blocks contain many layers of activities, organized by topography and traditional street form. I used a stepped cluster design to allow the residential quarters to adapt to the topographical constraints, following the natural contours and the need to orient the buildings towards the Haram al-Sharif. My design also responds to the local context ecologically, reflecting the Islamic view of being in harmony with the environment. I have tried to use technology to improve on traditional solutions, particularly in the critical area of water conservation, through conservation at the source (xeriscape) and recycling.

Specific proposals

The view corridors leading to the sacred places resulted in five north-south spines that defined boundaries, provided gates and employed new technologies to conserve on water use. In addition to this Badran proposed a radial geometry that recognized the Ka'bah as the centre of this religious universe, echoing the movement of worshippers around it (*tawaf*). He proposed praying areas and *suqs* along the north-south spines, and hotels higher up the slope to allow better views.

Stage Two

Once these general parameters were set, he began to identify the character of the residential units, testing the compatibility of his proposals with the authentic parts of the existing residential context, as well as with the new urban fabric he was promoting. He balanced the scale of the residential blocks with the size of the sectors and the interplay between residences and hotel towers. Along with the choice of the tower form for the multi-storey apartments, he decided on three specific features to help establish a connection between the old and the new. The first of these was an open roof, conceived as a courtyard in the sky, which had a clear historical precedent. In the past, before the advent of air conditioning, stone walls kept the interior of old Makkah tower houses cool, but the intractable physics of thermal log meant that after dark the heat trapped in the heavy walls could eventually find its way inside, making the interior spaces very hot. The entire family would usually sleep on the roof, since the nights in this region are cool most of the year and even cold for several months. The second feature was the *rawashawn*, a local variant of the *mushrabbiya* mentioned earlier. The *rawashawn* differs from the *mushrabbiya* in detail only; it is usually built on a much simpler design with thin strips of intricate wood pieces turned on a lathe. It works in the same way, however, as a projecting window that allows residents to see out without being seen, and also allows natural ventilation into the house. It could be prosaically

described as a window seat, but it has a much more complex social function, since it was historically used primarily by the women of each household to talk back and forth during the day. The third feature of the tower house was the base, which was faced in local granite to conform to the older structures.

Lastly, Badran proposed fabric tents for the prayer platforms of his master plan, close to the Haram al-Sharif. These were designed to order the spaces between the various sectors to be developed. In the 1980s, Sami Angawi, then of the *Hajj* Research Centre, proposed using tents to provide shade for pilgrims during the *Hajj*, but his scheme located them further up the sides of the mountains surrounding the city. Badran's fabric structures stand between the Haram al-Sharif and the new housing. These were intended to increase the number of prayer areas, in commercial sites and on rooftops throughout the new development, as an important part of the architect's open space plan.

A dialectic

Before and since the Jabal Omar proposal, Badran was determined 'to foster a deeper appreciation of the values, knowledge, and aesthetics inherent in traditional architecture and to do this within the parameters of a contemporary vision.' The duality that is implicit in this pairing is present in other obvious dichotomies that he established here: heritage versus inheritance, the sacred and the secular, the cosmological and the geophysical, the constant and the variable, the amorphous and the cluster, the visual and the historical, and space versus place. The apparent dichotomy of heritage versus inheritance, which is perhaps the most obscure of

these pairs, helps to explain the counterpoint that Badran sought to achieve in Jabal Omar. The best Western example of this is the devastation of the Great Fire of London in 1666, which offered an excellent opportunity to change the traditional pattern of confusing Saxon cow paths and trails that had become the city's streets. Several architects made proposals to the Crown to improve the city plan, but legal covenants took precedence and could not be broken. John Nash later found a way to offer a compromise that worked within and between these; the result amplifies the traditional urban context and street pattern in a new addition to the city. This is the kind of fit Badran seeks to find.

The Beirut experience is evidence of that way of thinking, as it recognizes the accumulated layers of history. The Jabal Omar competition has paved the way for Badran's team's involvement in another much larger, new mega development in Makkah, the Jabal Al-Shamia Project, which was also awarded as a joint venture with another large American architectural firm, Gensler, to complete the pre-used final planning scheme for implementation.

Above
A computer-generated image of the roofscape.

Opposite
Axonometric drawing of a portion of the Jabal Omar project.

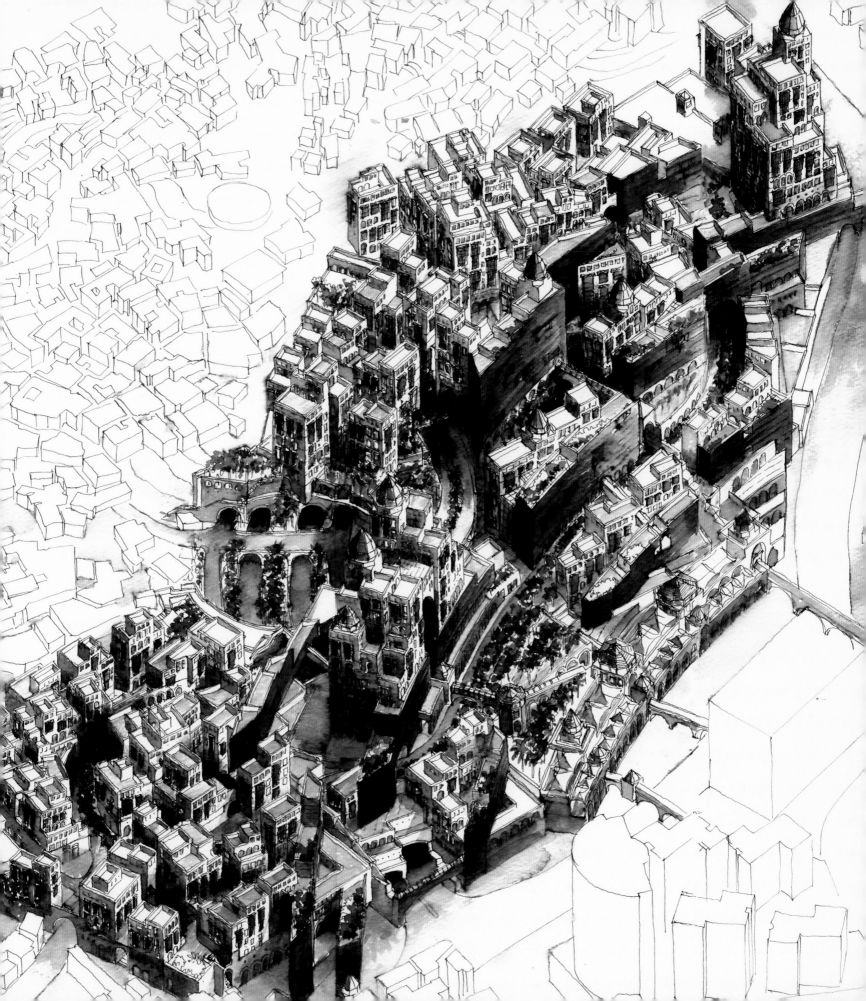

From the mountains to the sea

Sana'a, Yemen and Makkah share rugged topography, extreme climatic conditions and established building traditions. Rasem Badran's involvement in planning projects with waterfront locations, as in Dubai in 1999, the Wadi Barakrag in Morocco in 2002 and in Kuwait 2003, has required a different mindset and design response for a number of reasons. First of all, countries with a seafaring tradition in the Islamic world have historically developed a much different architectural legacy, primarily because of environmental constraints. While sea breezes are cool, they generate more humidity, which calls for alternative cooling strategies. Also, the primary relationship to the water, based on trade, has created different formal configurations which focus on functional variety.

Urban planning has increasingly become an important part of Badran's activities. Water is a source of sustained development; it provokes the socio-cultural encounter and, as a source of life, represents vitality.

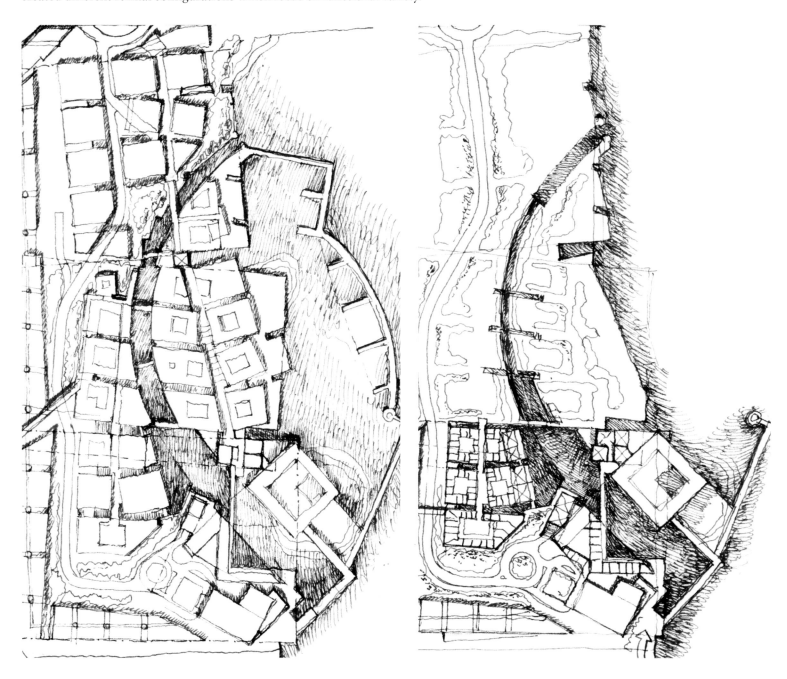

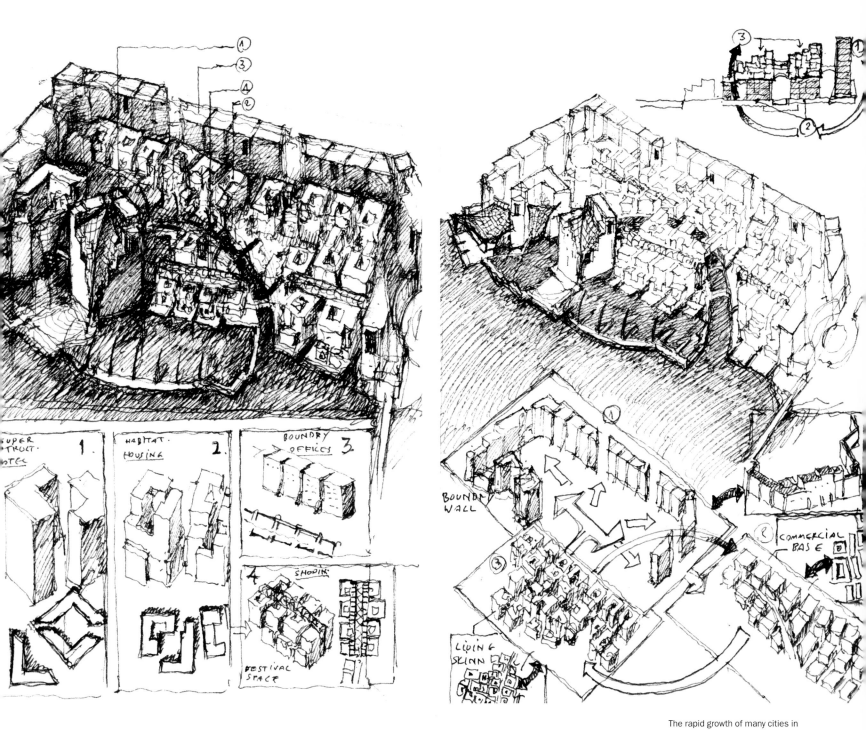

The rapid growth of many cities in the Gulf region has offered many new opportunities to offer fresh design ideas, transforming water as a source of sustained development through a man-made physical development.

Dubai Creek

The traditional architecture in Dubai has evolved in much the same way as that of other waterfront cultures in the Gulf region and, like theirs, it is under the threat of complete destruction from modernization. Dubai is perhaps the most obvious example of this shift, since it has embarked on an international public relations campaign to promote tourism, reinventing itself as a commercial, entertainment, shopping paradise.

Dubai Creek has always been a part of the main port, a wide arc of water running behind the elongated island on which the quays for the ships are located. Taking his cue from the official desire to transform the image of this Emirate, Badran chose to test the limits of the traditional-contemporary dialectic to find new ways of translating heritage. He was inspired in this attempt by the region's original source of livelihood, fishing with nets from dhows, which are marvels of marine design in themselves. He thought of the skeleton of fish, and of the spine as a structural element that could also be a conduit for conditioned air. The ribs became trusses with glazed infill, used as a counterpoint for the time-tested quali-

The internal nature of Dubai Creek made it possible to study it as a self-contained canal. The folding of the external skin as a hybrid skin reflects the city's motion pattern.

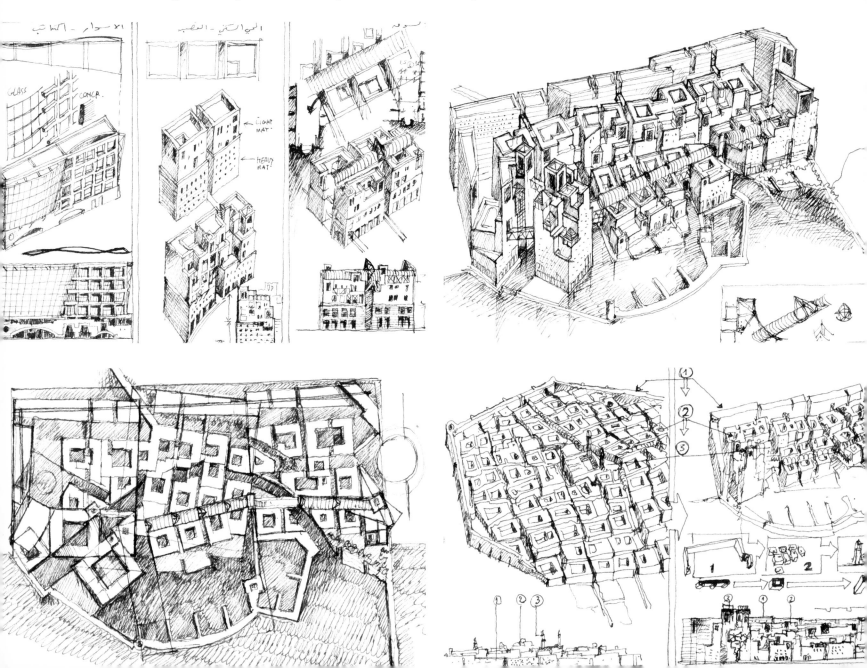

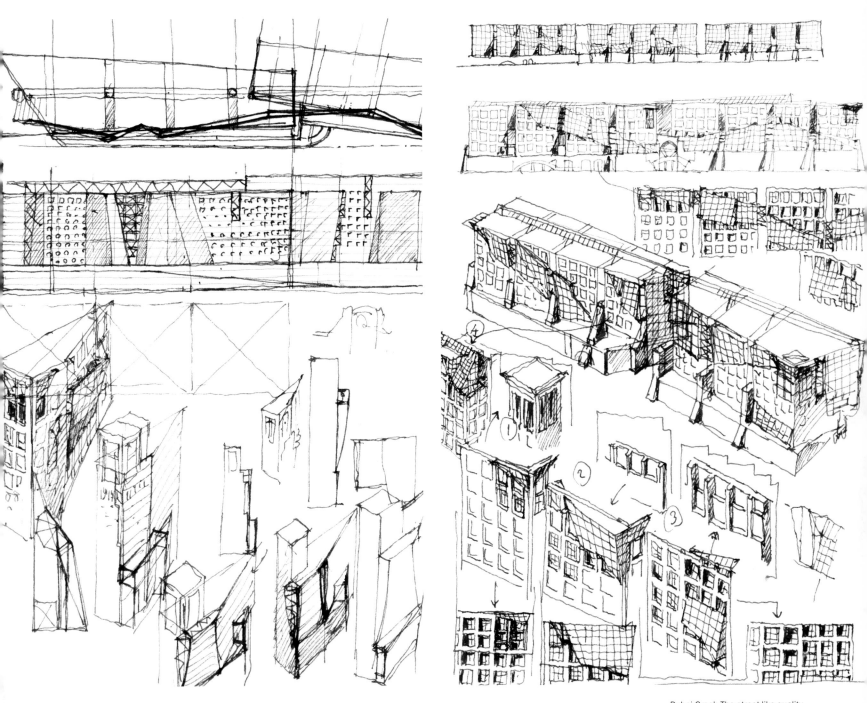

Dubai Creek. The street-like quality
of the canal prompted a
continuous structure, with glass
tilted out over the water shaded by
the roof above.

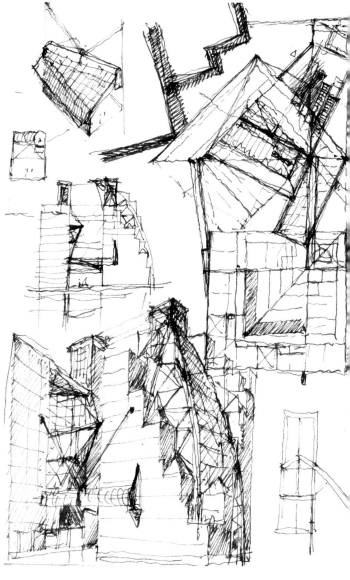

The sketches for Dubai Creek provide some of the most creative formal diagrams yet seen in Badran's work, inspired by the lateen sails of dhows and fish gills and skeletons.

ties of thermal mass, which he designed as a containing wrapper. The image that emerges is one of time passing in an instant, of past, present and future described architectonically.

The Dubai Creek proposal can be considered part of the *suq* morphology which Badran has successfully designed in several different contexts throughout the region, in Amman and Riyadh with Dr Abd Al -Haleem from Egypt and recently in Kuwait, in the Al-Manshar complex, now under construction.

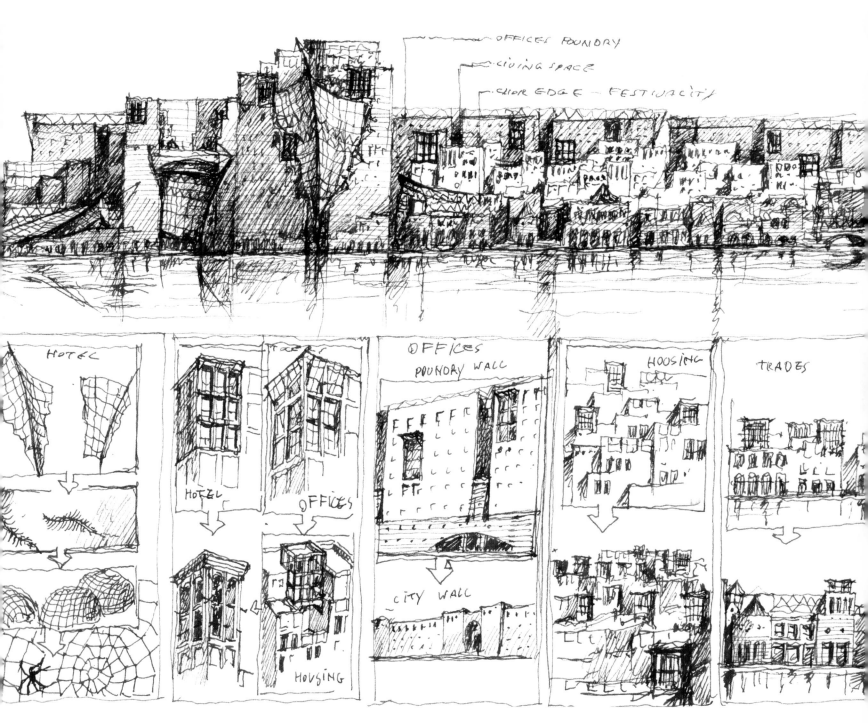

The dramatic elevation of Dubai Creek with the various parts described. The sea front recalls the city's memory, and is celebrated through the approach of the man-made structure.

More detailed sketches showing
internal and external views of the
glass canopy and the water side.
Shown top right is the overlal
image of the development.

Opposite
White on black plan and finished
elevation of Dubai Creek. The
power of water shapes the urban
fabric of the entire structure.

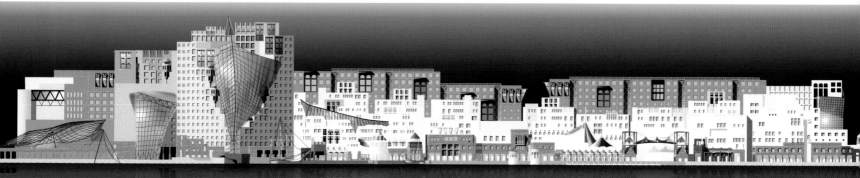

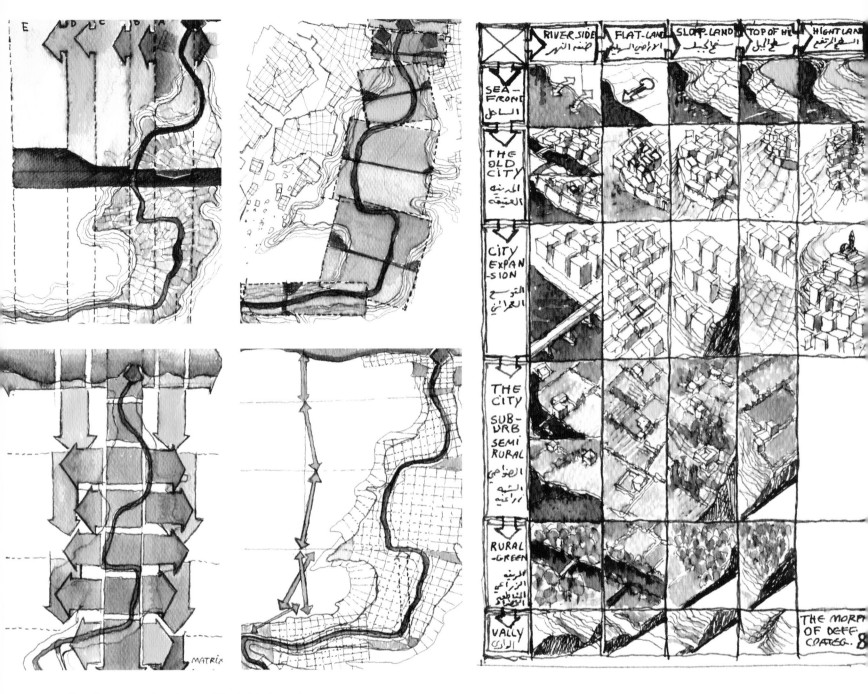

The study above shows the matrix, with columns labelled RIVERSIDE, FLAT-LAND, SLOPE-LAND, TOP OF HILL, HIGHLAND (with Arabic equivalents) and rows labelled SEA-FRONT, THE OLD CITY, CITY EXPANSION, THE CITY SUBURB SEMI RURAL, RURAL-GREEN, VALLEY (with Arabic equivalents). Lower right: THE MORPH OF DIFF. C.P.ATEG.

A regional master plan, uniting old rivals in a common purpose

In the Wadi Barakrag on the Atlantic coast of Morocco, improving economic conditions for survival took precedence over the reinvention of a national image. Badran was looking for ways to ameliorate the standard of living in this valley in a master plan that focused on the river running from a newly constructed dam, along the Atlantic Coast between Rabat and Sillah. His task was to find methods to promote cooperation between the two cities, which have been bitter rivals in the past with marked social and cultural differences.

He began his planning process with what he describes as 'a matrix of narrow readings' to achieve this *rapprochement*. It showed that re-establishing the agri-

The Wadi Barakrag master plan is systematic and poetic at the same time, reflecting these complementary components of the architect's character. Robert Venturi and Denise Scott Brown were also invited, among others, to propose alternative concepts for Wadi Barakrag. The study above shows the y–z matrix, which contains specific criteria that reveal a variety of combinations and possibilities in producing different patterns.

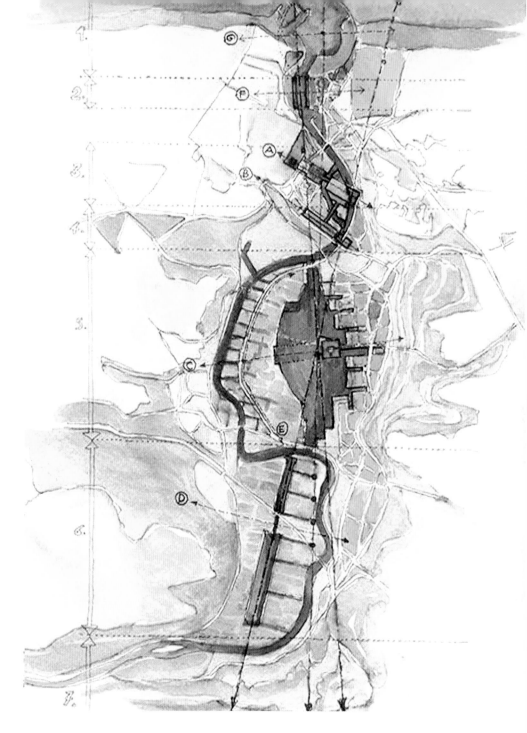

Wadi Barakrag master plan. Intended to bring together two feuding factions that share the waterway, this is truly social planning at its best. The production of various fragmented patterns guides the incremental growth of the valley's urban development.

cultural productivity of the land on each side of the river with better irrigation systems, and redeveloping the Atlantic port to benefit both, should be his first priorities. He then turned his attention towards public amenities on the river, to encourage interaction and exchange. One of these is an enclosed public plaza on Al-Qasba Island linked by bridges to each side of the river, allowing people to meet on neutral territory. Another device was the design of water tanks or ponds, which would serve each city, and a 'sea gate' to announce the port.

In this post-global age, this project offers hope that the built environment can promote positive change and make a significant contribution to altering and improving people's lives.

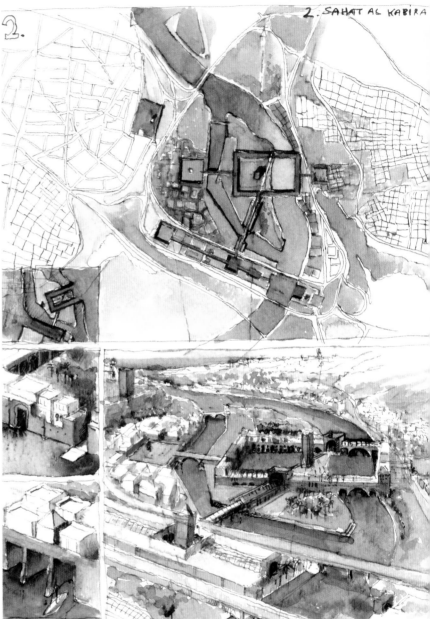

Wadi Barakrag master plan.
The meeting ground in the neutral
middle of the river, an important
symbolic representation of
rapprochement.

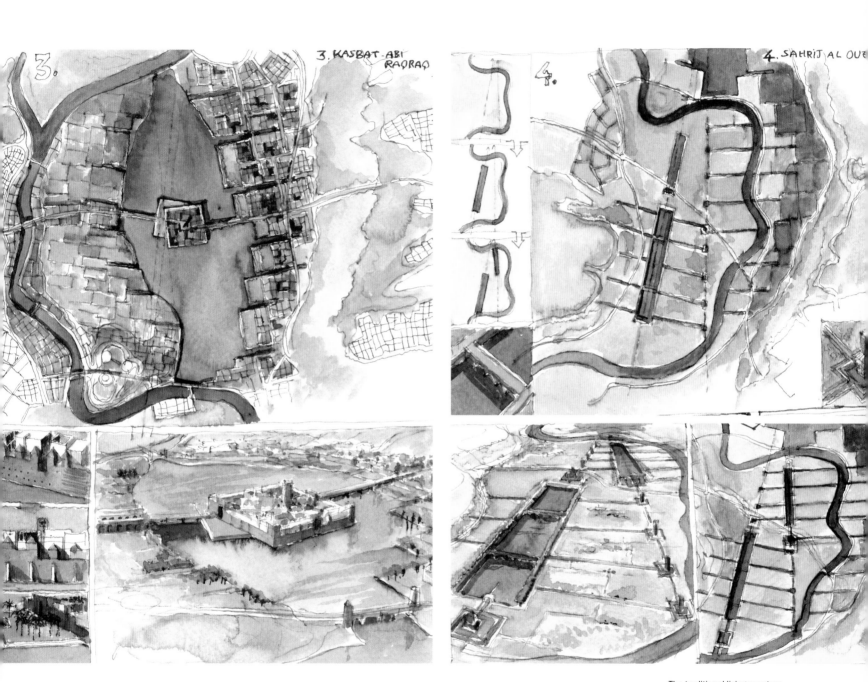

3. KASBAT-ABI RAQRAQ

4. SAHRIJ AL OUE

The traditional living quarters
(Al-Qasaba) and the water ponds,
with towers and canals for
irrigation. The plan is also
intended to improve the
environment and the livelihoods
of those living in the valley, and
so it has ambitious goals.

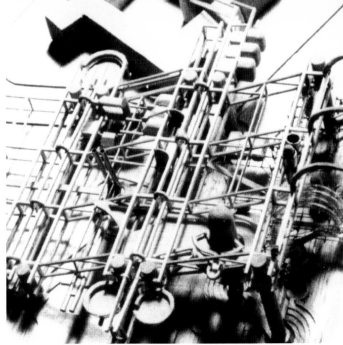

A Heritage Village and several *suqs* in Kuwait

Kuwait shares a Gulf-based history with Dubai, and many of the same growing pains, which have resulted in a progressive separation from its sea-going history. In 2003 Badran became involved in the design of a 'Heritage Village' to help maintain a connection with its history and point the way to the future, as he did in Dubai. He achieved this in Kuwait by starting with his architectural team to engage in a literal historical translation along the waterfront, complete with a corniche softened by trees and landscaping, which Badran then built up to a far more abstract, contemporary reading as the village grew inland. The fragmented roof forms, rendered in glass on the landside, reveal the influence of his diploma dissertation of 1969 in Kuwait – published in *Architecture aujourd'hui* in 1973,

Heritage Village, Kuwait.
The more progress that is made in making Gulf cities meet modern requirements, the more people seem to long for reminders of what they have lost. In this project Badran has tried to predict the possible changes of the urban pattern through time, introducing the water canal to locate hotel property within the proposed concept of rebuilding the old city quarter of Kuwait.

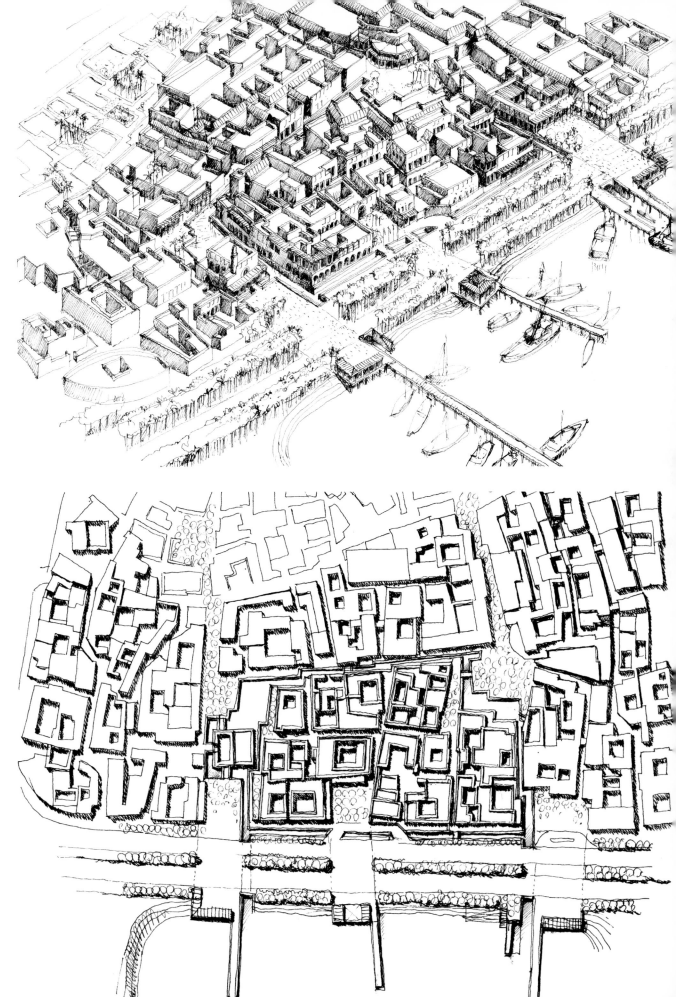

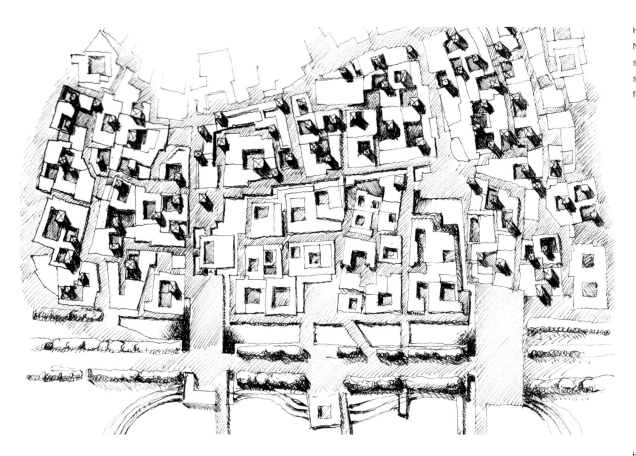

Heritage Village, Kuwait.
New geometries continue to
surprise Badran's followers. He
seems to have an infinite capacity
for constructive invention.

Heritage Village, Kuwait.
That invention typically includes
systems approaches, of an ever-
increasing scale.

Heritage Village, Kuwait.
Images of the city's evolution (the vertical accumulation of the activity and the changes in the spatial pattern). While many of these latest proposals may seem fanciful, they do indicate a deliberate intention to try new things, explore new technologies and attempt new means of expression.

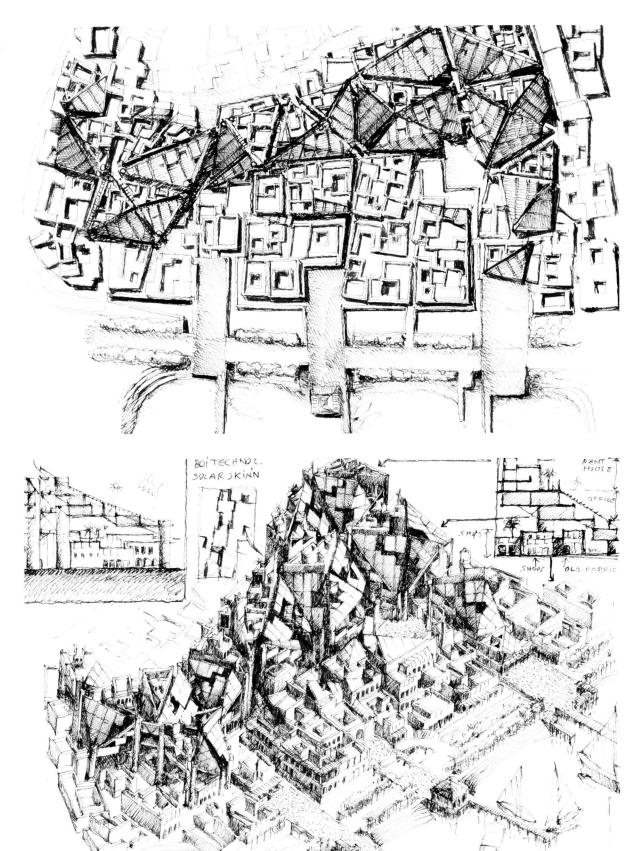

in which he proposed a living ecological hanging skin over the existing old city quarter. This reinforces his consistency and favours futuristic images that sharply contrast with his traditional reading in Dubai, all with the aim of developing an urban bio-system.

Suqs for the future

Malls have never really been popular in the Middle East. In spite of modernization many people still prefer the random informality of the *suq*, which has a venerable history in the region. There have been few serious attempts to update this much-loved commercial institution, but Badran and his architectural team have done just that in Kuwait, in two projects. At Al-Fheheel he designed an entire seafront complex around a cluster of contemporary *suqs*, connected to a marina and breakwater. The *suqs* combine several building technologies, organized by a rhythmical, orderly arcade, creating a protected internal street that is reminiscent of grand bazaars like the Khan al Khalili in Cairo, or Damascus and Istanbul. The rendition differs in its ease of access; the cluster also surrounds an internal court like a parking lot that is broken down in scale to prevent the familiar syndrome of asphalt around a huge, box-like mall.

The entire Al-Manshar complex, a remodelling of an existing shopping facility built in the 1960s, is a tour-de-force of cosmopolitan planning. It demonstrates the timeless principles of a spine acting as a demarcation line between land and water and a roundabout that connects the piers of the Al-Fheheel complex with inland Al-Manshar. It is seen as a circular terminus in which the change of scale that is necessary to transfer from vehicular to pedestrian movement occurs gradually. The entire composition is evocative of its place: it has balance and a sense of appropriateness consistent with the best contemporary examples of ocean-front planning. This project is a good example of his anti-grid morphology based on the 'fluidity of the fractal'.

Experimentation with new ways of improving on the traditional *suq* form by the Badran design team continues at Al-Fheheel, with the exception of the fabric structures used at Al-Manshar as a fluid roofing element. But at Al-Fheheel, he uses glass domes inside *badgirs*, which shade them, converting what has conventionally been a source of air into one of light.

The Sidon Sea Front Development master plan

In his the coastal master plan in Sidon, Lebanon, which Badran was again able to design as a result of winning an international competition – he has taken on the same issue: the harmonious integration of old and new with the accommodation of future growth. The challenge here was that he was now presented with a *tabula rasa* as in Kuwait, but had to work within an existing city context to provide urban infill, including an integral series of landscaped plazas and public gardens. While the texture of his approach is of a finer grain, the scope of work demands nothing less than a study of the Sidon port and old city, as well as a master plan for the entire five-kilometre seafront. This incorporates five pilot projects along its length to establish typical architectural typologies to be used in the city's future growth. He has submitted a proposal for reorganizing the coastline, rebuilding the waterfront portion of Sidon, and revitalizing the old city through incremental restoration. At the socio-cultural level, Badran undertook a drawing exercise for schoolchildren, with the support of Bahia Al-Hariri, in

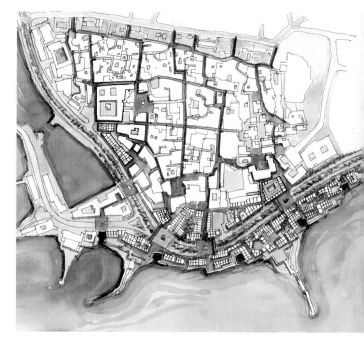

The Sidon Sea Front Development provided an exciting challenge for Badran, inspiring him because of the many possibilities open to him. This scheme is a source of social and cultural development, and has a powerful impact in preserving the fabric of the city.

As always, Sidon is also based on painstaking research, thorough scholarly background studies and intimate knowledge of his client base. The child's drawing on the left represents Sidon as perceived in the cultural memory.

order to identify their semiotic memory of the city, and thus to develop a visual matrix for the reconstruction of the demolished Sidon sea front.

A methodology that allows diversity

The methodology that Rasem Badran has used since the Al-Beit Foundation project in Jordan in the 1980s, and fine-tuned in Sana'a, Yemen, has obviously served him well. His design process of an initial graphic dissection of the topography, assessing pre-existing urban factors and the historical context of each civic condition, helps him to determine social and cultural differences within a uniform religious framework and to express them in built form. Since these differences have developed through environmental changes, his readings include these variations as well. The results shown here demonstrate the breadth of expression that this method has made possible.

Chronology of Work: Rasem Badran

Key to competition projects:

*	Competition won the First Prize	***	Competition won the Third Prize
**	Competition won the Second Prize	#	Competition Evaluation is not announced yet

1968

'Theatre of the Future'
Germany
Student project at the Technical
University of Darmstadt
Architect: R. Badran (Student)
Tutor: Prof. J. Jourdan

International Airport of Amman
Germany
Diploma student project at the
University of Darmstadt
Architect: R. Badran (Student)
Tutor: Prof. G. Behnisch

1969

Reconstruction of Kuwait
Diploma project at the Technical
University of Darmstadt
Architect: R. Badran (Student)
Tutor: Prof. Romero

1970

Olympia Park
Germany
Client: German Olympic
Committee
(1970–1972)
P. A.S. Design team: J. Jourdan,
B. Müller, R. Badran

1971

**P. A.S. Performing Art
Space in Sound Performance**
Darmstadt, Germany
Architectural Design Team of P. A.S.
J. Jourdan, B. Müller, R. Badran
The project was studied in
collaboration with the International
Workshop for Vanguard
Experimental Music in Darmstadt

**P. A.S. Cultural Activities
Art Exposition**
For Mrs C. Kowalski, G. Schweisser

1972

Low Cost Housing
Germany
Ministry of Housing –
Former West Germany
(1972–1974)
Architectural Design Team of P. A.S.
J. Jourdan, B. Müller, R. Badran

1973

**Development of Housing Scheme –
Alami Complex**
Amman, Jordan
Architect: R. Badran

Dr Suhail Khouri Residence
Amman, Jordan
Dr Suhail Khouri
(1973–1975)
Architect: R. Badran
Associates: Engineer Emil Shaker

Between 1973 and 1980, Badran
designed a series of houses in
Amman that effectively redefined a
local residential prototype, mixing
the customary use of local stone
with new forms. This series of
houses is especially significant
because of his re-interpretation of
the traditional indirect entry or
maqaz and central courtyard
sequence typically found in this
region. His experimentation with
venerated patterns, in a respectful
and thoughtful way in these
houses, came to characterize
his approach.

Housing Bank Headquarters*
Amman, Jordan
Client: Housing Bank
(1973–1977)
Architectural Design Team:
R. Badran, M. Alnamari

1974

Madi Residence
Amman, Jordan
Client: Mrs Moceenat Hekmat
Kalemat
(1974–1979)
Architect: R. Badran

1975

Al-Sa'ed Residence
Amman, Jordan
Client: Mr Falah Al-Sa'ed
(1975–1979)
Architect: R. Badran

Handal Residence
Amman, Jordan
Client: Mr George Handal
(1975–1979)
Architect: R. Badran

**Ministry of Planning and Housing
Corporation Headquarters***
Amman, Jordan
(1975–1977)
Architectural Design Team:
R. Badran, M. Alnamari

1976

Kamel Quwar Residence
Amman, Jordan
Client: Mr Kamel Quwar
(1976–1978)
Architect: R. Badran

1977

Al-Manhal Schools (6 Stages)
Amman, Jordan
Client: Al-Manhal Educational
Foundation
Architectural Design Team:
R. Badran, H. Mansour and
Mrs Rita Mansour

King Abdullah Mosque*
Amman, Jordan
Client: Ministry of Awqaf
Architect: R. Badran

1978

Talhouni Tower
Aqaba, Jordan
Client: Mr Khalil Talhouni
(1978–1982)
Architect: R. Badran

1979

Abu Ghouweilah Housing Complex*
Amman, Jordan
Client: Ministry of Awqaf
Architectural Design Team:
R. Badran, H. Mansour

Amman Commercial Centre*
Amman, Jordan
Client: Ministry of Awqaf
Architectural Design Team:
R. Badran, H. Mansour

Hatahet Residence
Amman, Jordan
Client: Mr Abdel Kareem Hatahet
(1979–1983)
Architectural Design Team:
R. Badran, H. Mansour

Irbid Commercial Centre*
Irbid, Jordan
Client: Ministry of Awqaf
Architectural Design Team:
R. Badran, Ms GH. Amr

1980

Protective Security Building
Amman, Jordan
Client: Public Security Directorate
(1980–1983)
Architectural Design Team:
R. Badran, H. Mansour

1981

State Grand Mosque*
Baghdad, Iraq
Client: Municipality of Baghdad
(1981)
Architectural Design Team:
R. Badran, Prof. O. Grabar, Prof.
J.Chika, A. Zuaiter, Ms GH. Amr,
B. Hammad, Y. Saqer

Public Security Officers Housing
Amman, Jordan
Client: Public Security Directorate
Architectural Design Team:
R. Badran, H. Mansour, Ms GH.
Amr, A. Almasri

Housing Security Office
Amman, Jordan
Client: Security Office Organization
Architectural Design Team:
R. Badran, A. Almasri, Ms GH. Amr,
Mrs M. Boderi

1982

**Queen Alia International
Airport Housing**
Zizia, Jordan
Client: Housing Authority
Architectural Design Team:
R. Badran, M. Abdulhadi, I. Kayali,
R. Abu Laban

**Administration Building of Cement
Factories Co.**
Al-Fuhais, Jordan
Client: Jordan Cement Factories Co.
(1982–1984)
Architectural Design Team:
R. Badran, H. Mansour,
Ms M. Boderi

**Cement Factory Employees
Housing, Al-Fuhais**
Al-Fuhais, Jordan
Client: Jordan Cement Factory Co.
(1982–1985)
Architectural Design Team:
R. Badran, Ms GH. Amr

Marto Residence
Amman, Jordan
Client: Mr Michael Marto
(1982–1986)
Architectural Design Team:
R. Badran, Ms GH. Amr

Hajjar Residence
Amman, Jordan
Client: Mr Radwan Hajjar
(1982–1986)
Architectural Design Team:
R. Badran, Ms GH. Amr

1983

Sati Residence
Amman, Jordan
Client: Mr Abdallah Sati
(1983–1986)
Architectural Design Team:
R. Badran, A. Almasri, E. Kayali

1984

Hisham Eziddine Residence
Amman, Jordan
Client: Mr Hisham Eziddine
(1984–1987)
Architectural Design Team:
R. Badran, Ms Z. Sabbagh
(Interior Designer)

Badran Residence
Amman, Jordan
Client: Dr Hassan Badran
(1984–1987)
Architectural Design Team:
R. Badran, R. Abu laban

Khorma Residence
Amman, Jordan
Client: Dr Sami Khorma
(1984–1988)
Architectural Design Team:
R. Badran, Y. Saqer

Special Police Dept. Building
Amman, Jordan
Client: Public Security Directorate
(1984–1988)
Architectural Design Team:
R. Badran, H. Mansour

Qattan Residence
Amman, Jordan
Client: Mr Tony Qattan
(1984–1989)
Architect: R. Badran and Ms GH. Amr

Opéra de la Bastille (study)
Paris, France
Client: De La Bastille
Architectural Design Team:
R. Badran, Prof. J.Chika

1985

Great Mosque*
Riyadh, Saudi Arabia
Client: Riyadh Development
Authority (ADA)
(1985–1991)
Architectural Design Team:
R. Badran, A. Zuaiter, Ms GH. Amr,
O. Amereh, A. Almasri, M. Abdul Hadi

**Al Al-Beit Foundation
Headquarters***
Amman, Jordan
Client: Islamic Study and
Research Centre
Architectural Design Team:
R. Badran, A. Zuaiter, Ms GH. Amr,
O. Amereh, A. Almasri

Ali Bin Abi Taleb Mosque*
Doha, Qatar
Client: Ministry of Public Works
Architectural Design Team:
R. Badran, A. Zuaiter

United Arab Emirates Embassy**
Amman, Jordan
Client: Ministry of Works, UAE
Architectural Design Team:
R. Badran, W. Alsayid

Umm Al Qura University*
Makkah, Saudi Arabia
Client: Ministry of Higher Education
Joint Design Team: Dr A. I.
Abdelhalim – Egypt, Turgut Ganzifer
– Turkey, Saud Consult – Saudi
Arabia, A. Mekia – London, Prof.
S. Bianca – Switzerland.

1986

Princess Nura Palace
Riyadh, Saudi Arabia
Client: H. R. H. Nura Bint Abdel Aziz
(1986–1988)
Architectural Design Team:
R. Badran, H. Mansour

Sheikh M. Dughaither Residence
Riyadh, Saudi Arabia
Client: Sheikh Moh'd Dughaither
(1986–1990)
Architect: R. Badran

Palace of Justice (Qasr Al-Hukm)*
Riyadh, Saudi Arabia
Client: Riyadh Development
Authority (ADA)
(1986–1992)
Architectural Design Team:
R. Badran, A. Zuaiter, O. Amereh,
Mrs H. Barkat, A. Mansour,
A. Almasri, A. Mansour,
Ms GH. Amr, M. Abdul Hadi

Prince Mashhoor Palace
Riyadh, Saudi Arabia
Client: H.R.H. Prince Mashhoor
(1986–1989)
Architect: R. Badran, H. Mansour

**Chamber of Commerce and
Industry Building****
Dammam, Saudi Arabia.
Client: Chamber of Commerce
and Industry
Architectural Design Team:
R. Badran, R. Abu Laban

**Prince Sultan Bin Salman Palace
(study)**
Riyadh, Saudi Arabia
Client: HRH Prince Sultan Bin
Salman
(1986–1989)
Architect: R. Badran

1988

Presidential Palace**
Baghdad, Iraq
Client: Ministry of Housing
Architectural Design Team:
R. Badran, S. Jarar, M. Muhasen,
R. Daher, S. Barakat
Associates: Architect Ihsan Fydi –
Baghdad

1989

**The Space and Science Oasis
Museum (Phase One)***
Riyadh, Saudi Arabia
Client: Riyadh Development
Authority (ADA)
(Schematic design 1989–1992)
Architectural Design Team:
R. Badran, M. Khashman,
M. Khalid, W. Alsayed, A. Bsaiso

**Imam Mohammad Bin Sa'ud
Islamic University (Interior Design)**
Riyadh, Saudi Arabia
Client: Imam Mohammad Bin Sa'ud
Islamic University
Architectural Design Team:
R. Badran, H. Mansour,
R. Abu Laban, Ms Z. Sabbagh
Associates: Ibrahim Abalkhel
Office, Saudi Arabia

Mango Residence
Amman, Jordan
Client: Mr Hassan Mango
(1989–1995)
Architects: R. Badran, E. Kayali

**Jordan Pavilion in Seville, Expo '92
(Interior Design)**
Amman, Jordan
Client: Jordan Commissioner of
Expo'92
(1989–1992)
Architectural Design Team:
R. Badran, B. Hammad, A. Abu
Hamdan, A. Zuaiter,
A. Al-Jabiri, Ms. A. Laham

1990

**Commercial and Housing
Complex Project***
Sana'a, Yemen
Client: Kuwait – Yemen
Investment Co.
Architectural Design Team:
R. Badran, W. Alsayed

Taha Residence
Amman, Jordan
Client: Mr Mahmoud Taha
Architectural Design Team:
R. Badran, Ms A. Laham

**B.M.W Showroom
(Interior Design)**
Amman, Jordan
Client: Mr Hani Abu Na'meh
(1990–1991)
Architectural Design Team:
R. Badran, Ms Z. Sabbagh

**Jordan National
Archaeological Museum***
Amman, Jordan
Client: Municipality of Amman
Architectural Design Team:
R. Badran, Dr A. I. Abdelhalim &
Architectural Team
from Amman – Cairo
Joint Venture with Dr A. I.
Abdelhalim, Cairo

University of Applied Sciences*
Amman, Jordan
Client: International Arab Co. for
Education & Investment
(1990–1994)
Architectural Design Team:
R. Badran, H. Mansour, R. Abu
Laban, A. Bsaiso, E. Kayali

Al Deek Residence
Amman, Jordan
Client: Mr Mohammad Al Deek
(1990–1994)
Architectural Design Team:
R. Badran, Ms. A. Laham

**The Space and Science Oasis
Museum
(Phase Two)***
Riyadh, Saudi Arabia
Client: Riyadh Development
Authority (ADA)
(1990–1992)
Architectural Design Team:
R. Badran, Dr. A. I. Abdelhalim &
Architectural Team from Amman –
Cairo
Joint Venture with Dr A. I.
Abdelhalim – Egypt

**Jordan University for Girls (Petra
University)***
Amman, Jordan
Client: Jordan University for Girls
Company
(1990–1993)
Architectural Design Team:
R. Badran, Dr. T. Rifai
Associates: ACE – Amman, Jordan –
Engineering services

1991

Madi Centre
Amman, Jordan
Client: Mr Hayder Madi
(1991–1995)
Architectural Design Team:
R. Badran, H. Mansour, R. Abu
Laban, I. Khrem

**The New International Islamic
University Campus (IIU)**
Kuala Lumpur, Malaysia
Client: University's Administration
(1991–1998)
R. Badran and A. I. Abdelhalim as
International Consultants

Issam Qattan Residence
Riyadh, Saudi Arabia
Client: Mr Issam Qattan
(1991–1993)
Architectural Design Team:
R. Badran, W. Alsayed

1992

**Al-Jamaliah District
Development Plan***
Cairo, Egypt
Client: Housing Authority
Architectural Design Team:
R. Badran, Dr. A. I. Abdelhalim &
Architectural Team from
Amman –Cairo
Joint Venture with Dr A. I.
Abdelhalim – Cairo

**Dr Abdel Razek Hussain
Residence**
Amman, Jordan
Client: Dr Abdel Razek Hussain
(1992–1995)
Architect: R. Badran

**The Nabatean Castle Hotel
(138 rooms)**
Petra, Jordan
Client: Nabatean Hotels Company
(1992–1996)
Architectural Design Team:
R. Badran, M. Khashman, I. Kayali

**Specialty Hospital
(3 Phases) (300 beds)**
Amman, Jordan
Client: Specialty Hospital Company
(1992–1995)
Architectural Design Team:
R. Badran, S. Sabbagh, M. Khalid,
T. Abu Hantash

Al- Talhouni Residence
Amman, Jordan
Client: Mr Khalil Al-Talhouni
(1992–1996)
Architectural Design Team:
R. Badran, Ms Z. Sabbagh
(Interior Designer)

Wahbeh Commercial Centre
Amman, Jordan
Client: Mr Mahmoud Wahbeh
(1992–1995)
Architectural Design Team:
R. Badran, S. Sabbagh, A. Bsaiso

Zahran St. Residential Building
Amman, Jordan
Client: Mr Hisham Ezz Eddin
(1992–1995)
Architectural Design Team:
R. Badran, S. Sabbagh, W. Alsayed

1993

Adnan Talhouni Residence
Amman, Jordan
Client: Mr. Adnan Talhouni
(1993–1995)
Architectural Design Team:
R. Badran, A. Laham

**The Shrines of the Prophets
Companions – Abu Ubayda
Mosque Complex**
Jordan Valley, Jordan
Client: Ministry of Awaf and
Islamic Affairs
(1993–1998)
Architectural Design Team:
R. Badran, Rami Arnaout, Raed
Arnaout, A. Bsaiso, W. Almasri,
Ms A. Zanoun (Landscape)

Al-Ta'meer Center*
Riyadh, Saudi Arabia
Client: Riyadh Development
Company (ADC)
(1993–1999)
Architectural Design Team:
R. Badran, Dr. A. I. Abdelhalim,
J. Batchlor, Assoc. Prof. L. Medlin,
S. Sabbagh, M. Abbas, A.Betros,
Ayhab & Architectural Team from
Amman – Cairo – Cambridge, Mass.
Joint Venture with Dr A. I.
Abdelhalim – Cairo, ARROW STREET
OFFICE Cambridge, Mass.

**Bethlehem Intercontinental Hotel
(240 rooms)**
Bethlehem
Client: Palestine For Tourism
Investment Co.
Architect: R. Badran

**The Shrines of
the Prophets Companions
(Sahaba/Al Mazar South)***
Al Mazar, Jordan
Client: Ministry of Awqaf
(1993–1998)
Architectural Design Team:
R. Badran, Dr. A. I. Abdelhalim,
A. Zuaiter, T. Abu Hantash,
M. Khalid & Architectural Team
from Amman – Cairo
Joint venture with: Dr A. I.
Abdelhalim (Cairo)

Islamic Shrines (Imam Bukhari)**
Samarkand, Bukhara
Client: The Centre for Islamic
Studies at Oxford University
Architectural Design Team:
R. Badran, Dr. A. I. Abdelhalim &
Architectural Team from
Amman - Cairo
Joint Venture with
Dr A. I. Abdelhalim (Cairo)

**Jordan Central Bank
(Building No.3)**
Amman, Jordan
Client: Jordan Central Bank
(1993–1995)
Architectural Design Team:
R. Badran, I. Shaheen, I. Khrem,
R. Abu Laban, Ms. Z. Sabbagh

Al-Manhal Elementary School
Amman, Jordan
Client: Al-Manhal Educational Est.
(1993–1996)
Architectural Design Team:
R. Badran, H. Mansour

**International Islamic
University/Medical Campus**
Kuala Lumpur, Malaysia
Client: Ministry of Education

Architectural Design Team:
R. Badran, Dr. A. I. Abdelhalim &
Architectural Team from
Amman – Cairo
Joint Venture with Dr A. I.
Abdelhalim

Irbid Specialty Hospital (100 beds)
Irbid, Jordan
Client: Irbid Specialty Hospital Co.
(1993–1996)
Architectural Design Team:
R. Badran, S. Sabbagh

**Al-Mashriq Hotel (Mövenpick)
(153 rooms)**
Petra, Jordan
Client: Levant Hotels &
Tourism Company
(1993–1998)
Architectural Design Team:
R. Badran, W. Alsayed,
Ms A. Laham

**Royal Palace (The Residence of
The Late King Hussein) (Study)**
Amman, Jordan
Client: Royal Court of
Queen Noor of Jordan (1994)
Architectural Design Team:
R. Badran, S. Sabbagh,
S. Moghrabi, W. Almasri

**Abu Loghod International Hospital
(80 beds)**
Amman, Jordan
Client: Dr M. Abu Loghod and
Partners
Architectural Design Team:
R. Badran, S. Sabbagh,
Ms A. Zanoun, Ms S. Bejawi

Labour Village
Riyadh, Saudi Arabia
Client: Mr Imad Hujailan
Architectural Design Team:
R. Badran, S. Sabbagh

Courts Complex**
Riyadh, Saudi Arabia
Client: Riyadh Development
Authority
Architectural Design Team:
R. Badran, Dr. A. I. Abdelhalim
Joint Venture with Dr A. I.
Abdelhalim

Jubilee School**
Amman, Jordan
Client: Queen Noor Al-Hussein
Foundation
Architectural Design Team:
R. Badran, S. Jarar, W. Alsayed,
H. Mansour, A.Bsaiso

1995

Dirar Bin Al-Azwar Mosque
Jordan Valley, Jordan
Client: Ministry of Awqaf
(1995–1999)
Architectural Design Team:
R. Badran, Rami Arnaout, Raed
Arnaout

Saudi Ceramic Co. Building**
Riyadh, Saudi Arabia
Client: Saudi Ceramic Co.
Architect: R. Badran

Sahab Hospital (120 beds)
Sahab, Jordan
Client: Ministry of Health
(1995–1999)
Architectural Design Team:
R. Badran, Ms A. Zanoun,
Mrs D. Shequwara

**Institute Of Diplomacy
(Remodelling)**
Amman, Jordan
Client: Ministry of Culture
(1995–1996)
Architectural Design Team:
R. Badran, Ms Z. Sabbagh

Amman City Hall
Amman, Jordan
Client: The Municipality
of Amman (1995–1998)
Architectural Design Team:
R. Badran, J. Touqan & Architectural
Team Associates: Jafar
Touqan Office

CitiBank
Amman, Jordan
Client: Mr S.Kassab
(1995–1998)
Architectural Design Team:
R. Badran, Rami Arnaout

King Abdul Aziz Mosque*
Al-Kharj, Saudi Arabia
Client: Riyadh Development
Authority (ADA)
(1995–1999)
Architectural Design Team:
R. Badran, M. Abbas, R. Al-Khatib,
Mrs Z. Sabbagh (Interior Designer)
Associate engineers: Omraniah,
Riyadh, Saudi Arabia

Abha Girls University*
Abha, Saudi Arabia
Client: Ministry of Higher Education
Architectural Design Team:
R. Badran, Dr A. I. Abdelhalim,
M. Khashman, A. Bsaiso &
Architectural Team from Amman –
Cairo Joint Venture with
Dr A. I. Abdelhalim

1996

**King Abdul Aziz Historic Centre*
(Phase 1 – Urban Design
Development)**
Riyadh, Saudi Arabia
Client: Riyadh Development.
Authority (ADA)
(1996–1999)
Architectural Design Team:
R. Badran, A. Alshuaibi
Associates: Al Bee'A Office,
Saudi Arabia

**King Abdul Aziz Historic Centre*
Phase 2 – Architectural Design**
Riyadh, Saudi Arabia
Client: Riyadh Development
Authority (ADA)
(1996–1999)
Architectural Design Team:
R. Badran, M. Abbas, S. Sabbagh,
Rami Arnaout, Ms Z. Sabbagh
(Interior Designer), Ms A. Zanoun
(Landscape)
Associates: Reich & Petch –
Ontario, Canada
Exhibit Design and OMRANIAH –
Riyadh, Saudi Arabia
(Engineering Design)

Islamic Bank Building*
Dubai, U.A.E.
Client: Islamic Bank
Architect: R. Badran

Al Rajihi Residence
Riyadh, Saudi Arabia
Client: Mr Abdullah Al Rajihi
(1996–1999)
Architectural Design Team:
R. Badran, M. Abbas, S. Sabbagh

**Chamber of Trading and
Industry Building****
Makkah, Saudi Arabia
Client: Chamber of Trading
and Industry
(1996–1999)
Architectural Design Team:
R. Badran, W. Alsayed, A. Bsaiso

Al-Mo'asher Residence
Amman, Jordan
Client: Mr Fares Al-Moasher
(1996–1999)
Architect: R. Badran

**Jordan Telecom
Administration Tower****
Amman, Jordan
Client: Jordan Telecom Company
Architectural Design Team:
R. Badran, A. Bsaiso, Rami Arnaout

Dead Sea Oasis Spa (schematic)
Dead Sea, Jordan
Client: The Jordanian Spa Company
Architectural Design Team:
R. Badran, Ms A. Zanoun

Al-Kazimi Mosque
Amman, Jordan
Client: Mohammad Al-Kazimi
(1996–2000)
Architectural Design Team:
R. Badran, Rami Arnaout

**Abdoun Hotel (Schematics Only)
(158 rooms)**
Amman, Jordan
Client: Al-Wadi Company for
Hotels & Investment Co.
Architectural Design Team:
R. Badran, Ms A. Taha

Amman Mall (C-Town)
Amman, Jordan
Client: American Department
Stores Company
(1996–1999)
Architectural Design Team:
R. Badran, S. Sabbagh and
Ms S. Bejawi, Ms Z. Sabbagh
(Interior Designer)

Headquarters of President Arafat
Nablus
Client: Palestinian
National Authority
Architectural Design Team:
R. Badran, A. Bsaiso

1997

**Jordan Second Tourism
Development Wadi Rum
Component**
Wadi Rum, Jordan
Client: Aqaba Regional Authority
(ARA)
(1997–2001)
Architectural Design Team:
R. Badran, Ms. A. Zanoun,
Ms A. Taha

Bethlehem Housing Complex
Bethlehem
Client: Association of
Bethlehem University
Architectural Design Team:
R. Badran, A. Bsaiso, I. Khrem

**Riyadh Development
Company Offices**
Riyadh, Saudi Arabia
Client: Riyadh Development
Company (ADC)
Organizer: Riyadh Development
Authority (ADA)
Architect: R. Badran, R. Arnaout

Museum For Islamic Arts / Qatar*
(Design Only)
Doha, Qatar
Client: Special Projects Office,
State of Qatar
Organizer: The Agha Khan Trust
for Culture (Geneva,Swiss)
(1997–1999)
Architectural Design Team:
R. Badran, R. Khatib, M. Abbas,
M. Hyari, A. Moamar,
Interior Design Team: Mrs
Z. Sabbagh, Ms I. Haram
Landscape Design Team:
Ms A. Zanoun, R. Bödecker
Associates:
Lord and Rome – Museumology,
Canada: R. Barnaett, J. Nicks
Event- Exhibit Design – London:
Mrs J. Ashworth
OMRANIAH – Engineering Design –
Saudi Arabia
Richard Bödecker – Landscape
Design – Germany

Prince Asem Bin Nayef Residence
Amman, Jordan
Client: HRH Prince Asem Bin Nayef
(1997–2002)
Architectural Design Team:
R. Badran, Mrs. S. Bejawi,
Mrs Z. Sabbagh

Modern Arab School
Amman, Jordan
Client: Modern Arab Company for
Private Education
(1997–2000)
Architectural Design Team:
R. Badran, Jafar Touqan
Associates: Jafar Touqan Office

Al-Yarmouk University
Central Library
Irbid, Jordan
Client: Al-Yarmouk University
(1997–2002)
Architectural Design Team:
R. Badran, S. Moughrabi,
J. Jayyousi, A. Moamar, B. Rashid,
Mrs R. Hatamlah, Mr. M. Salman

Sidon Sea Front Development
(Master Plan)*
Sidon, Lebanon
Client: Civil Organization
Directorate and
Mrs M.P. Bahia Al Hariri,
(1997 till now)
Architectural Design Team:
R. Badran, S. Sabbagh, M. Abbas,
M. Hyari, Mrs S. Bejawi

Ali Al-Sehebani Villa
Riyadh, Saudi Arabia
Client: Mr Ali Shebani
Architectural Design Team:
R. Badran, S. Sabbagh

1998

Ruler's Private Residence#
Dubai, U.A.E.
Client: Municipality of Dubai
Architectural Design Team:
R. Badran, Rami Arnaout

Al-Hamriya Mall Development
Scheme#
Dubai, U.A.E.
Client: Municipality of Dubai
Architectural Design Team:
R. Badran, GH. Alsayed, A. Wardat,
A. Aljasme
Associates: Al-Burj Office – Dubai

Ruler's Palace#
Al-Ain, U.A.E.
Client: Municipality of Al-Ain
Architectural Design Team:
R. Badran, M.Abbas, Rami Arnaout

Dubai Creek Complex#
Dubai, U.A.E.
Client: Dubai Municipality
Architectural Design Team:
R. Badran, J. Patchclor (from Arrow
Street), GH. Alsayed, A. Wardat,
W. Alnuri
Associates: Arrow Street, USA

School for the Gifted*
Riyadh, Saudi Arabia
Client: Ministry of Education
Architectural Design Team:
R. Badran, S. Sabbagh
1999

Al-Hudaida University
Hudaida, Yemen
Client: University's Administration
(1999 till now)
Architectural Design Team:
R. Badran, GH. Alsayed, Ms A. Taha

Court Complex, Sharja**
Sharja, U.A.E.
Client: Ministry of Public Works
Architectural Design Team:
R. Badran, M. Abbas

Al-Ain Museum
Al-Ain, U.A.E.
Client: Municipality of Al-Ain#
Architectural Design Team:
R. Badran, R. Arnaout
Associates: Event, Exhibit Design –
London: Mrs J. Joy-Alsworth

Granada Shopping Mall***
Riyadh, Saudi Arabia
Client: G.O.S.L., Riyadh,
Saudi Arabia
Architectural Design Team:
R. Badran,Rami Arnaout, M. Hyari,
Ms A. Zanoun

Ramallah City Center
Master Plan***
Ramallah
Client: Municipality of Ramallah
Architectural Design Team:
R. Badran, M. Abbas

NESSCO Office Building*
Tripoli, Libya
Client: NESSCO, Tripoli, Libya
(1999 till now)
Architectural Design Team:
R. Badran, W. Almasri, M Abbas,
Mrs N. Tayem, Ms. A. Zanoun

Jordan University of Science and
Technology (Library, Deanery,
Admissions and President's Office)
Irbid, Jordan
Client: Jordan University of Science
and Technology
(1999 till now)
Architectural Design Team:
R. Badran, R. Arnaout, M. Abbas,
A. Moamar, GH. Alsayed, M. Hyari

Wadi Saleh Housing
Jerusalem
Client: Jerusalem Engineering
Establishment
Architectural Design Team:
R. Badran, Z. Alsoghayer
Associates: Ziyad Alsoghayer
Architectural Office, Bethlehem,
Palestinian National Authority

Museum for Children
Amman, Jordan
Client: Royal Court, Amman
Municipality
Architectural Design Team:
R. Badran, Mrs S. Bejawi
Associates: Mrs H. Alkurdi –
Museology

2000

Al-Fheheel Water Front
Development (Phase One –
Preliminary Design Stage)
Al-Fheheel, Kuwait
Client: Tamdeen Real Estate Co.
Architectural Design Team:
R. Badran, W. Almasri, M. Abbas,
Ms A. Zanoun
Associates: C. 7. Cambridge, Mass.
– Preliminary Design Stage

Jabal Omar – Makkah
Development#
Makkah, Saudi Arabia
Client: Makkah Construction &
Development Co.
Organizer: Millennium,
Beirut, Lebanon
Architectural Design Team:
R. Badran, W. Almasri,
M. Abbas & Others

Associates: Consult – Canada –
Traffic Expert

Al-Fheheel Water Front
Development (Phase Two –
Architectural Design
Development)
Al-Fheheel, Kuwait
Client: Tamdeen Real Estate Co.
(2000–2004)
Architectural Design Team:
R. Badran, W. Almasri. A. Moamar,
Rami Arnaout, M. Abbas, Ms
A. Zanoun (Landscape)

Al-Manshar Complex
Al-Fheheel, Kuwait
Client: Tamdeen Real Estate Co.
(2000 till now)
Architectural Design Team:
R. Badran, W. Almasri, Mrs
N. Tayem, M. Abbas, Ms A. Zanoun
(Landscape)

Jordan University of
Science and Technology
(Administration Bldg, President's
Bldg, Students Affairs Bldg)
(Design Only)
Irbid, Jordan
Client: Jordan University
of Science & Technology
(2000–2002)
Architectural Design Team:
R. Badran, R. Arnaout, M. Abbas,
M. Moamar, GH. Alsayed, M. Hyari

Private Residence
Dubai, U.A.E.
Client: Sheikh Khalid Bin Zaied
Architectural Design Team:
R. Badran, M. Abbas, Ms
A. Zanoun, and Mrs Z. Sabbagh
(Interior Designer)

2001

Qathafy Islamic Minaret
(Kano Great Mosque)
Kano, Nigeria
Client: World Islamic Call Society
Architectural Design team:
R. Badran, Ms A. Zanoun,
Mrs S. Bejawi

Moh'd Al-Sheikh Residence
Riyadh, Saudi Arabia
Client: Mr Mohammad Al-Sheikh
Architectural Design Team:
R. Badran, S. Sabbagh, M. Hyari

Jordan University of Science and
Technology Gateway
Irbid, Jordan
Client: Jordan University of Science
and Technology
(2001–2003)
Architect: R. Badran, B. Rashid

Hussein Bin Talal
University Gateway
Ma'an, Jordan
Client: Hussein Bin Talal University
(2001–2003)
Architectural Design Team:
R. Badran, W. Almasri, GH. Alsayed,
Mrs N. Tayem
Associates: Arrow Street, USA

2002

Sharif Al-Saee'd Villa
Amman, Jordan
Client: Mr. Sharif Al- Saee'd
(2002–2005)
Architectural Design Team:
R. Badran, Mrs N. Tayem, Mrs
Z. Sabbagh (Interior Designer)

Al-Suwaidi Villa (Design Only)
Abu Dhabi, U.A.E
Client: Mr Mohammad Al-Suwaidi
(2002–2004)
Architectural Design Team:
R. Badran, S. Sabbagh, Rami
Arnaout, Mrs Z. Sabbagh (Interior
Designer)

Wadi Baraqraq Development
Scheme (Advisory)
Misseelah, Kuwait
Client: Kingdom of Morocco
(2002–2003)
Architectural Design Team:
R. Badran, W. Almasri
Associates: Collaboration Bureau
– Morocco: M. F. Bin Abdullah,
A. Montasir, R. Andaloussi,
S. Moulin, T. Aloufer

Al-Hudaida University
Central Library
Al-Hudaida, Yemen
Client: Al-Hudaida University
(2002–2004)
Architectural Design Team:
R. Badran, GH. Alsayed

Al-Amin Mosque
Beirut, Lebanon
Client: Ministry of Awqaf and
Islamic Affairs – Beirut
Architectural Design Team:
R. Badran, M. Hyari

Yousef Al-Saee'd Villa
Amman, Jordan
Client: Mr. Yousef Al- Saee'd
(2002–2004)
Architectural Design Team:
R. Badran, Mrs N. Tayem,
Mrs Z. Sabbagh (Interior Designer)

2003

Abu-Ghazaleh Mosque
Amman, Jordan
Client: Mohammed Abu-Ghazaleh
(2003–2004)
Architectural Design Team:
R. Badran, Rami Arnaout

Heritage Village (Main Scheme)
Sharq, Kuwait City
Client: Kuwait Government
Architectural Design Team:
W. Almasri, Ms A. Zanoun,
M. Abbas, M. Hyari

**Heritage Village (Alternative
Proposal)**
Sharq, Kuwait City
Client: Kuwait Government
Architect: R. Badran

**Sana'a Conference Palace
(Design Proposal)**
Sana'a, Republic of Yemen
Client: The Foreign Ministry of
State, Qatar
Architectural Design Team: R. Badran,
A. Moamar, H. Khyat, F. Akkelah

**Wadi Abu Jamil Housing
Development Scheme**
Beirut, Lebanon
Client: Solidere
Architectural Design Team:
R. Badran, W. Almasri, M. Abbas,
GH. Alsayed

**Qatar Embassy and
Ambassador's Residence**
Amman, Jordan
Client: Ministry of Foreign Affairs,
Qatar
Architectural Design Team:
R. Badran, GH. Alsayed,
N. Yaravase, Ms A. Qattawi

**Damascus University Central
Library**
Damascus, Syria
Client: Damascus University
Architectural Design Team:
R. Badran, GH. Alsayed, M. Moamar

**National Bank of Kuwait
(Remodelling)**
Amman, Jordan
Client: National Bank of Kuwait
(2003–2004)
Architectural Design Team:
R. Badran, Mrs N. Tayem,
H. Khyat, Mrs Z. Sabbagh
(Interior Designer)

**Al-Shamiya Development Project
(Three Phases)**
Makkah, Saudi Arabia
Client: Makkah Real
State Company
Architectural Design Team:
R. Badran, W. Almasri, M. Abbas,
Mrs N. Barkat, Ms S. Ghzawi,
Ms R. Al-Ashhab
Associates: Gensler, USA
(in Phase Three only)

2004

Kordofan Trading Tower*
Khartoum, Sudan
Client: Kordofan Company Ltd
Architectural Design Team:
R. Badran, Rami Arnaout

Housing Bank (Design Proposal)
Amman, Jordan
Client: Housing Bank
Architectural Design Team:
R. Badran, J. Badran Jr
Associates: Gensler, USA

**Sudan Cotton
Company Building****
Khartoum, Sudan
Client: Sudan Cotton Company
Architectural Design Team:
R. Badran, Rami Arnaout

Ministry Of Finance Complex*
Amman, Jordan
Client: Ministry of Finance
Architectural Design Team:
R. Badran, M. Hyari, H. Khyat,
Mrs S. Ghzawi, Mrs R. Al-Ashhab

**Al-Fateh University Central
Library#**
Tripoli, Libya
Client: Al-Fateh University
Architectural Design Team:
R. Badran, A. Wardat

Beirut Martyr's Square#
Beirut, Lebanon
Client: Solidere
Architectural Design Team:
R. Badran, R. Daher, R. Arnaout,
J. Badran Jr
Associates: Rami Daher

Dubai Creek Development#
Dubai, U.A.E
Client: Dubai Development and
Investment Authority
Architectural Design Team:
R. Badran, M. Hyari

**Al-Qouz Land Project, Workers
Housing Development**
Dubai, Jabal Ali, U.A.E
Client: The Executive Office
Architectural Design Team:
R. Badran, Rami Arnaout,
O. Rosan, N. Yaravase,
H. Khyat, F. Akkelah, M. Hyari,
Mrs N. Barkat
Joint venture with MECON,
Dubai, UAE

**Ministry of Pilgrimage,
Preliminary Design**
Riyadh, Saudi Arabia
Client: Ministry of Pilgrimage
Architectural Design Team:
R. Badran, R. Al-Khatib,
S. Sabbagh

**Doha Great Mosque (Preliminary
Design)**
Doha, Qatar
Client: Special Office of the Doha
Government
Architectural Design Team:
R. Badran, Rami Arnaout

2005

**Berlin Expo (The Narrative of an
Arab Family) (the Badran Family
1909–2005)**
Mobile Exhibit System
(2004–2005)
Client: Ministry of Foreign
Affairs, Berlin

**IFA Gallery, Berlin,
Stuttgart Exhibition
R. Badran's Architectural Work –
a Biography**
Mobile Exhibit System
(2004–2005)
Client: IFA (Institut für
Auslandsbeziehungen)
Designed by: R. Badran, Mrs
Z. Sabbagh, J. Badran Jr
Coordination team – Amman:
B. Rashid, J. Malhas, Ms A. Khdier
Coordination team – Germany:
Dr A. Prinz, Mr A. Nowak,
Dr B. Barsch, Mrs I. Lenz
Beate Ekstine,
Architect: Mr A. Ramadan.

Supporting team for Ministry of
Foreign Affairs and IFA:
Ms N. Othman, Ms H. Msallam,
Ms H. Khammash, Ms A. Zuaiter

Notes by chapter

**Chapter 1. A Narrative on People,
Place and Culture**
1.IASTE 2004 Conference Brief
Frederic Jameson. *Post-
Modernism, or, The Cultural Logic
of Late Capitalism*, Durham
University Press, 1985.
2.Daniel Bell, *The Social
Framework of the Information
Society*, MIT Press, Cambridge
Mass., 1980
3.John Ralston Saul, 'The
Collapse of Globalism and The
Rebirth of Nationalism', *Harpers*,
March 2004 p. 35
4.Ibid. p. 36
5.Ibid. p. 37
6.Robert Wade, 'Global Inequality'
The Economist, 20 April 2001,
p.74
7.Ibid. p. 75
8.Rasem Badran, *Reflections on
the Narrative of Place – The Infinite Conversation*. Unpublished,
no pagination
9.Ibid.

**Chapter 2. Creative Heritage and
the Return to the East**
This chapter is based on a short
biography written by Rasem
Badran, translated from the Arabic
by Rami F. Daher. All quotes are
taken from this translation, which
was completed in Amman in
January 2004 and made available
to me then.

**Chapter 4. The Fourth Dimension
is the Spirit**
1.Dogan Kuban in Ismail
Serageldin and James Steele, *The
Contemporary Mosque*, Academy
Editions, London, 1994, p. 37
2.Ibid. p.46
3.Ibid. p.57
4.John D. Hoag. *Islamic
Architecture*, Academy Editions,
London, 1977, p. 34

**Chapter 5. Preserving a Living
History**
1.Mumford, Lewis, *The City in
History*, Penguin, London, 1975,
p. 64
2.Two Centuries as a Museum,
www.louvre.fr
3.Giebelhauser, Michaela, ed.
The Architecture of the Museum,
Manchester University Press,
2003, p. 6

4.Douglas, David, *The Museum
Transformed*, Abbeville Press, New
York, 199, p. 26
5.Giebelhauser, Michaela, op.cit.
p. 4
6.Steele, James, *Orientalism and
the Other*, PhD Thesis, University
of Southern California, 2000.
Unpublished, p. 16
7.Weil, Stephen, *Rethinking the
Museum*, Smithsonian Institute
Press, Washington D.C., 1990, p.
140
8.Ibid. p. 51
9.Harria, Neil, Midwest Museum
Conference Proceedings, University of Chicago, 1986, p.32
10.Weil, Stephen, op.cit. p. 60
11.Weil, Stephen, op.cit. p. 57
12.Weil, Stephen, op.cit. p. 52
13.Weil, Stephen, op.cit. p. 61
14.Douglas, David, op.cit. p. 6

Chapter 6. An Earthly Paradise
1.Victoria Meinecke-Berg 'Outline
of the Urban Development of
Cairo'
2.Islamic Cairo: 'Architectural Conservation and Urban Development
of the Historic Centre', ed. Michael
Meinecke, Proceedings of a
Seminar organized by the Goethe
Institute (Cairo), 1–5 October
1978, p. 8
Jaquelin Tyrwhitt was fond of using
the term 'human-scale intermediary' in her studies of city planning.
3.*Minarets as Landmarks in
Islamic Cairo*, unpublished doctoral dissertation, Nezar Al-Sayyad
UCLA (Berkeley), 1978. In the dissertation, Nezar al-Sayyad shows
how mosques were not only
located within the reach of the
muezzin's call, but also served as
visual markers to guide people
through the maze of streets.
4. Omar al-Farook, John Norton,
Wendy Etchells et al., 'Report on
Islamic Cairo', Architectural Association (London), 1987.

Bibliography

Akram Abu Hamdan: 'Profile, Rasem Badran', *Mimar* 25, September 1987, pp. 50–57

Salim Al-Faquih, 'Islamic Style in Contemporary Arab Architecture', *Mimar* 3, June 1989, pp. 48–52

Rasem Badran: 'Historical references and Contemporary Design' in Theories and Principles of Design in the Architecture of the Islamic Societies. Symposium (1987), The Aga Khan Program for Islamic Architecture, Cambridge Mass. (1988), pp. 149–159

Rasem Badran: 'The Jama Mosque, Qasr Al-Houkm' in *Al-Bena'a* 36 (September 1987), pp. 74–80 [in Arabic]. English translation pp. 4–5

Rasem Badran: 'Chamber of Commerce And Industry in Dammam' in *Al-Bena'a* 44 Vol. 8 (December 1988), pp. 37–39 [in Arabic]. English translation pp. 14-15

Rasem Badran: 'Architect of the Issue: Rasem Badran from Jordan' in *Al-Bena'a* 23 Vol. 4 (June—September 1985), pp. 115–119

Doris Behrens Abouseif, *The Islamic Architecture of Cairo*, Brill, Leidon, 1989

Stefano Bianca, *Urban Form in the Arab World; Past and Present*, Thames and Hudson, London, 2000

S. Blair and J. Bloom, *The Art and Architecture of Islam; 1250-1800*, Yale University Press, New Haven and London, 1994

Rifat Chadirji, *Concepts and Influences: Towards a Regionalised International Architecture*, KPI, London, 1984

Oleg Grabar and Richard Ettinghausen, *The Art and Architecture of Islam 650–1250*, Yale University Press, New Haven and London, 1994

Edward Said, *Orientalism*, Vintage Books, New York ,197.

James Steele, 'The New Traditionalists', *Mimar* 40, September 1991, pp.43–45

Glossary

adhan the daily call to prayer, delivered by the muezzin

badana family group within a tribe

badgir wind-tower

baratsi lightweight roof truss constructed as a folded slab from woven wire, reeds and cement

bayt palace

chahar-bagh a structure in which four arches support a dome

caravanserai inn with large inner court

claustra pierced divding wall

dahliz antechamber

dikka raised platform from which the words and actions of the imam are relayed to members of the congregation

diwan al-harim sitting room

diwan hasil sitting room reserved for women

durqa'a central space of the **qa'a**

Fatimid descended from Fatima, daughter of Mohammad; dynasty ruled Egypt 969–1171

feddan measure of land equivalent to approx 1. acre (0.405 hectare)

hajj pilgrimage, especially to Makkah

hammam public bath

haram private quarters of a house or sanctuary of a mosque

imam leader; any adult male who leads prayers during congregational worship in a mosque

iwan ancillary space, often adjoining a **qa'a**

jami congregation

Jumah congregational mosque

kamariyya stained-glass window joined with plaster

khan accommodation for travellers

khayma flat-roofed loggia

külliye complex of buildings associated with a mosque, including those used for medical, teaching and charitable purposes

maidan a large open space for ceremonial use

madresa Islamic school, often attached to a mosque

magaz indirect or offset entry

maghribi North African horseshoe arch

majlis reception hall for male guests

malkaf wind catch

Mamluk dynasty, ruled Egypt 1250–1517

manthara guest sitting room

manzil large house

maqa'ad loggia, open 'room'

mastaba step or bench

masjid a district or neighbourhood mosque

mihrab the recess or niche in a mosque indicating the direction of Makkah

minbar the pulpit in a mosque

mojabab see **magaz**

muallim benna master mason

muqarnas honeycomb vaulting

mashrabiya screen or grille of turned wood

palestra public area for teaching or display of wrestling, etc.

pishtaq a monumental portal forming the open side of an **iwan**

qa'a main hall of a house, comprising a **durqa'a** and two **iwans**, usually reserved solely for male guests

qibla direction of prayer

qubba dome; the term is sometimes applied to a mausoleum

ribat fortified monastery

riwaq portico; living quarters for teachers

sahn the courtyard of a mosque

salamlik pavilion (sitting room for men)

salsabil water-fed cooling plate, usually of marble, used in conjunction with a malkaf

Sassanid dynasty descended from Sasan, which ruled the Persian Empire 226–651

sharia the law of Islam

shukshaykha vented or fenestrated lantern of a dome

suq open-air market

squinch arch-shaped element spanning a corner, resolving square supporting walls with the circular base of a dome through an 8- then 16-sided transitional zone

takhtabush covered outdoor sitting area between two courtyards

umriyad coloured glass inserted in a dome

ziyada an enclosure around, or an extension of a mosque

Index

Page numbers in *italic* refer to illustrations

Abdul Aziz Ibn Saud, King 89
Abu Obaida Mosque, Jordan Valley *3*
Abha 75
Adorno, Theodor W. 11, 13
Aga Khan 38, 41, 87
Aga Khan Award for Architecture 40, 47, 106
Aga Khan Trust for Culture 98, 123, 130, 179
Ahmad ibn Tulun 198
Ain Jalut, Battle of 188
Akbar, Jamel 197, 203, 204
Ala-Iddeen, Fatima 31
Al-Ain Museum, United Arab Emirates 148, 150, 156, 174, 206; *149–55, 175–77*
Al-Alami housing project, East Jerusalem *39*
Al-Amin Mosque, Beirut 118, 121; *118–21*
Al-Aqmar Mosque, Cairo 183, 184
Al-Aqsa Mosque, Jerusalem 31
Al-Askar 180
Al-Azhar Garden, Cairo 41, 179, 187–91, 194–200; *182–83, 186–91, 196–201*
Al-Beit Al-Kamal, Sana'a, Yemen 41, 207, 210, 213, 217; *208–9, 211–15, 217*
Al-Beit Foundation, Amman 38, 39, 54–55, 58, 144, 204, 205, 248; *54–55*
Al-Dara Complex 41, 161; *122, 161–73*
Alexandria 179
Al-Fheheel 248
Al-Fustat 180, 187, 198
Al-Guyushi Mosque, Cairo 184
Al-Haleem, Abd 236
Alhambra, Granada 179
Al-Hariri, Bahia 248
Ali Bin Abi Taleb Mosque, Qatar 114, 118; *114–115*
Al-Kharj 40, 108–11, 114; *108, 109, 111*
Al-Khore Mosque, Qatar 114, 118; *116–17*
Al-Manshar complex 248
Al-Mansur 84, 86
Al-Qarawiyin Mosque, Fez 75
Al-Qasba Island 241
Al-Qatai 180
Al-Rajhi house, Riyadh *73*
Al-Sa'ed residence, Amman 49
Al-Salih Talai Mosque, Cairo 184
Al-Sayyad, Nezar 75
Al-Shamiya development, Makkah 41
Al-Sheikh, Mohammad 40
Al-Siqelli, General Gawhar 180
Al-Talhouni, Khalil 43, 71
Al-Talhouni residence, Amman 71; *70–71, 178*
Alte Nationalgalerie, Berlin 124
Al-Yarmouk University Central Library 43; *45–47*
Amman 10, 37, 38, 39, 41, 43, 49, 51, 53, 54, 55, 71, 204, 205, 236
Amri Ibn al-As, General 179
Angawi, Sami 229
Anthemius 87
Archigram group 36
Architectural Association, London 184

Assem, Prince, residence of *48*
Aswan High Dam 187

Babylon, fortress of 179, 180
Badran, Jamal 8, 31, 33, 70; *32*
Badran, Jamal (Jr) 43, 44
Badran, Ola 43, 44
Badran, Samina 43
Baghdad 82, 204, 206
Baghdad State Mosque 10, 38, 40, 47, 51, 58, 80–88, 98, 114, 121, 144; *79–85*
Behnisch, Günther 36, 37
Behrens, Peter 37
Beirut 118
Beit Al-Kadi, Cairo 77
Beit Al-Suheimi, Cairo 27; *28*
Bell, Daniel 16
Berger, Geiger 37
Bianca, Stefano 98
Blue Mosque, Istanbul 77
Bofil, Ricardo 10, 38
Bonn 36
Britton, John 124
Brown, Denise Scott 10, 38, 40, 88, 240

C. Town Mall, Amman *16*
Cairo 27, 41, 49, 52, 55, 75, 77, 78, 114, 183, 184, 185, 187, 188, 189, 190, 195, 196, 197, 198, 199, 200, 204, 205, 206, 213; *180, 184, 194, 195*
calligraphy 134, 183; *128–29*
Chadirji, Rifaat 38, 80, 38
Circassia 197
Citadel, Cairo 55, 78, 185, 187, 190
City Hall of the Municipality of Greater Amman 41; *42, 43*
Committee for a New Museology 127
Cook, Peter 36

Damascus 31, 33, 34, 43, 49, 188, 204, 248; *202*
Dar al-Omran 40, 88, 102, 106, 148
Darmstadt, Technical University of 13, 35, 37, 38
Darriyah 69, 89; *90*
Darriyah Mosque 89, 90, 92, 98
David, Douglas 130
Diderot, Denis 123
Doha 41, 130, 133–36, 138, 141–44, 148; *131–35, 137–43, 145–46*
Dome of the Rock, Jerusalem 134
Dubai 234, 236, 244, 248; *14*
Dubai Creek 206, 234, 236; *234–39*
Durand, Jean-Nicolas 123

East Jerusalem housing project 38
Edirne 78
Egypt 9, 35, 41, 81, 179, 188
Elementa 72, Bonn 36; *36*
Enlightenment 11, 13, 37, 123
Euphrates 81, 86

Fathy, Hassan 9–10, 11, 41, 43, 71, 187, 198, 204
Fez 75
Fuhais 38, 53, 204; *52, 53*

Gensler 230
Gerasa 204

Germany 36, 49, 73, 86
Grabar, Oleg 38
Great Mosque, Cordoba 86
Great Mosque, Damascus 78, 86
Great Mosque, Riyadh 40, 101–2, 106; *91*; see also Palace of Justice, Riyadh; Qasr al-Hukm Complex, Riyadh
Great Mosque, Samarra 78, 83, 84

Hagia Sophia 76, 87
Hajj Research Centre 229
Hakim, Besim 197, 203, 204
Handal villa 49
Harnoncourt, René d' 127
Hasht Behesht Palace, Isfahan 27
Henri VI 124
'Heritage Village', Kuwait 207, 244; *245–47*
Hijaz region, Saudi Arabia 210, 218
Historic Cities Suppport Programme 98
Horkheimer, Max 11, 13

Ibn Tulun 180
India 197, 211
Iran 27, 28, 114
Iraq 40, 41, 81, 84, 198
Irbid 43
Isfahan 27, 28, 114
Isidorus 87
Isozaki, Arata 13
Istanbul 77, 199, 248

Jabal al Shamia development scheme, Makkah 218, 230
Jabal Omar housing development, Makkah 41, 47, 206, 210, 218–19, 221, 226–30; *219–27, 229, 230–31*
Jameson, Frederic 15–16
Jantar Mantar Gardens, Delhi 131
Jeddah 210, 211, 218
Jencks, Charles 11
Jerusalem 37, 38, 41, 43, 49, 53, 204, 205
Jordan 10, 37, 38, 40, 43, 49, 69, 248
Jordan Cement Factory Employees Housing 38, 53, 204; *52, 53*
Jourdan, Joachim 35, 36

Kabala 198
Kahn, Louis I. 9
Khaled Bin Zied, Sheikh, residence of *14*
Khan al Khalili, Cairo 248
Khan Mirjan, Baghdad 84, 86
Khor Dubai 41
Khore Mosque, Qatar 114, 118; *116–17*
Khouri residence 49
King Abdul Aziz Historic Centre, Riyadh 40, 161
King Abdul Aziz Mosque, Al-Kharj 40, 108–11, 114; *108, 109, 111, 113*
Kuala Lumpur 80
Kuban, Dogan 76
Kuwait 41, 206, 232, 236, 244, 248; *244*
Kuwaiti National Bank, Amman *12*

Laugier, Abbé 123
layering 49; *48*
Le Corbusier 144
Lebanon 38, 41, 206, 248
Lefebvre, Henri 19
Legitte, George 36
Linneaus, Carl 123
Louis XIV 124
Louvre, Paris 124
Lybia 33

Madi residence, Amman 49; *50*
Madinah 76, 134, 180
Makkah 41, 77, 98, 180, 206, 210, 211, 218–19, 221, 226–30, 232; *218, 219–26, 228, 229, 230–31*
Malaysia 41, 78
Masjid al-Tami'i Mosque, Sana'a, Yemen 213
Masjid Negara, Kuala Lumpur 80
Mehmet (the Conqueror) 77, 199
Meinecke-Berg, Victoria 181, 183
Mendelsohn, Erich 37
Mesopotamia 87
Mies van der Rohe, Ludwig 37
Modernism 9, 10–11, 15, 37, 51, 87, 88
Moore, Charles 106
Morocco 41, 75, 213, 232
Mosque of Ahmad ibn Tulun, Cairo 76, 78, 180, 183, 185, 199
Mosque of Al-Hakim, Cairo 183, 195; *194*
Mosque of Iman Turki Abdullah, Riyadh 89
Mosque of Mohammad Ali, Cairo 55
Mosque of Shaykh al-Mu'ayyad 184
Mosque of Shaykh Lutfallah, Isfahan 114
Mosque of Sinan, Bulaq 187
Mosque of Sulaiman Pasha, Cairo 187
Mosque of Sultan Baybars 185
Mosque of Sultan Hasan, Cairo 78, 184, 187, 199
Mövenpick Hotel, Petra *71*
Mu'awiya 78
Muhammad 'Ali 187
Müller, Bernhard 36
Muqattam Hills 180, 187, 190
Museum for Children, Amman 156; *156–59*
Museum of Islamic Arts, Doha 41, 123, 130, 133–36, 138, 141–44; *131–35, 137–43, 145–47*
Museum of State, Doha 148
Musmak fortress, Riyadh 88, 98, 101

Najd 28, 88, 161
Najdi style 41, 98, 101, 102, 106, 108; *104*
Napoleon 124
National Museum, Doha 130, 148
National Saudi Museum 40
New Gourna Village 11, 187
New Urbanist theory 98
Nile 81, 179, 180, 187, 189, 195
Noble, Joseph Veach 127
Noor, Queen 41
North Africa 78, 188

Olympia Park, Munich 37; *36*
Orientalism 125–27, 133, 203
Otto, Frei 37

P.A.S. 36
Palace of Justice, Riyadh 40, 88, 92, 98–101, 104, 106; *98–101*; see also Great Mosque, Riyadh; Qasr al-Hukm Complex, Riyadh
Palestine 31
Popper, Karl 125
Post-Modernism 10–11, 15, 40
Prophet's Mosque, Madinah 76, 134
Putrajaya 78

Qairawan 206
Qasr al-Hukm Complex, Riyadh 40, 88–107, 108, 121; *40, 74, 92–107*; see also Great Mosque, Riyadh; Palace of Justice, Riyadh
Qatar 41, 130

Rabat 240
Ramallah *6*, 31, 43
'Reflections on the Narrative of Place – the Infinite Conversation' 18–29
Regensburg *35*
Riyadh 40, 47, 69, 88, 89, 98, 102, 108, 161, 236
Riyadh Development Authority 88, 89, 92
Royal Court, Amman 41

Sabil-Khuttub *194*
Sahara 188
Said, Edward 125
Salah ad-Din 31, 32, 183, 197
Sana'a, Yemen 41, 58, 205, 207, 210, 213, 216, 217, 232, 249; *205, 206, 208–9, 211–15, 217*
Saudi Arabia 9, 10, 28, 40, 41, 69, 75, 88, 161, 211, 218
Schinkel, Karl Friedrich von 37, 124
Science Oasis *4*
Sea Front Development, Sidon 206, 248; *248–49*
Selim, Sultan 187
Selimye Mosque, Edirne 78
Serageldin, Ismail 77
Serai Burnu Palace, Istanbul 77
Sharia Port Said 183
Shubeilat, L. 38
Sidon 41, 206, 248; *248–49*
Sillah 240
Sinan 76, 78
Sinno, Anas 38
Sir John Soane's Museum, London 124
Stockhausen, Karlheinz 36
Sultan Hasan Mosque, Cairo 55
Sultan Qala'un, *maristan, madresa* and mausoleum of, Cairo 185
Syria 31, 188

Takasaki 13
Tange, Kenzo 37
Tangiers 206
Taurus mountains 81
'Theatre of the Future' project 36; *35*
Tigris 81, 86
Topkapi Palace, Istanbul 77, 199
Transjordan 204
Tripoli 33–34, 43
Tunisia 213

Ukhaidir Palace, Kabala 84, 198
United Arab Emirates 41

van Mensch, Peter 127
Venturi, Robert 10, 11, 13, 18, 38, 40, 88, 240
VIP Rest House, Saudi Arabia *68, 69*
Vivant Denon, Dominique 124

Wade, Robert 17–18
Wadi Abu Jamil Housing project, Beirut 58–59; *58–67*
Wadi Barakrag master plan, Morocco 232, 240; *240–43*
Wadi Hanifah 68, 89; *68–69*
Wadi Saleh Housing project *56–57*
Wahabi sect 98
Weelus airbase, Tripoli 34
White Temple, Warka 82, 85
Wright, Frank Lloyd 37

Yeang, Ken 47

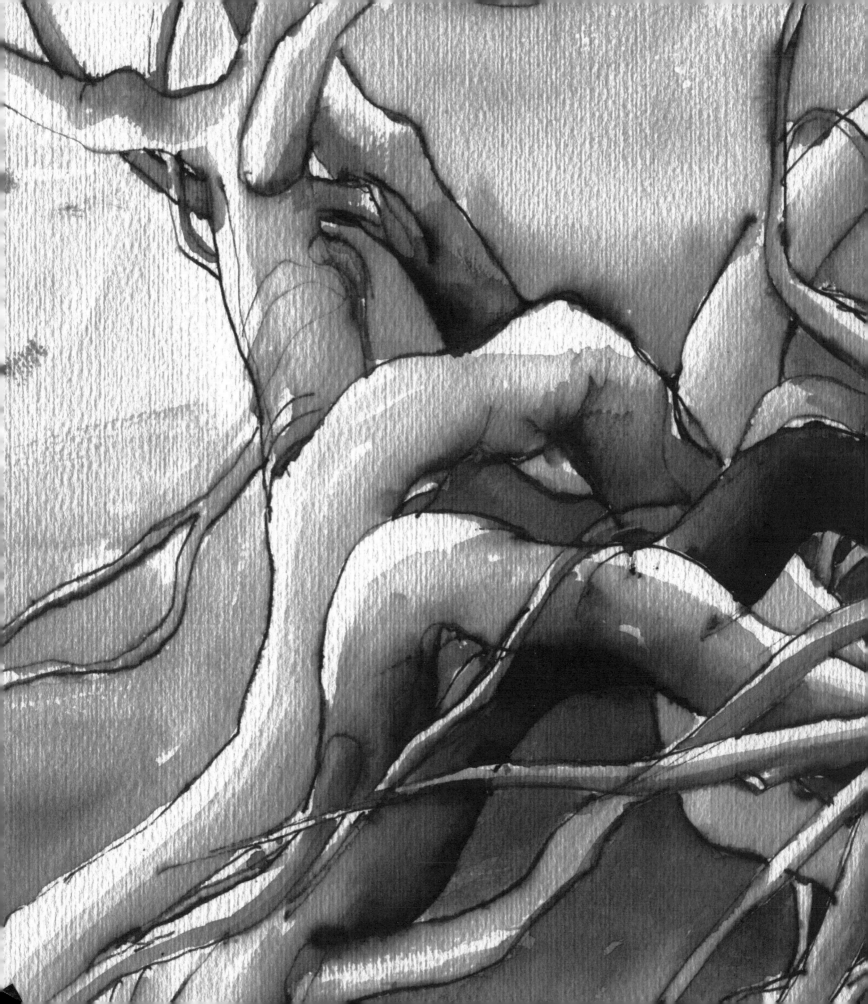